THE HIDDEN GARDENS OF IRELAND

OF IRELAND

Where to find them

THE HIDDEN GARDENS
OF IRELAND

Where to find them

Revised Edition

Marianne Heron

Gill & Macmillan

Gill & Macmillan Ltd
Goldenbridge
Dublin 8
with associated companies throughout the world

© Marianne Heron 1993, 1996
0 7171 2427 4

Illustrations by Michael Fewer

Index compiled by Gloria Greenwood

Print origination and design by Identikit Design Consultants

Printed by ColourBooks Ltd, Dublin

A catalogue record is available for this book
from the British Library.

1 3 5 7 6 4 2

CONTENTS

To David, with love

AUTHOR'S NOTE

T his is a highly personal guide. In addition to verbal pictures designed to set the mood for each garden there is the kind of information that I would give to friends visiting from abroad or from another part of the country. There are suggestions for intriguing places to visit en route to gardens. There are also listings of places to stay and places to eat which reflect personal preference.

The houses mentioned are not typical hotel or B & B bungalow accommodation. Often, in charming homes which may have colourful owners and histories, the establishments offer the atmosphere of a country house party. The pubs and restaurants have been chosen for their pleasing surroundings and good, original food.

The prices and other details are correct at the time of going to print, although obviously these may be liable to change. Those gardens which are open by appointment only, belong to gardeners who are kind enough to share their enthusiasm, so please do arrange your visit in advance. Don't turn up on the doorstep unannounced.

What constitutes a group? This is one of those 'How long is a piece of string' questions! The reduced group rate usually applies to groups of over 20, although this may be negotiable. In some cases there is a special minibus rate. Private gardens open by appointment welcome garden clubs, special outings and so on, but a carload of several people may also constitute a perfectly acceptable group in some cases.

The
Rhododendron
Road

The Wee North

The Lakelands

Fair City

The Garden
of Ireland

The Normandy
of Ireland

Waters
and the Wild

Earthy
Delights

A GROWING PASSION

Introduction

G arden visiting has become a favourite leisure activity. This book is designed as a guide to gardens in the thirty-two counties of Ireland which are open full time, part time or by appointment. Some of the gardens are impressive legacies from the past, a testimony to landowners' enthusiasm for decorative demesnes and pleasure gardens. Others are the glorious fruits of passionate collectors who subscribed to plant expeditions to the four corners of the globe, or private gardens whose secrets were previously hidden away behind concealing boundaries. An increasing number, like Jim Reynold's lovely creation at Butterstream, are gardens born of the new wave of enthusiasm for gardening.

In Ireland we are tremendously lucky to have a veritable paradise for plants. The mild climate, tempered by the Gulf Stream, allows a wider range of plants to be grown here than anywhere else in Europe. Tender species from five different continents, normally grown under glass, can be found flourishing outdoors here. There is an amazingly rich variety of gardens drawn from different traditions: from Mount Congreve's 100 acres of dazzling colour, with one of the finest rhododendron collections in the world, to the magical island of Ilnacullin, and from Lutyens's architectural jewel at Heywood to the Himalayan rhododendron forests at Ard na Mona in Donegal.

There are historic estates like Killruddery in County Wicklow with its rare baroque garden, romantic wild gardens like Annes Grove in County Cork, the collections of dedicated plantspeople like Helen Dillon, and unforgettable gardens like Mount Stewart in County Down. Their settings - like Bantry House with its stairway to the sky or the sub-tropical luxuriance of Derreen - are often incomparable. What is more, they are wonderfully unspoilt. Even the most popular of gardens seldom has more than a dozen or two visitors at a time. And perhaps too Irish gardens have their own brand of magic, a certain romantic waywardness and colourfulness of expression missing from their more manicured counterparts elsewhere.

The tradition of the wild garden has its roots in Ireland. William Robinson, author of the influential *Wild Garden*, began his career at Ballykilcavan. Mount Usher, County Wicklow, and Rowallane, County Down, are some of the loveliest examples of his philosophy, which celebrated the natural profusion of plants.

Since the first version of this book was published in 1993 a quiet, green revolution has been unfurling. The number of people visiting gardens has increased significantly and, in response to burgeoning interest, more gardens have opened to the public and are included in this guide.

Marketing groups like Gardens of Ireland - a group of over thirty distinguished gardens open to the public - have sprung up. Gardeners have come together to organise local garden routes, and garden festivals like those in County Wicklow and Cork are now well established.

Timotei, the original sponsors of this book, are involved in a happy example of conservation of the natural gardens of Ireland. Since their products rely on natural ingredients, the Timotei people believe in giving something back to nature. In conjunction with the Irish Wildlife Federation they have bought two meadows: one in the unique Shannon Callows area, the other in the West. They are also involved with schools in a number of meadow projects, designed to heighten the awareness of the need to conserve grasslands and wild meadows.

Gardens may once have been the Cinderellas of Irish heritage, receiving negligible support. Happily this situation has begun to change, as the potential of gardens as a leisure and tourism resource is more fully appreciated. Where heritage buildings can survive decades of neglect before they crumble irredeemably to dust, gardens are ephemeral things. They are readily snatched back by rampant nature, often preserved only through the heroic efforts of families or individuals. Now heritage gardens open to the public qualify for tax breaks and a £4 million Great Gardens of Ireland Restoration Scheme, launched in 1994, will aid the restoration of up to thirty gardens by the year 2000.

The perception that the great gardens were a legacy of ascendancy landowners best forgotten has altered gradually. Now the surviving great gardens are seen more as a valuable heritage resource. Several important gardens which had gone into decline have been restored, including the fairytale demesne at Ballinlough, County Meath, and the gardens at Hilton Park, County Monaghan. The walled garden at Strokestown

Park, County Roscommon, has been recreated and the delightful eighteenth-century Kilfane Glen and waterfall at Thomastown, County Kilkenny, have been rediscovered and restored by Nicholas and Susan Mosse, with the help of European Union funding. The Office of Public Works has taken a number of important gardens, including the Lutyens gardens at Heywood and Emo, into its care. In the Six Counties the peace dividend combined with a new enthusiasm for garden visiting has produced a lovely crop of gardens. These gardens are promoted by the National Trust Ulster Gardens Scheme and by the *Guide to Gardens and Historic Demesnes* provided by the Northern Ireland Tourist Board.

However, the picture isn't always positive. The Shackleton garden, Beech Park, which was included in the first edition, with its important herbaceous collection and described as fourth in importance in these islands, had to be sold by the Shackletons and the opportunity to acquire the garden for the nation was missed.

Kilmacurragh, County Wicklow, also included previously, still remains a poignant reminder of the plight of once great gardens teetering on the brink of extinction as they revert year by year to wilderness.

Garden visiting used to be a popular pastime and has a rich history involving many colourful characters. When the ladies of Llangollen – Eleanor Butler and Sarah Ponsonby from Kilkenny – lived out their romanticised ideals at their *ferme orné* at Plas Newydd in the 1780s, Sir Walter Scott and Wordsworth were among those who flocked to visit them. The remarkable Mrs Delaney loved to show her friends – including Dean Jonathan Swift – the now vanished naturalistic garden she created at Delville near Glasnevin. Records from the period show that well over 100 eminent gardens were visited. The pendulum has now swung back again and gardening has become the growing edge of leisure.

Ireland could, in future, become recognised as the garden of Europe. In one sense, the countryside as a whole has all the ingredients of a wonderful natural garden: lush greenness, woods, hills, ever-present water and the constant changes of scenery that so enrapture visitors. Where else in the world would you find an exotic Italianate garden like Ilnacullin in the heart of a wild Atlantic island?

Having had a wonderfully enjoyable experience researching this book and its predecessor, I can thoroughly recommend the Irish garden experience.

EARTHY DELIGHTS

I f ever there was an area equipped to be a garden of earthy delights, Cork is the place. With a mild, damp climate, fabulous scenery and an enthusiastic gardening tradition it has to be the gardening county.

There are two very different sides to Cork: the demure landscapes and gentle hills around Cork city and the wonderful scenery of West Cork which veers from the wild to the exotic, often within the space of a few miles. The extraordinary contrasts between bare mountains and lush inlets continue on into Kerry with the lakes and mountains of Killarney and the subtropical luxuriance of Kenmare.

Cities with hills have a whole added fascination. Rome has them, Florence has them and so does Cork. Gardeners grumble about having to work with the ups and downs of hilly terrain, but slopes open up all kinds of opportunities for garden design which capitalises on changing levels.

Cork now has a fledgling garden festival which features contemporary gardens around the city. They are the kind of gardens people can relate to easily, modest in size and created with one or two pairs of hands. They feature the sort of imaginative, intimate planting which can transform a suburban garden, and quite a number of these generous gardeners are prepared to expose their creations to public view by appointment.

Things are definitely stirring in County Cork. Darina Allen now hosts gardening seminars at her cookery school at Kinoith. Gardening consultant Brian Cross has contributed to the design of a number of lovely gardens, and the choice of plants available from exciting outlets like Neil Williams's Carewswood Garden Centre at Castlemartyr in County Cork has never been better.

The level of activity around Cork proves the point that the gardening bug is catching. There's more behind the existence of good gardens than favourable climate, there has to be a gardening ethos. Some areas of the country have a paucity of good gardens which can't be explained away by conditions. Elsewhere they exist in great satisfying clumps and Cork vies with Wicklow in having the biggest concentration of gardens.

The majority of Cork's gardens are around the coast, but a trip to an inland garden like Annes Grove provides the motivation to see the gorgeous lush countryside where rich dairyland, woods and water form an incomparable tapestry.

ROUND AND ABOUT

C ork is a fabulous city for shopping and for eating. If you don't know the city, the main shopping area is around Patrick Street and in the small streets running between Patrick Street and South Mall. The English Market (behind Oliver Plunkett Street and Princes Street) selling every imaginable food from the local delicacy of drisheens to hot buttered eggs, has recently undergone a revamp but remains a shrine to traditional fishmongers and butchers; here you will see pyramids of pigs' tails and more exotic imports such as olives and sun-dried tomatoes.

Several Cork restaurants deserve mention. Michael Clifford is one of the bright lights of the Irish food renaissance and his restaurant, Clifford's, at 18 Dyke Parade is the kind of place to go for a special dinner, tel. 021-275333. The Arbutus Lodge run by the Ryan brothers Declan and Michael has a long-established reputation with food enthusiasts; traditional Irish dishes are served as well as *haute cuisine*, tel. 021-501237. The Oyster Tavern, dating from 1792 and quaint as the name suggests, is in Market Lane off Patrick Street and serves wonderful steaks and seafood.

For more casual meals, the Crawford Gallery Café, Emmet Place, attached to the art gallery and run by one of the Allens of Ballymaloe, offers interesting food at reasonable prices. Café Paradiso on 16 Lancaster Quay serves delicious Mediterranean/vegetarian style food for lunch and dinner and is a great place to drop in for morning coffee and crumpets or afternoon tea. Lots of organic foods are used on the menu and everything from the olive bread to the pasta is made on the premises.

5

Cobh, with its steep hills and picturesque past, is dominated by St Colman's Cathedral and is a colourful spot full of equally colourful characters. You can get it all in perspective by taking a one-hour tour of the harbour from Kennedy Pier. Barryscourt Castle, seat of the Barrymore family and dating back to the thirteenth century, is just outside Carrigtwohill; it is being restored and there is a tea room and craft shop there. Open April-Oct. 10.30am-6.30pm. A tour wouldn't be complete without a visit to Ballymaloe House, where Myrtle Allen, the matriarch of the Allen clan, presides over the country house and restaurant; most of the food is produced on the family farm, tel. 021-652531. Nearby at Shanagarry Pottery, distinctive brown/white, grey/blue ware is on sale; seconds can also be bought at bargain prices. While in the Ballycotton area do not miss the Carewswood Garden Centre at Castlemartyr. Neil Williams has a huge selection of unusual plants, travels to England regularly and showed me a newly imported *Corydalis cashmeriana*. There is a conservatory tea room.

Kinsale (18 miles/29 km from Cork), a pretty fishing village boasting over a dozen restaurants, is the home of the Kinsale Gourmet Festival and winner of the European Tourism Development award. The only difficulty is deciding which restaurant to choose. Among them are Man Friday, Blue Haven Hotel, the Trident, and the White House. The Oystercatcher restaurant in nearby Oysterhaven specialises in original seafood dishes, including oyster sausage.

Blarney Castle, home of Cormac MacCarthy (who gave the word 'blarney' to the language in Elizabethan times) and of the infamous Blarney Stone, is very much on the tourist trail, while the Blarney Woollen Mills shop, owned by the Hayes family, has beautifully designed Irish fashions. Nearby the Rock Close Gardens, laid out with huge stones by the St John Jefferyes family, are worth a visit if you are in the vicinity. Admission £2.50, open June-mid Sept. Mon.-Sat. 12noon-6pm.

Doneraile Court, an early eighteenth-century house, has a beautiful setting on the Awbeg River with formal vistas of lakes and trees. The house - restored by the Georgian Society - has many stories about the St Leger family woven around it, including the 1710 tale of Elizabeth St Leger who was made a Mason after she eavesdropped on a Masonic meeting. A ceiling painted to look like the sky is one of the intriguing features at Dunkathel, in Glanmire. Open May-mid Oct. Wed., Sun. 2-6pm.

The ceiling at Riverstown House depicting Time rescuing Truth is one of the first pieces of work done in the 1730s by the Francini stuccodores. The house, which dates back to 1602, is at Riverstown near Glanmire, open May-Aug. Thurs.-Sat. 2-6pm.

PLACES TO STAY

F riends have come back several pounds heavier and singing the praises of Jeremy and Merrie Green's hospitality at Ballyvolane House. Dating back to 1728 and Italianised the following century, Ballyvolane belongs to the Hidden Ireland organisation and is in the Blackwater Valley, B & B £35-£44.00, dinner £20.00, tel. 025-36349. The Old Presbytery is another haven recommended by friends. An old Victorian town house, it is in the village of Kinsale and provides nice old-fashioned touches like linen sheets, brass beds and cooking of the standard you would expect in the epicentre of gourmet Ireland. B & B from £16-£24.00, tel. 021-772027, run by the McEvoy family.

The creeper-clad former rectory known as The Glebe House, at Ballinadee, Bandon, is run by Gillian and Tim Bracken. It is furnished with antiques and surrounded by extensive gardens which provide produce for the table. And it is close to beaches. B & B £25.00, dinner £16.50, tel. 021-778456. Courtmacsherry is an attractive fishing village on the Adrigeen estuary, and Georgian Travara Lodge, which belongs to the Friendly Homes of Ireland organisation, overlooks the bay. Mandy Guy, proprietor, specialises in seafood. B & B £18-£20.00, dinner à la carte £15.00, tel. 023-46493.

Longueville House, Mallow, epitomises all that is best about Irish country houses. The 1720 house is run by the O'Callaghan family. Michael O'Callaghan grows his own wines and produces wonderful lamb, vegetables and fruit, Jane O'Callaghan makes sure that all the guests are spoiled rotten, and William O'Callaghan, the son of the house, produces the most wonderful original dishes. Expensive but memorable, B & B £53-£80.00, dinner £28.00, tel. 022-447156. Set in an award-winning garden, seventeenth-century Assolas House is run by the Bourke family. Tennis, boating and fishing are among the peaceful pleasures. Open March-Nov. B & B £110-£150.00 for two, dinner £28.00, tel. 029-50015.

KINOITH

Ballymaloe Cookery School,
Shanagarry, Midleton, County Cork

VEGETABLE GARDEN

A delightful new creation, with potager,
vegetable garden and fruit garden, laid
out in the formal manner.

Gardening is going to be to the '90s what cooking was to the '80s, predicts Darina Allen. To prove the point, the next growing edges of the Allens' highly successful Ballymaloe Cookery School are the gardens. They are 'simply delicious' both in concept and content just like Darina's cookery books and TV series of the same name.

Tim and Darina Allen's herb garden at Kinoith sprang from a visit to the glorious gardens of Vilandry. Flower-shaped beds of lemon balm, bronze fennel, purple sage, lovage, summer savory, sweet cecily, parsley, chives and angelica are laid out in a formal parterre edged with box and set in gravel. The herbs are planted in patterns of contrasting colour and clumps of Jerusalem artichokes and scarlet runner beans grown on decorative stands are used to give height to the design.

The garden is set in a compartment of ancient beech hedges with arched entrances, part of Kinoith's once neglected nineteenth-century garden. Along the sides of the garden herbaceous borders and beds of sea kale - complete with terracotta forcing pots - are punctuated by the dark exclamation marks of Italian cypress. At the centre of the garden is a *Myrtus ugni* planted in honour of Myrtle Allen, the inspiration behind the Ballymaloe House restaurant. There is a bird's eye view of the plan from a specially created vantage point atop a rustic shelter.

Often thought by visitors to be an old garden, the area was created just eight years ago but it belongs to a very ancient tradition, for herb plots were one of the earliest forms of garden. In medieval times they were an essential feature of any large household and herbs were used as remedies, for cookery and for strewing on floors to sweeten the air.

Hidden inside a screen of trees with a wicket gate to exclude a flock of free range hens is the *potager*. Laid out in a series of diamonds and squares with herringbone paths of old brick, the formal layout shows just how decorative vegetables can be. Scarlet-stemmed chard, lacy *frisée* lettuce, old-fashioned potatoes like Pink Fir Apple and Sharp's Express, radishes, edible flowers and asparagus spears are planted in neat rows. The only drawback, says Darina, is that it almost seems a sacrilege to spoil the design by picking vegetables.

The newest area is the ornamental fruit garden outside the converted apple packing station which houses the cookery school. The formal layout, designed by Jim Reynolds, is intended to provide a shade-dappled haven with trellised walks and spring-flowering bulbs like snowdrops and *Chionodoxa*.

The gardens, just one of the multi-faceted family concerns at Ballymaloe, which gives employment to 130, are immaculately kept by Darina's sister Elizabeth, Eileen O'Donovan and Haulie Walsh, and some of the ornamental ironwork is by Tim and Darina's son Isaac. There are further plans afoot - one for a pool at the far end of the old garden which will mirror a temple created from an old portico. Another is for a memory garden with an arboretum planted in honour of people and places.

Mrs Delaney - that indefatigable eighteenth-century visitor of houses and gardens - would thoroughly approve of the Allens' 'improvements' at Kinoith. Several years ago, Darina started collecting shells to decorate an old apple bunker; instead, a new idea took shape and a hexagonal grotto with gothic windows now stands in the middle of a field. Every inch of the walls, reflected in a little fountain, have been shelled by Darina and Blot Kerr Wilson. Nearby there will be a maze in an allegorical pattern by friend Peter Lamb whose celtic design incorporates the Allen family's initials.

Admission £3.00, open April-Sept. Mon.-Sat. 9am-6pm by appointment only; teas, £4.00, feature a plate of five freshly baked goodies including scones warm from the oven, tel. 021-646785. Directions: Look for the signs to Ballymaloe in Castlemartyr on the main Waterford Cork Road. Follow the road to Ballycotton until you see the signs for the cookery school.

CLANABOY

Woodleigh Park, Model Farm Road, Cork

FLOWER GARDEN

An enchanting small garden to inspire townies.

Showers of Kiftsgate roses and philadelphus bursting over the wall distinguish Aileen Kennedy's garden from her neighbours'. Mrs Kennedy has been gardening here for 40 years and began collecting plants and shrubs long before local nurseries had much of interest.

This may be a small garden in a quiet cul-de-sac but it is so packed with treasures that it takes longer to admire than one ten times its size. In the back garden, filled with the scent of roses and the sound of a trickling pool, you could be in a green Eden miles from anywhere.

The effect is of glorious profusion. In midsummer clematis, honeysuckle, old roses: 'Madame Isaac Pereire', *R.* 'Belle de Crecy', 'Grootendorst', 'William Lobb',

fling their blooms over shrubs and perennials. The more you look, the more you see: interesting foliage shrubs: *Mahonia nervosa* with its changing leaves, tender *Melianthus major*, golden *Hydrangea*, *Acer vitifolia*, *Pittosporum tobira*, vying with herbaceous numbers like the chocolate plant *Cosmos atrosanguineus*, *Tovara* 'Painter's Palette', willow gentians, magenta

Admission £2.50, open by appointment only, April-Sept. tel. 021-541560. Directions: Going out of Cork heading for West Cork on the western road, turn right at Dennehy's Cross, left at the traffic lights on Model Farm Road opposite the Rendezvous Bar, turn second right, past Highfield rugby club and the house is the fourth on the left.

Primula vialii, the cowls of *Arisema candidissimum* and the devilish scarlet *Crocosmia* 'Lucifer'.

There is a fernery beside the pool with curiosities like the Irish tatting fern, the crested fern and the bead fern. Gardens always have a growing edge - this one is no exception and the latest addition is a scree bed for such Alpine treasures as *Lilium pricea*, lapeiroasia corms and *Iris pallida*. There is even a secret garden within a hidden garden at the end of the plot and a surprising number of trees, the tricolour beech with its flashes of pink, an umbrella pine and a *Cryptomeria* 'Sekkan-sugi'. Mrs Kennedy is a very knowledgeable plantswoman and can tell you about every plant in her garden, and it is a garden with year-round interest.

LAKEMOUNT

Glanmire, County Cork

FLOWER GARDEN

An intensively planted, intricately planned two-acre garden with excellent spring to autumn colour.

The neat hedge-topped wall at the summit of an exposed hill high above Glanmire gives little hint of the riches to be found inside this beautifully planned garden.

Developed over a 20-year period by Brian Cross and his mother Mrs Margaret Cross, the garden consists of a series of gardens within the two-acre site. Cleverly defined without formal compartments, each area has a mood of its own so that every few yards there is a sense of anticipation followed by a delightful reward.

To one side of the house the pool area, complete with small temple, has an almost picture-postcard brilliance, the pinks and apricots of camellias, azaleas, rhododendrons and a collection of

Admission £3.00, open by appointment only at weekends, tel. 021-821052. Mostly accessible to wheelchairs. No children. Directions: Go through the village of Glanmire from the Cork direction, leave the bridge on your right and take the first turn left up the very steep hill; the house is at the top of the hill on the left. If coming to Glanmire from the new Cork Road, turn right at the bridge just before you enter the village. This approach brings you past Dunkathel - a house in the Palladian style with a fine bifurcated staircase - which is open to the public May-Oct. Wed.-Sun. 2-4pm.

primulas predominating. A shady green area creates the transition to lush lawns and island beds filled with herbaceous plants which provide a wonderful object lesson in planting. Strongly shaped evergreens make a framework and the impact is achieved by using the colour and form of plants in a punchy contrasting way.

A single bush of glowing yellow *R. macabeanum* is echoed by golden *Aralia elata*, a collection of acers provides autumn colour and *Brachyglottis* and a Japanese banana tree flourish in the central beds despite the exposed site. The mood of the pond garden - paved with Liscannor stone and defined by rock beds full of Alpine treasures - is more formal. Nearby the jasmine-scented conservatory, full of tender plants and unusual climbers - *Sollya heterophylla* and *Dendromecon rigida* -

overlooks a small formal garden. Brian's latest addition to the garden is a small-scale forced perspective created with a beech *allée*.

The exposed site means that plants have to keep their heads down and shrubs are either pruned or chosen for their modest height. A huge variety of choice plants is concentrated in a relatively small area. Among the rarest is a *Restio subverticallatus* (S. African rope grass), and among the many covetables are a *Picea breweriana* (weeping spruce), *Acer* 'Senkaki Sotidium', *Dianella tasmanica* and *Dicksonia antarctica*. Brian, who combines his work as an art teacher with garden consultancy, has deservedly been three times overall winner of the Bord Fáilte/National Gardens Association competition and his garden features in *In an Irish Garden* by Helen Dillon and Sybil Connolly.

FOTA ARBORETUM

Fota Island, County Cork

ARBORETUM

Handsome grounds well maintained with many fine specimens.

Gardening is meant to soothe the soul and it certainly had a calming effect on the Smith Barry family. The seventh Earl of Barrymore squandered the family fortunes, the fast-living eighth Earl was known as 'Hellgate'. But by the 1820s James Smith Barrymore had begun the tradition of gardening enjoyed by his descendants until the family left Fota in the 1970s.

The 27 acres of pleasure grounds surrounding Fota House, the splendid Regency mansion designed by Richard Morrison, form the centrepiece of the estate on Fota Island. Sheltered by the inlet of Lough Mahon and protected by belts of trees the island provides very favourable conditions for tender species. Date palms flourish and bananas have been known to fruit within the arboretum there which contains a historic collection of over 1,000 trees. The Smith Barry family began planting the garden in the 1820s; some of the oldest trees date from this period and the layout has changed little in 200 years.

Collections of plants from Chile, Japan and China are particularly well represented and specimens have been planted individually so that they can be admired from every angle.

The entrance to the garden is through a modest gate near the car park and this first part of the arboretum contains a large collection of rare conifers, the planting crossed by a grid of walks. Paths lead around a large pond and a rock garden to a fernery under a sheltered canopy of beeches planted with the tree fern *Dicksonia antarctica*. There are very large collections of individual genera, with up to 15 species of magnolia alone, a large number of camellias, 10 japonica hybrids. Among the more unusual shrubs are the scarlet-flowered Australian Waratah and the *Lomatia ferruginea*. Given their great age some of the specimens like the *Magnolia campbellii* and tulip trees have grown to enormous size.

Additional features in the L-shaped gardens include an orangery, scheduled for restoration, and the walled Italian garden - now, alas, virtually empty. Nearly all the trees and shrubs are clearly labelled with their date of planting and country of origin. There are some wonderful sights to be seen: a huge tree of Granny's Ringlets or *Cryptomeria japonica* 'Spiralis', a large collection of *Pieris* varieties with their flame-tipped branches and lily of the valley blossoms, myrtles – among them *Myrtus lechleriana* frothing with cream-scented blossom, enormous tulip trees, and the weeping spruce *Picea breweriana*, with its enchanting drooping habit.

Many of the trees are very early introductions to Ireland – like the *Sequoia*, planted just two years after they first reached these islands in 1845 – and must have been a source of great wonder in their day. Coming on the stunning sight of a handkerchief tree (*Davidia involucrata*) aflutter with thousands of pale bracts, it is possible to experience some of the excitement Père David must have felt when he first caught sight of this beautiful tree on a hillside in China.

There has been considerable controversy over the future of Fota. The estate was bought from the Smith Barrymore descendants by University College Cork in 1975. The University then sold part of the estate to a developer.

Currently LET, a different developer, is involved and 115 acres of land including the arboretum and house are held by the Fota Trust.

Replanting both within the arboretum and in the shelter around it is being carried out. The arboretum *per se* is now secure but the problem is that its future well-being depends not only on its immediate surroundings but on the delicate balances within the island and its shelter belts as a whole. In the same way, the beauty of the estate lies in the total relationship between parkland, house, grounds and sheltered island setting. The future of that relationship is uncertain.

Admission free, car parking £1.00, open 17 Mar.-3 Nov. weekdays 10am-6pm, Sundays 11am-6pm, tel. 021-812678. Suitable for wheelchairs and children. Fast food restaurant. Directions: Take the Cobh turn off the main Cork Waterford Road and follow the signs for Fota. There is a wild life park in the estate; the house was closed at the time of writing.

HILLSIDE

Annmount, Glounthane, County Cork

FLOWER GARDEN

*An original young garden, very
rewarding for the plantsperson.*

C ork has two great advantages:
one is the Gulf Stream warming
its flanks, the other is its enthusiastic
women gardeners. Mary Byrne's
garden at Annmount is one of the
exciting new gardens which became

a founding member of the Cork
Gardens Festival.

Work on the four-acre hillside
garden began around 6 years ago
and the terrace and rockery area
were designed for Mary by Brian
Cross. The terrace links the house to
the garden and is surrounded by
raised beds of plants so that their
scent and colour can be enjoyed
from the sunny south-facing rooms.
The rockery area makes a feature of
the steepest part of the garden and
provides a transition from terrace to
lawns and shrubs.

Within the shelter of
surrounding woodland, the garden is

designed to make the most of changing levels. A series of pools and cascades tumble down through the rockery which has an enviable planting of dwarf conifers and Alpines. A gold theme predominates with phormiums providing strong architectural shapes. At the beginning of July various Alpine gentians were about to flower.

There are many choice plants to catch the eye in the herbaceous beds around the terrace. A pink-patterned *Campanula punctata*, *Callistemon splendens* with gold on its scarlet bottlebrushes, *Lobelia tupa*, golden oats or *Stipa gigantea*, the Chatham Island forget-me-not *Myosotidium*. *Pseudopanax* and *Dodonaea* are among the covetable collection.

Rhododendrons, azaleas, *Cornus kousa*, *Acer kinshi*, the summer-flowering *Magnolia sieboldii*, *Viburnum* 'Mariesii' and many other appealing shrubs are already well established in the informal beds in the lower part of the garden. Near the house there is a pale herbaceous border where blues predominate amid pinks and white, and where *Alstroemeria* is a speciality. New areas of this promising garden under creation include a woodland area planted with shade-loving plants, ferns, hostas and hellebores. The garden was a National Gardens Association award winner in 1991.

The half shade of the woodland also provides ideal conditions for rhododendrons, azaleas and camellias. The latest addition to the garden is an extensive scree bed - the previous planting of dwarf conifers and heathers went out of favour - which is filling up with alpines, Mary Byrne's latest passion.

Open to groups by appointment only, admission £3.00 April-Sept. tel. 021-353119. Directions: Leaving Cork on the Waterford Road, turn left up the hill at Glounthane church. Pass under the bridge, turn right through pillars marked Annmount, and go up the first drive on the left.

KADUNA

Maryborough Hill, Douglas, County Cork

FLOWER GARDEN

A well thought-out garden with a particularly fine collection of shrubs.

This 25-year-old garden is included in the Cork Gardens Festival (for dates and other information tel. 021-353119) and has won many accolades for Elizabeth Kavanagh in garden contests. The three-quarter-acre plot is informally planted with many unusual shrubs, with particularly attractive foliage reflecting the owner's enthusiasm for flower arranging.

Carefully laid, so that its secrets are revealed only as you walk around it, the design is centred on a number of focal points. In the front garden a *Cornus alternifolia variegata* shelters two scree beds of Alpines guarded by a little lead figure. The eye is also caught by a *Viburnum plicatum* 'Mariesii' and a rustic gateway in a stone wall leading to an area of lawn and raised beds planted with herbaceous plants including penstemons, salvias and small shrubs – azaleas and *Cornus controversa*.

A terrace behind the house with a lily pond and bridge feature provides a pleasant vantage point overlooking the rest of the garden. The paving is softened with a spreading juniper, an *Abies* and *Acer palmatum* 'Dissectum Atropurpureum' and containers of plants. The layout of this garden should provide an inspiration for anyone trying to soften the uncompromising outline of a suburban garden. The projecting bed which divides the back garden disguises its square shape and gives an illusion of much larger space. Planted with richly contrasting foliage – *Stipa gigantea*, *Lomatia tinctoria*, a bronze hazel, *Acer brilliantissimum*, the Adam's needle Yucca, *Photinia* and golden and copper beech – the curving beds hide a lichen wooden seat under the shelter of a weeping pear and a statue of Pandora tucked away in a little sylvan glade.

The garden was developed bit by bit over the years, and among the tender plants flourishing there are *Cytisus battandieri* the pineapple broom, *Trachycarpus fortunei*, the herbaceous *Clematis integrifolia* as well as a number of plants particularly appreciated by flower arrangers: species of *Phormium*, *Helleborus*, *Alchemilla mollis*, *Echinops* and *Miscanthus*.

Admission £2.50, by appointment only, tel. 021-893560. Suitable for wheelchairs and well-behaved children. Directions: Go through Douglas village and the roundabout, the house is the fifth entrance on the left after the golf club.

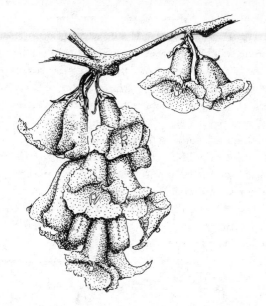

AMERGEN

Walshestown, Ovens, County Cork

ORNAMENTAL GARDEN

An intriguing young garden with much to delight the plantsperson.
Year-round interest.

Incredible as it may seem, ten years ago there was nothing but a field on the hill above the Inniscarra Lake where Christine Fehily's stunning garden now stands. After a digger had carved out what was to become a terrace and a long sweep of lawn between two gently curving borders, Chris set to work with a pick-axe in the dry summer of 1984 and began planting trees before her new home took shape.

The terrace in front of the house has a lovely prospect across the lake to the distant Derrynasaggart Mountains. The two-acre garden seems almost like an island floating high above the water and is full of the most enviable plants. The lawn is a green ribbon between two beds banked with shrubs and herbaceous plants. There are many choice plants: a bronze elder, *Sambucus* 'Guincho Purple', *Aristotelia variegata*, a cut-leaved alder *Alnus glutinosa* 'Imperialis', a contorted robinia *Robinia Pseudocacia* 'Tortuosa', *Abies spectabilis* with blue cones, *Picea spinulose*, the peeling barked *Acer griseum*, pretty pink-flowered *Indigofera*, scrambling pale blue *Codonopsis*, and the David Austin rose 'Abraham Darby' among many other old and modern roses.

Where the ground falls towards the lake, rock has been uncovered to create a natural feature with pockets of planting amid a wild dell where paths twist back and forth. Podophyllums grow among wild plants, the green-belled *Nicotiana langsdorfii* with blue stamens, the pink-flowered *Buddleia colvilei* and a *Styrax japonica* with a carpet of fallen white scented bells were some of the pleasing plants I saw in July.

Other features include a short avenue lined with a collection of birches and hollies, including the large-leaved *Ilex castaneafolia*, *Eucalyptus cordata* and the powdery blue *E. pulverulenta* grown from seed, a secret scented garden and a fruit garden. The terrace area is a riot of colour with penstemons, watsonias and angels' fishing rods (*Dierama*) among the bright hues.

Admission by appointment only. April-Sept. Donations towards upkeep accepted, tel. 021-331326. Directions: Go through Ballincollig on the N22; five miles/8 km on turn right up the hill at Tatler Jaks and Mother Kelly's pubs. Take the second turn on the right up a cul de sac. One mile further on look for the white gate piers with 'Amergen' on the wing wall.

ANNES GROVE

Castletownroche, County Cork

WILD GARDEN

*A Robinsonian garden of great
atmosphere, with many fine specimens.*

The lush wooded valley of the Awbeg River provided both the inspiration and the backdrop for the historic garden at Annes Grove. The earlier parts of the garden are of the same date as the charming creeper-covered eighteenth-century house. And the walled garden with its intriguing 'mount' or vantage point and the 'ornamental glen' mentioned in Arthur Young's tour of Ireland in the 1770s constituted the first embellishments of the estate.

The later garden was created by R.A. Grove Annesley, a keen plantsman and grandfather of the present owner, over a 60-year span. Some major gardens were created in Ireland during this period and gardening was one of the few expansive things in Ireland to emerge from the death of the Edwardian era. It may be that the exciting new species introduced through the great plant expeditions of the time provided the stimulus. Perhaps, too, at a difficult stage of history the estate owners poured their energies into their gardens.

There are three contrasting areas within the 30 acres of pleasure grounds - the walled garden, the glen and the riverside garden. Grove Annesley was a subscriber to the Kingdon Ward expeditions and the Robinsonian garden in the glen includes some of the earliest Kingdon Ward rhododendron introductions to Ireland, many of them grown from seed. Dozens of different species of rhododendrons and azaleas grow much as they would in the rhododendron forests of the Himalayas providing dazzling glimpses of colour and wafts of perfume amid the sheltering trees. Sadly, recent storms have caused damage in this area and some replanting is being carried out.

Among the choice specimens to be found along the woodland walks are *Hoheria*, *Cornus kousa*, *Camellia*, *Embothrium* and *Eucryphia*. And among the most spectacular of the huge collection of rhododendrons is a *R. cinnabarinum* var. blandiiflorum, its drooping red trumpet-shaped blossoms lined with gold, a stately *R. barbatum* with cinnamon bark and early crimson flowers (almost certainly from Kingdon Ward seed) and a *R. Wardii* named for Kingdon Ward with splotches of red inside its rich yellow flowers. Shrubs and trees from all over the world are planted as prescribed by William Robinson (who, we have seen, started out at Ballykilcavan) as though they had taken root naturally in a single garden of Eden.

The river garden, where *Lysichiton*, *Gunnera*, the umbrella plant *Peltiphyllum peltatum* and *Primula florindae* grow to enormous size, is almost tropical in its luxuriance. British soldiers stationed at the Fermoy barracks before World War I helped with the construction of rustic bridges which cross the river and lily pond to an island. Above the river there are limestone cliffs where the almost Mediterranean vegetation forms a complete contrast to the riverside jungle.

Inside the walled garden the features include a central path flanked by double herbaceous borders with purple drifts of *Thalictrum aquilegiifolium* (meadow rue) and the scarlet-flowered *Tropaeolum* (creeping nasturtium) climbing through the yew hedges. The rustic summer-house on the mount looks down on ribbon beds of clipped box and in a secluded corner there is a pond surrounded by water-loving plants. Tender plants like *Abutilon*, *Melianthus major* and *Corokia* flourish in this sheltered area.

Admission £2.50, £1.50 OAP, £1.00 children, open 17 March-30 Sept. Mon.-Sat. 10am-5pm, Sun. 1-6pm. Suitable for children. Groups by appointment, tel. 022-26145. Directions: Castletownroche is half-way between Mallow and Fermoy. Annes Grove is signposted from the village.

LISMORE CASTLE

Lismore, County Waterford

HISTORICAL INTEREST

A beguiling seven-acre garden with a romantic setting that should not be missed.

There could hardly be a more romantic setting for a garden than at Lismore Castle. The honey-coloured towers and turrets of the castle appear to float above the tree-clad banks of the beautiful Blackwater Valley. And although the entrance to the castle is in the centre of the market town the grounds are a haven of peace screened by encircling conifers and beeches.

Layer upon layer of history links Lismore Castle with Prince John of England, Sir Walter Raleigh, the Elizabethan adventurer Richard Boyle, and the Dukes of Devonshire.

The entrance to the gardens is through the outer defence of the Riding House and the Gate House which guards the entrance to the main courtyard. These and the fortified walls around the gardens are part of the castle stronghold built by Richard Boyle, first Earl of Cork, in 1620 on the site of two previous castles. The first, built by Prince John, was destroyed in 1190. The second, an episcopal palace, was leased by the notorious Bishop of Lismore Myler MacGrath to Sir Walter Raleigh, who in turn sold it to Richard Boyle.

The present castle, which forms a magnificent backdrop to the garden, is in the Victorian romantic tradition, designed by Joseph Paxton of Crystal Palace fame for the sixth Duke of Devonshire, whose grandfather inherited the castle from the Earls of Cork in 1753.

The sixth Earl, known as the 'Bachelor Duke', was also responsible for the Pleasure Grounds in the lower garden. Informally planted with wonderful flowering cherries, magnolia and rhododendron, the garden is filled with the scent of azaleas and bluebells in spring, when it is especially lovely. I like to imagine the Duke and Paxton, who began his career as the under-gardener and became the Duke's friend and adviser, supervising the making of special beds of peat brought from the Knockmealdown Mountains. At the lower end of the garden is the dark aisle of an ancient yew walk dating back to 1707.

The upper enclosure - a rare surviving Jacobean garden - is delightfully linked with the grounds by a staircase through the Riding House. Laid out by the first Earl of Cork in the 1620s the garden would originally have included walks through 'flowery meads', the existing Jacobean 'terras' and orchards of nectarine, peach, pear, cherry and apple. The range of flowers available then was much smaller - probably no more than a few hundred varieties - whereas now gardeners can choose from over a quarter of a million plants. It would be intriguing to suppose that Edmund Spenser wrote his amoretti sonnets to his second wife, Elizabeth, the golden-haired daughter of Richard Boyle, in this garden.

The present compartmentalised garden combines vegetable and flower gardens in the Victorian manner; some of the vineries designed by Paxton are still in use and a new orchard traversed by meadow paths has been planted by the present Duchess of Devonshire. A view of St Carthage's Cathedral is framed by the yew hedges and herbaceous borders of the central walk. The Broghill Tower at the south end of the terrace, where one of the Earl of Cork's sons fought off a siege in 1642, provides magnificent views of the castle and the Blackwater River.

Admission £2.50, £1.50 children, groups by appointment only, open daily mid May-Sept. 1.45-4.45pm except Sat, tel. 058-54424. Suitable for children but steps rule out wheelchairs. Directions: Entrance is off the main Waterford Youghal Road in the centre of the town.

TIMOLEAGUE
CASTLE GARDENS

Timoleague, County Cork

FLOWER GARDEN
Pleasant old-world garden, a good spot
for a family outing.

There is something wonderfully wicked about picking raspberries from someone else's garden (they have done the work and you get the pleasure). That is just what is on offer in the Travers' delightfully old-world garden on the shores of Courtmacsherry Bay. There is a soft fruit picking scheme there in season, in the walled kitchen garden.

The garden is on the edge of Timoleague village which takes its name Tigh Mo-Laga from an early monastic foundation. A frame of specimen trees on one side and views of the sea and a ruined thirteenth-century Franciscan friary on the other make an idyllic setting for the garden. There is a 'stump' of a thirteenth-century Barrymore castle in the grounds.

In front of the creeper-covered Edwardian house a wide games lawn with a picnic and play area overlooks the bay. Behind the house there are two walled gardens, one for fruit and one for flowers with a fine collection of old-fashioned herbaceous plants. A pretty feature has been made of potted *Dierama* which hang their angel's fishing rods over a bird bath. Palm trees and frost-tender shrubs grow in the shelter of the ruins of the old castle behind the house. Many of the trees and plants are helpfully labelled.

Admission £2.00, OAP £1.50, June-Aug. daily, 11am-6pm, other times by appointment, tel. 023-46116 or 021-831512. Directions: Timoleague is on the coast between Bandon and Clonakilty on the 602 Bandon Courtmacsherry Road.

THE GARDEN OF IRELAND

During the last century the Glens of Wicklow vied with the Ring of Kerry and the Lakes of Killarney as Ireland's most popular tourist attraction. Visitors would arrive by the trainload at the resort of Bray, then booming as the Brighton of Ireland, thanks to the rail link with Dublin and Dun Laoghaire built by William Dargan, a nineteenth-century entrepreneur, and completed in 1854.

Hackney carriages and horse-drawn cars lined up outside the station ready to take visitors to see Powerscourt waterfall and demesne, Glendalough, the Vale of Avoca, the Dargle Glen and other natural wonders. Many of the sightseers would base themselves in the fashionable hotels lining the seafront. The largest of them, the International, stood opposite Bray station and in 1882 charged the grand sum of two and sixpence a day for bedrooms, two shillings for luncheons and two and sixpence for dinners.

The attractions of the town included ballrooms and sea bathing as well as the Turkish baths (now gone) and the esplanade, both built by the enterprising Mr Dargan. But the greatest draw of all for Victorian tourists was the scenery: the dramatic grandeur of vales, glens, lakes and waterfalls created by Wicklow's short swift rivers and which appealed so much to nineteenth-century sensibilities. It is easy to see why sightseers were enchanted.

There is a wonderfully eccentric quality about Wicklow; maybe it has something to do with the extreme contrasts in scenery. The Mediterranean sweep of Killiney Bay is juxtaposed with the stark volcanic silhouette of the Sugarloaf Mountain. Within a few minutes of the idyllic woods and water of the Glencree Valley you come upon the twin lakes of Lough Bray, black and forbidding in the shadow of beetling escarpments. In the splendid isolation of the Cloghoge Valley,

Luggala Lodge appears like a sugarspun gothic fantasy beside the peat-brown water of Lough Tay. Drive across bleak, empty mountainscape through the Sally Gap, take the road that runs west beside the young River Liffey and you emerge beside the Blessington Lakes surrounded by parkland and pasture.

There is a slightly schizophrenic nature to the county too. Wicklow has two sides to its character; the exotic coastal strip where Mediterranean trees like mimosa and arbutus grow and rare plants flourish contrasts with the wild expanse of the Wicklow Hills which takes up most of the county. You can stand on the summit of Djouce, look south west and see nothing but fold upon fold of empty hills rolling to the horizon and to Lugnaquilla, the second-highest mountain in Ireland.

To this day the military road built by the British forces after the rebellion of 1798 in order to rout the rebels from their mountain hideaways is the only road running north/south through the heart of the hills. The former barracks at Glencree and at Glenmalure are a reminder of the way the hills have always provided a refuge to rebels and a threat to the Pale - the English enclave around Dublin.

The county's two different names are another indication of its turbulent past. The Irish name Cill Mhantain dates back to the landing of St Patrick and his companion Mantan in the fifth century at the mouth of the Vartry River. Their arrival sowed the seed which led to the establishment of Glendalough. Rumours of gold and the rich pickings to be had from Christian settlements brought the Vikings to exactly the same spot, and the name Wicklow derives from Vykingalo, the ninth-century Viking settlement established there.

Few counties in Ireland can offer such a variety of attractions: there are the great estates like Russborough and Powerscourt, the early Christian settlement of Glendalough, wonderful gardens like Mount Usher and Killruddery, Kilquade and Graigueconna, as well as several dozen gardens open during the Wicklow Gardens Festival (tel. 0404-69117) in late May and June, the fabulous strand at Brittas Bay, Avondale, the home of Charles Stewart Parnell, a dozen top-class restaurants and wonderful riding and walking in scenery every bit as spectacular in its own way as the west of Ireland.

ROUND AND ABOUT

The seafront at Bray still evokes its Victorian heyday with sugar almond coloured villas stretching beside the esplanade between the Martello Terrace (where James Joyce once lived with his parents), and the rocky hill of Bray Head. Right at the southern end of the front is an establishment where you can dine in great style - The Tree of Idleness, which takes Greek-based cuisine into the realms of the sublime. The late Akis Courtellas fled the Turkish invasion of Cyprus in 1974 and opened his Bray restaurant in 1977 naming it for his family's former restaurant overlooking the sea among the citrus groves near Kyrenia.

Tucked away in an alley just beside Bray station there is a very different brand of ethnic cuisine - a pizzeria called Pizzas and Cream, and although it is Irish run, the pizzas are the real thing, baked to order.

The Victorian tourist trail from Bray, the N11, runs beside the Dargle River through the Valley of Diamonds, so called because of the sparkling water created by the confluence of the Dargle and Cookstown Rivers.

There is a spectacular walk above the Dargle Glen along a road which was specially created by the Powerscourt family for a visit of George IV so that he could see the river raging through the deep ravine from the comfort of his carriage. He never used the road, but a track remains, starting above the beautiful riverside garden created by Sir Basil and Lady Valerie Goulding, winding past the 300-foot/91.5 m drop of Lover's Leap and ending beside the main gates of the Powerscourt estate.

Enniskerry village is very much a landlord village, carefully planned and laid out by the paternalistic Wingfields. Poppy's - a cheerful coffee shop furnished in country kitchen style - is excellent for light meals and has the most sinful cakes. There are several other sources of temptation in the village in the shape of gift and clothes shops. About two miles/ 3.2 km up the Glencree Road the Kilmolin nursery, signed to the right from the peak of the hill, has reasonably priced hardy plants and shrubs. Further up the Glencree Valley with wonderful views across to Powerscourt and Tonduff Mountain is Enniscree Lodge, a favoured spot for dinner after a day in the hills, or Sunday lunch.

The Avoca Handweavers shop on the N11 at Kilmacanogue is

another source of temptation. The attractive centre in the grounds of Glencormac House has a restaurant serving imaginative light meals. (To get to it you have to run the gauntlet of a shop packed with gorgeous clothes and gifts.) To work off the after-effects, the walk through Djouce Woods (on the Enniskerry Roundwood Road) and up Djouce Mountain can make one feel on top of the world. The Devil's Glen (take the Annamoe Road from Ashford) has a lovely walk through the woods beside the Vartry River. The Bel Air Hotel signed from Ashford on the road to Rathdrum is a colourful watering spot frequented by horsey characters, and scenes reminiscent of the *Irish RM* can develop.

My favourite discovery in Wicklow town is the Church of the Vine on Church Hill, where the Vikings used to light beacons. Built on the site of an earlier church and incorporating some of its stones, the baptismal register dates back to 1655, the roof trusses are an unusual sunburst design and the strange tower was added by the Eaton family in 1777. Below it is the Murrough, its sheltered waters once a haven for Viking ships but now a wild fowl sanctuary.

Just outside Laragh, Glendalough, site of the sixth-century monastery founded by St Kevin with its spectacular lakeside remains, is a must on every tourist's list and is well described elsewhere. The drive from Laragh to Rathdrum through the wooded Avonmore Valley and the Meeting of the Waters in the Vale of Avoca are especially lovely.

Roundwood is regarded as having the distinction of boasting the highest pub in Ireland and the Roundwood Inn has been in business since the seventeenth-century and offers an original restaurant menu which can include dishes like Wiener schnitzel and crayfish.

Newtownmountkennedy is a favourite stopping-off point for lunch at Harvey's Bistro, tel. 2819203 (which makes a point of serving the best of potatoes - real balls of flour), and a browse at the Wicklow Fly Fishers (source of waxed jackets, cords, knits and smart Continental outfits).

The prettiest part of west Wicklow on the other side of the mountains is around the Blessington Lakes which make an idyllic setting for Russborough House, Richard Castle's Palladian masterpiece built for the first Earl of Milltown in 1741 and now open to the public, tel. 045-65239. The Poulaphuca Inn to the right just after the bridge on the main Blessington Baltinglass Road retains some of the character it used to have in the days when it catered for passengers travelling out by tram from Dublin to the lakes.

The Wicklow Gardens Festival, running from the last weeks of May to the third week in June, is now a hardy annual. It makes a specially good start or finish for overseas garden tours and includes a combination of Heritage properties, special events and private gardens which are open on specific days during the festival. They range from old-world gardens like Warble Bank, Newtownmountkennedy - with wonderful old roses and a cutting garden - to a tiny garden packed with unusual plants at Sidmonton Square, Bray. Some of these, encouraged by the enthusiastic response of visitors, are now open by appointment during spring and summer. One of my favourites is Knockmore, above the Dargle River near Enniskerry. The century-old garden has a Robinsonian dell with a cascade, a potager, fountains of old roses backing double herbaceous borders, a cowslip meadow and even a genteel gardening ghost. Tel. 2867336. For a brochure on the festival, contact Wicklow County Tourism, St Manntan's House, Wicklow Town, County Wicklow, tel. 0404-66058, fax 0404-66057.

PLACES TO STAY

Hunter's Hotel in Rathnew (run by the incomparable Mrs Gelletlie) is an old coaching inn. The dining room, where the Irish version of *cuisine grandmère* is served on starched white tablecloths, looks out over an old knot garden and lawns sloping down to the Vartry River. There are 17 old-world bedrooms with the comfiest of beds (I spent my honeymoon night in one of them). Hunter's is a splendid place for afternoon tea and everything is home-made down to the jelly made from apples grown in the kitchen garden. B & B from £45.00 per person, dinner from £21.50, open all year, tel. 0404-40106.

Tinakilly House, Rathnew, is a magnificent monument to Victorian enterprise built by Captain Robert Halpin who made his fortune laying the first transatlantic cable. The impressive double oak staircase and gallery in the hallway are reminiscent of the bridge of a ship. William and Bee Power have enhanced the feeling of Victorian opulence. In the 1870 house there are 26 rooms. B & B £58-£74.00, dinner £28.50, tel. 0404-69274.

TINAKILLY HOUSE

At the Old Rectory just on the outskirts of Wicklow town Linda and Paul Saunders have made a virtue of green cuisine. Delightfully original dishes like Dublin lawyer (lobster sautéed in cream and whiskey sauce), or smoked salmon parcels tied with chives come to the table garnished with fresh flowers and herbs, seafood is caught locally and vegetables are organically grown. Staying there is like being a guest in a country home. Maximum 10 guests. B & B from £46.00, dinner £27.00, tel. 0404-67048.

Converted from a former Queen Anne stables, Rathsallagh House is a long creeper-clad building set in a 500-acre estate. There is an old walled garden and fine old specimen trees; a country house atmosphere prevails with happy touches like log fires and an indoor swimming pool. Open all year except for Christmas. B & B £55-£85.00, dinner from £27.00, tel. 045-403112.

Derrybawn House is set in a beautiful wooded valley just outside Laragh. It is reasonably priced and family run, tel. 0503-75282.

BALLYORNEY HOUSE

Enniskerry, County Wicklow

FLOWER GARDEN

An old summer garden showing sensitive restoration.

The Sugarloaf Mountain, framed by the formal gardens at Powerscourt Demesne, is surely the best-known view in County Wicklow. At Ballyorney, thought to have been the dower house of Powerscourt, the conical mountain is also a focal point for the garden.

The delightful two-acre compartmentalised garden at Ballyorney has, in a sense, come full circle. Originally created in the 1920s by Colonel and Mrs Claude Raill, the garden has been restored by their daughter, the distinguished gardener Mrs Rosemary Brown, for the new owner of the house, Mark Kavanagh.

The garden is a good object-lesson for anyone facing the sensitive task of restoring an old-fashioned garden. And although there has been major reconstruction and replanting around the main features, the garden looks as though it has always been there.

The original double herbaceous and shrub borders have been

Admission: House and gardens, £2.50; garden only, £2.00. Open during the 3-week Wicklow Gardens Festival (tel. 0404-69117) 2-4pm. The house and gardens are also open to the public on weekdays for three weeks in June, the first week in July and the last two weeks in September, 11am-3pm, groups by appointment. Not suitable for wheelchairs. Directions: Two miles/3.2 km from Enniskerry on the Roundwood Waterfall Road.

retained and realigned so that they frame the Sugarloaf in one direction and an imposing Venetian doorway in the other. The transition between the classical severity of this architectural feature and the informal planting of the garden is bridged by a newly created formal terrace paved in granite. In the shelter of a restored beech hedge new herbaceous beds and lawns have supplanted the former kitchen garden, and climbing roses have been trained through the old apple trees in the orchard.

The garden paths were laid out so as to take full advantage of mountain vistas. From the stone bench at the top of the herb garden with its topiaried yew and box hedging you are rewarded with a distant view of Djouce Mountain. The banks of a deep stream running through the garden have been uncovered, cascades and steps created and new terracing planted with hostas, ferns, bamboo, primulas and other damp-loving plants. The rustic theme is echoed by cottage *orné* effect, designed by architect Johnny O'Connell, which cleverly disguises a blank wall of the house.

The garden at Ballyorney provides a great deal of interest and variety in a small area and won the Bord Fáilte award (private garden category) in 1990. Work on the garden, carried out by landscape contractor Philip Brightling and maintained by Frank Lynch, is ongoing. Thousands of bulbs are being planted under the trees and in the long term Mark Kavanagh hopes to reintroduce many of the old-fashioned plants which were a feature of Irish gardens in the pre-war era.

KILLRUDDERY

Bray, County Wicklow

HISTORICAL INTEREST

A rare insight into seventeenth-century gardening in the grand manner in a most entrancing setting.

There is a naive painting in the study in Killruddery House which shows the layout of the estate as it was in the early eighteenth century. All the main features shown in that painting are still there nearly 300 years later.

The grounds present a rare example of a Baroque design. The twin canals, the fountain pool, the geometric clipped hedges known as the Angles, and the sylvan theatre are the almost unique survivors of a style that was swept away by the vogue for romantic landscaped grounds in the eighteenth century. The emphasis during the Baroque period was on grand formal design and grounds were seen as an extension of the geometry of buildings. Trees, hedges, water and paths were laid out in a geometric fashion and embellished with classical statuary, pavilions, terraces and fountains. Pleasure grounds were designed to entertain and impress those who strolled within their confines with their harmony and order. Gardening on this scale was not for those of slender means: the gardens at Longleat in Somerset, laid out at the same time, cost £30,000.

Killruddery estate has been owned by the Earls of Meath for 350 years and the garden, laid out by Monsieur Bonet in 1682, shows strongly the formal French influence. (The nearby garden of Powerscourt laid out a century and a half later in the more flamboyant Italian style makes an interesting contrast.)

The pair of canals, known as the Long Ponds, are over 500 feet/ 152 m long and resemble those at the Chateau de Courances. They stretch out to the south of the house, their impressive perspective continued by a venerable avenue of limes. To the east the ground rises in a series of terraces to the rocky outcrop at the foot of Bray Head, and between these two features are the Angles. Laid out in five avenues radiating from a circle they are in the design known as *patte d'oie* or goose foot. These devices, designed either as vantage points for riders or to offer walkers different vistas, are now extremely rare.

The sylvan theatre is enclosed by beech hedges and the audience sits on the tiers of a grass amphitheatre. It would make a most perfect place to perform *A Midsummer Night's Dream*. The circular fountain pool is encircled by double beech hedges with cast iron statues of the four seasons standing guard at each entrance. Behind the pool, with a lovely vista of the Little Sugarloaf as a backdrop, is the rectangular wood known as the Wilderness, crossed by a grid of paths.

The splendid Victorian conservatory to the west of the house was designed by William Burns in 1852, and had a dome designed by Richard Turner. The two parterres beyond the conservatory are also nineteenth-century additions and the ornamental dairy built against the garden wall and designed by Sir George Hodson is a charming feature. The house, Killruddery, an 1820s Tudor revival design, enclosing an earlier house and designed by Richard Morrison and his son Vitruvius, is still the home of the Earl and Countess of Meath.

Admission £2.50, open daily May, June, Sept. 1-5pm. At other times by special arrangement for groups. Suitable for children, partially suitable for wheelchairs. The house may also be seen by groups by special arrangement, tel. (Dublin) 2863405. Directions: Just outside Bray on the right-hand side of the Greystones Road.

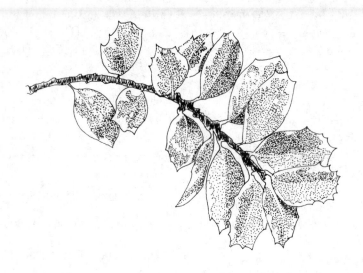

STILEBAWN COTTAGE

Crowe Lane, Kilmacanogue, County Wicklow

FLOWER GARDEN AND ARBORETUM

A cleverly planned informal garden with a wonderful collection of trees.

When they moved to Stilebawn Cottage it was a toss-up whether the Austens would graze a horse or make a garden from a rocky wilderness. Plants won. And

25 years later a wonderfully varied garden has taken shape in the two-acre site. A small formal garden planted with old shrub roses, herbs and bearded irises, an informal arboretum and a shrub and herbaceous garden are the main features. With lots of spring bulbs and good autumn colour the garden provides year-round interest.

The young specimen trees are particularly rewarding and there is a good collection of weeping trees: Perry's weeping silver holly, weeping lime and ash. Among the several varieties of birch are the lovely white *Jacquemontii* and the pink-barked *Albo sinensis*. Other intriguing trees include *Prunus serrula* with its coppery peeling bark, the golden-tipped *Picea orientalis* 'Aurea', and the Siberian spruce (*Picea omorika*) with its upturned tips. There are over 90 different varieties of rhododendron in the garden.

The shrub and herbaceous area is cleverly planned with two long beds of hybrid tea roses with the lovely droopy arms of a *Cedrus atlantica* 'Pendula' at their head as an unexpected focal point. There is a hidden pond, splendid contrasts between the colour and form of shrubs, and a herbaceous border full of sun-loving plants. Many of the trees and shrubs are labelled and the Austens are knowledgeable about a collection which has a great deal to interest the plantsperson. Hens pecking in the orchard and a vegetable garden add to the cottagey feel of the place.

Admission £2.00, groups by appointment, open April-Sept. Teas by arrangement, tel. (Dublin) 2867185. Level grass areas should be accessible for wheelchairs, fine for children. Directions: Turn off the Dublin Wexford Road at Kilmacanogue, take the right fork for Enniskerry, 109 yards/ 100 metres on take a sharp right-hand turn up the Rocky Valley Drive and look for three letterboxes on the left-hand side. Stilebawn is a quarter-mile/.4 km down the laneway on the left.

AVONDALE

Rathdrum, County Wicklow

ARBORETUM

*A favourite place for family outings
and picnics.*

The Avonmore Valley - known
as the Vale of Clara - is one of
the most beautiful in Wicklow. The
swift golden brown river tumbles
along a wide bed between the
ancient oak woods climbing the
sides of gentle mountains -
Derrybawn, Cullentragh and Kirikee

to the west and Trooperstown Hill
to the east.

Avondale, the home of Charles
Stewart Parnell, is situated at the
southern end of the vale, flanked by
one of the loveliest stretches of the
river. The champion of home rule
was born in the house and lived
there all his life. It is a pleasant
house of modest size completed in
1779 with some elegant features - a
Bossi fireplace, a splendid hall with
handsome plasterwork - and has
been beautifully restored. Filled with
Parnell memorabilia including some
fine cartoons from the period, it is
open to the public.

Trees are the great glory of the
523-acre estate at Avondale, which

became a forestry school when the estate was handed over to the then British government in 1904. A magnificent ride with views of the valley and hills is laid out as a 'forest' garden with trees planted in square-acre plots. This section was planned by A.C. Forbes, Director of Forestry in Ireland, who worked closely with the famous plant collector Augustine Henry, and there is a grove at Avondale (between the house and the forest plots) dedicated to his memory. Among the many interesting specimens are some of his own introduction, including *Rhododendron henryi* and *Pinus armandii*.

Some of the stateliest trees are to be found down by the river, where the whispering of giant Sequoias and the graceful Tsuga mingles with the burbling water. There is also an arboretum dating back to the early 1900s where there are some rare trees including the *Picea koyamae* native of Japan. The oldest trees on the estate are the beeches, which are now over 200 years old and were planted by Samuel Hayes, the original owner of the house. There

is a pleasant three and a half mile/5.6 km walk beside the river.

Further down the valley Castle Howard looks out over the Meeting of the Waters made famous in the Percy French song, and behind it is Cronebane Hill topped by the Mottee Stone, the legendary hurling stone of Finn McCool. The annual Parnell Summer School is held at Avondale.

Admission £1.00, cars £2.00, open daily 10am-1pm and 2-6pm, tel. 0404-46111. Tea shop, toilet facilities. Wonderful for children, partially accessible to wheelchairs. Directions: From Dublin take the N11, turn off at Rathnew and take the R752 to Rathdrum; Avondale is signposted one mile/1.6 km south.

VALCLUSA

Waterfall Road, Enniskerry,

County Wicklow

FLOWER GARDEN

Charming hillside garden with plenty to reward the plantsperson.

I n still weather the sound of the Powerscourt waterfall drifts across the deer meadow to this intriguing garden at the foot of Long Hill. A spring which flows through a series of small pools, and the sloping site, add to its character.

Valclusa House dates back to around 1830 and may have been built as a dower house for the Powerscourt estate. The ornamental trees in the four-acre grounds - redwoods, silver firs and Lawson cypress - date from the same time as extensive planting of north-western American conifers, carried out at Powerscourt to provide relief during one of a succession of potato famines.

A venerable tulip tree with

Clematis armandii growing through it, a fine *Cornus capitata* and early-flowering rhododendrons provided the framework for the plan laid out during the 1960s by Eithne MacWeeney, which included a hillside rockery, a small pool garden and two strategically placed rustic summer houses which afford vistas of the garden beside the tinkling stream. The garden has been restored and extended by the next generation: Susan and Duncan Forsythe.

The planting in the garden is carefully planned so that there is year-round colour. Around trees and shrubs are planted hundreds of spring bulbs, snowdrops, crocuses, scillas and daffodils; these are overplanted with a huge selection of more than 400 herbaceous perennials which take over when the bulbs have died back.

A golden yew, an *Olearia forestii* and a *Magnolia sieboldii* are among the shrubs providing contrasting form and colour beside the paths winding through the rockery. And a lawn flanked by irregular beds and the stream winds up the hill to an arched gateway. The colour scheme in this area of the garden changes completely between spring when *Azalea mollis, Corylopsis,* daffodils and narcissi create a yellow and white scheme, and summer when blue, pink and silver colours predominate among *Lobelia* 'Dark Crusader', *Anaphalis, Aconitum,* foxgloves and perennial geraniums.

There are particularly good collections of old shrub roses, perennial geraniums and hostas. One of the very pleasing things about this garden is that all of the unusual perennials growing there can be purchased *in situ,* and there is also a choice collection of uncommon shrubs.

A new area at the top of the garden includes a butterfly garden which attracts insects from four different types of habitat nearby, and a number of interesting and covetable plants including turtle head or *Chelone obliqua, Acanthus* 'Lady Moore', *Celmisia* and *Strobilanthes atropurpureum.* The waterfall terrace has a wonderful view across the valley to the cascade. Interesting planting ideas in the garden include the use of variegated bamboo (*Sasa veitchii*) around the base of trees to provide winter colour, and combinations like the blues of lacecap hydrangea and monkshood mixed with the glaucous foliage of *Kniphofia caulescens.*

Throughout the year there is an unfolding display of more than 400 different varieties of herbaceous perennials, among them over eighty different types of perennial geraniums, from the palest silvery pink *G. endressii* to the double purple *G. himalayense,* and over thirty different varieties of hosta.

Admission £2.50, open May-Aug. Sat.-Sun. Unusual plants for sale, suitable for children but not wheelchairs. Teas. Tel. (Dublin) 2869485. Directions: Turn off the N11 for Enniskerry, take the Roundwood Waterfall Road and follow the signs for the waterfall. Valclusa is on the left at the bottom of the steep hill just before the entrance to the waterfall.

POWERSCOURT GARDENS

Enniskerry, County Wicklow

FORMAL GARDEN,

HISTORICAL INTEREST

A magnificent formal garden in an incomparable setting.

Powerscourt must be the best known of all Irish gardens. Breathtaking even on picture postcards, the dramatic view of its terraces and fountain with the perfect cone of the Sugarloaf Mountain as a backdrop must have dropped through letterboxes all over the world inspiring untold numbers of visitors to come and see it for themselves.

Richard Castle (Cassel), architect of Leinster House and Russborough, designed the imposing Palladian palazzo for Viscount Powerscourt in 1741. To provide a fitting frame for the house within the spectacular landscape, he created a series of terraces around a circular lake enhancing the view across the valley to the Sugarloaf.

A century later Daniel Robertson was employed to embellish the landscape in the fashionable Italian manner. The garden at Powerscourt is believed to be based on the Villa Butera in Sicily. The main features remained but they were accented by a broad terrace in front of the house with a great staircase down to a very grand fountain, and a statuary walk leading down to the pool. Classic urns, the black and white pebble mosaics of the stairs and a pair of winged pegasi guarding the pool all add to the grandeur of the design.

Daniel Robertson was in a bad way at the time; he occasionally had to hide in the attics of the house to avoid debt collectors and sought inspiration for his work in drink. He suffered from gout and had to direct gardening operations from a wheelbarrow, bottle in hand. He never completed his design, though this was not because of his habits but because the sixth Viscount Powerscourt died and his successor did not come of age until some time later. The design was eventually completed by another Robertson - Alexander - who came to Powerscourt as a gardener, followed Daniel's plans and added rare plants and trees, statues and ornamental gates.

The prelude to this wonderful garden is a drive through stately 200-year-old beeches with views down into the Dargle Valley. The drive sweeps past the remains of the great house, which was tragically gutted in a fire in 1974 just as the current owners, the Slazenger family, were planning to open the house to the public. The entrance to the garden is beyond the south wing of the house through an ornate gateway which came from Bavaria. A broad walk leads past a rose garden and lawns with ornamental beds. To the right a walk between magnificent double herbaceous borders leads to another decorative gateway wrought with gilded roses, thistles and shamrocks symbolising England, Scotland and Ireland.

Beyond this gateway a pool mirroring evergreen shrubs and conifers sets the mood for the less formal areas of the gardens. Further afield there is an Edwardian 'Japanesey' garden, the main claim to oriental influence being a red lacquered bridge, stone lanterns and groups of acers around a pleasant dell.

A woodland walk planted with rhododendrons and interesting conifers, including *Pinus coulteri* with its ten-inch cones, blue cedars and golden larches, has as its focal point a pepper-pot tower atop a hill. A monkey puzzle avenue is a splendid reminder of Victorian taste. The gardens are particularly lovely in spring when flowering shrubs and trees - magnolias, prunus, rhododendrons and azaleas - are in bloom. The grounds are in the wider setting of a magnificent estate with woodland walks and the River Dargle running through the valley. Plans are being floated to re-instate Powerscourt House, which incorporates the massive walls of an earlier castle built by the de la Poers.

Admission £2.80, open mid March-end Oct. 9.30am-5.30pm. Suitable for children, partially accessible to wheelchairs. Garden centre, restaurant, toilet facilities, shop, tel. (Dublin) 2867676. Directions: Turn off the N11 Dublin Wexford Road for Enniskerry, in the village take the Roundwood Road; the gates are at the top of the hill on the right.

MOUNT USHER

Ashford, County Wicklow

WILD GARDEN

An unforgettable garden with a splendid collection of trees and shrubs combined with naturalised flowers in the Robinsonian manner.

Mount Usher is a perfect example of the kind of naturalised garden William Robinson had in mind when he published *The Wild Garden* in 1870. The 20 acres of grounds have a marvellous location on the banks of the Vartry where the river, crossed by graceful bridges and sparkling with cascades, affords the most beautiful vistas.

The planting works superbly on two different levels. There are breathtaking displays of colour and enchanting prospects to appeal to everyone: maple walks which blaze crimson and gold in autumn, azalea avenues with a scented haze of pinks, yellows and whites. There are meadows carpeted with a succession of naturalised flowers, snowdrops, daffodils, tulips and lilies; and winding paths reveal new vistas and eye-catching plants at every turn.

For connoisseurs there is a fascinating array of rare specimens awaiting discovery among the more showy plants. And among the 5,000 trees and shrubs there are three collections for which Mount Usher is particularly noted: *Eucalyptus* (there are about 40 different species with the tallest growing to 111.5-124.7 ft/34-38 m), *Nothofagus* (southern hemisphere beeches) and *Eucryphia*.

A series of delightful vistas has been created around the garden. The first is the maple walk which frames a view of the river where the banks are planted with three different varieties of skunk cabbage. Meandering paths then lead through the woodland area where rhododendrons, magnolias, tree ferns and unusual specimens are sheltered beneath a canopy of oak. Species of *Erythronium*, *Trillium* and *Helleborus* carpet the glades. Among the sights to delight plantspeople are a *Gevuina avellana*, *Lapageria rosea* and in spring spectacular clumps of deep crimson *Trillium chloropetalum*.

The azalea ride is the next delight and although this is at its most spectacular in May/June there is a great deal of interest during the rest of the year including one of the jewels of this garden: the silvery blue Montezuma pine and some of the 150 species of rhododendrons which feature throughout the garden. Cross the river via a narrow rainbow arc of a bridge and if you search carefully you will find the secret fern garden where you can experience the sensation of walking on water without getting your feet wet.

The arboretum at the far end of the garden is divided by the Vartry with the evergreen thickets of *Eucryphia* on one side and the soaring *Eucalyptus* on the other. Under them I found my favourite sight in spring: a carpet of *Fritillaria* nodding their checked heads in the breeze. The palm walk provides a further vista back towards house and river.

In the island area of the garden the herbaceous collection which had fallen away is being built up once more. New species are being introduced, brought back from the wild by plant expeditions to the four corners of the globe.

The garden also has an important scientific side behind the scenes. There are specimens on the threatened plant list - like the Japanese *Trochodendron aralioides* -

which are being propagated and shared with other botanical collections. The garden's rare species of *Podophyllum* is being researched as a cancer cure.

The garden was created by the Walpole family. Edward Walpole fell in love with the beautiful valley and bought the lease on the old mill beside the river in 1868. He gave the acre of land and the mill to his sons, Edward, George and Thomas, who added more land and carried out extensive planting; the work was continued in the next generation by Horace Walpole and the property was sold by his son Robert to Madeline Jay in 1980. The garden is

Admission £3.00, OAP £1.50, groups £1.70, open 17 March-31 Oct. Mon.-Sat. 10.30am-6pm, tel. 0404-40116. Suitable for children, partially accessible to wheelchairs. Pleasant tea rooms, clothes and craft shops. Directions: On the main Dublin Wexford Road at Ashford.

now cared for by a team of three, headed by John Anderson, who trained at Kew Gardens. A book in which the genus and origins of every plant introduced to the garden between 1870 and 1916 has been recorded was recently returned to Mount Usher by the Walpole descendants. Many of the earliest additions came from the now threatened collection of the great plantsman Thomas Acton at Kilmacurragh.

Part of the charm of the garden is the way wild and exotic plants are mixed together. No chemicals are used, strimmers have been banned, the meadows are mown just once a year six weeks after the last wave of bloom when the seeds of the flowers have scattered. William Robinson would have approved.

NATIONAL GARDEN EXHIBITION CENTRE

Kilquade, County Wicklow

HISTORICAL INTEREST

Fourteen contrasting garden designs interlinked in a pleasing plan to provide inspiration for new and seasoned gardeners alike.

The idea behind the exhibition centre beside Calumet nurseries is a novel one. If there are display centres for kitchens and bathrooms, why not a centre where people can see plants and garden features in situ, reasoned Tim Wallace of Calumet. 'The biggest problem was that people could not imagine what their gardens were going to look like,' says Tim. He also felt that it was important to demystify gardening for people who were new to it.

Tim and his wife Suzanne shared the idea with designer Gordon Ledbetter one winter night, and two years ago and £180,000 later the National Garden Exhibition Centre was born. Fourteen contrasting gardens took shape where the plastic tunnels for the nursery once stood, each one designed by a leading contractor or designer. The gardens are now coming into their own, as plants and shrubs begin to mature and fill out the designs. They range from low budget, low maintenance gardens that can be created for as little as £700, like Richard Joyce's Periphery Garden, to a water extravaganza with a recycled stream flowing endlessly down rocky

Admission £2.50.

Open Mon.-Sat. 10am-6pm,

Sun. 1-6pm. Directions:

Turn left at Kilpedder off the

N11 heading south. The centre

is clearly signposted.

cascades into a lake, or to Robert Myerscough's acid garden which cost £10,000 to create.

The latest addition to the display solves the challenge of fitting a fountain, play area, paths, grass, a barbecue area and borders into an average size town garden, without breaking the bank. The attractive plan, which won the Bord Gais competition for a family garden, also includes a sand pit (for later conversion into a pond), and provides the 'tinkle factor' in the shape of a cascade falling into a stone trough – all within a budget of £2,500.

The centre illustrates the point that gardens do not have to be grand or expensive to be deeply satisfying. With good planning and interesting plants the smallest garden becomes a place in which to relax. Tim finds that people relate most readily to the smaller gardens, especially the town garden, with its pool, lush planting and raised beds ingeniously edged with sleepers by Philip Brightling and the country garden with its spring burbling through a millstone and pretty herbaceous planting designed by Andrew Collier.

My absolute favourite is Verney Naylor's Contemplative Garden which has a strong Japanese influence. Stepping stones set in pale granite gravel create paths which wind around irregular raised beds filled with soothing green foliage plants: hostas, *Acer*, ferns and grasses. The design is very low maintenance. There isn't a blade of grass to be mown and the idea could be adapted to all kinds of locations, from the smallest front garden to a separate area within a larger garden.

There are gardens for specific types of conditions: the acid garden which is intriguingly constructed out of blocks of cut turf, a seaside garden with salt tolerant plants and a relaxed water and woodland garden, planted with shrubs like the foxglove tree *Paulownia tomentosa*, dogwoods, the bronze beech *Fagus riversii* and drifts of spring bulbs. The Irish garden, featuring native Irish plants and Irish crafts from thatching to basket-making, may be of particular interest to overseas visitors.

There are all kinds of eye-catching features and plants at the centre. The herb knot designed by Susan Maxwell, which combines the idea of a medieval knotte or geometric garden with a herb plot, shows that flowering plants are not the only way of creating colour. Lavender, variegated sage, rosemary and crimson *Berberis bagatelle* provide a wonderfully contrasting pattern.

Among the other intriguing services on offer at Calumet are garden design by post (Andrew Collier creates plans for a fee of £85 to fit individual requirements), a forty-minute guided tour of the gardens (for no extra charge), and a new conservatory centre particularly good for shrubs and for plants which will tolerate seaside conditions.

SHEKINA

Kirikee, Glenmalure, County Wicklow

FORMAL GARDEN

A magnificent formal garden in an incomparable setting.

Talking with visitors touring gardens during the June Wicklow Gardens Festival about the new gardens they had seen, the name 'Shekina' kept coming up. 'Interesting and different,' my informants said. And Shekina is very different. Its concept reaches back to the paradise gardens of the Middle Ages and biblical times, which were created to foster peace of mind and dedicated to worship. Situated in one of the most beautiful valleys in Wicklow, beside the Avonbeg River, Shekina is about spirituality, not in the strict religious sense, but rather in fostering a level of deeper awareness.

'It is a garden for using your senses,' says its creator Catherine McCann. The pleasures in this garden come not from traditional arrangements of flowers and shrubs, but from the peaceful surroundings and a collection of unusual sculptures - each representing a particular aspect of the mystery of the Creation. It is not just what you see, but what the sculptures say to you that makes them special.

At present there are ten works of art sited around the pleasant, sloping garden with its meandering stream, miniature waterfalls, lily pools and backdrops of multi-coloured foliage. All of them are by Irish sculptors and each in its own way is symbolic. Among them is a fascinating naturalistic sculpture in 4,000-year-old bog yew by Michael Casey, the grains and knots brought more vividly alive by regular anointment with linseed oil. Other favourites with visitors include Dreamer's Rest - a fractured bench in which the faces of a mother and child are revealed in Kilkenny limestone - by Noel Scullion, and Lovers - the hand of a man and a woman, steepled in union - by Imogen Stuart. Catherine's latest acquisition, the second Fred Conlon piece in the collection, has the intriguing title

'Níl mar a shiltear bitear' (Things are not what they seem).

Catherine McCann has developed her own personal philosophy around each of the works and printed them in a leaflet as thought provoking as the garden is inspirational. I am sure that more than a few visitors leave determined to include a sculpture in their own gardens in future. They may also leave with some intriguing new perspective on life. Gardens are as much about gardeners as they are about plants. Catherine McCann is one of life's catalysts. A writer, physiotherapist and counsellor, she uses the garden as an aspect of teaching stress management and when I met her was working on a book about retirement called *Falling in Love with Life*.

When she came to Shekina – the name comes from the biblical concept of the presence of God in a place – there was a strip of grass and a barn filled with wrecked cars. The present acre with its breakfast arbour, miniature Japanese bridge and gazebo was won back from wilderness. Catherine dug out the ponds herself, using a crowbar to prise out the rocks, and does all her major gardening projects in winter – a great way of keeping warm!

Admission, which includes a cup of tea, is by donation, which goes to charity.

Open by appointment, tel. 0404-46128 or 2838711. Directions: Via Laragh/Glenmalure turning left at the Glenmalure crossroads; or via Rathdrum/Greenan. At Greenan veer right and continue for one and a half miles/2.4 km. Shekina is painted green and is the first house on the left.

GRAIGUECONNA

Old Connaught Avenue,

Bray, County Wicklow

HISTORICAL INTEREST

A mature old-world garden packed with interest.

The garden at Graigueconna belongs to that loveliest of breeds: the multi-generational garden, and has the best of all possible combinations: old bones graced by a mature garden created by dedicated plantspeople. Not only time but inherited knowledge and plants combine to make it very special.

The bones were contributed by the present owner's great-grandfather, Phineas Riall, and his grandson, Lewis Meredith, an alpine enthusiast. The latter went to extraordinary lengths to cater for his passion and actually built a railway line down the middle of the garden to carry stones for his one-and-a-half acre rock garden. The line of

the tracks is there to this day and now forms a grass path running down the centre of the garden between two breathtaking borders.

However, by the time Lewis' granddaughter, Rosemary Brown, and her husband, John, inherited the garden twenty-six years ago, the alpines of the rock garden had long disappeared and little remained apart from venerable crinodendrons, cordylines, mature trees and a myrtle, symbol of fertility, grown traditionally from a sprig in a bride's bouquet.

Admission £3.00, strictly by appointment, for groups of four or more, May-July, tel. 01-2822273. The garden is at its best in June.

Directions: Last house on the left going up Old Connaught Avenue from Bray.

Today the garden is full of unusual plants, many of them grown from seed or cuttings. The herbaceous walk, which forms the central axis of the garden, is like an aisle celebrating happy marriages between leggy, old-fashioned roses with veils of clematis and handsome herbaceous plants and select shrubs.

One of the things that makes Graigueconna so special is the way that plants are used to form a whole series of painterly compositions that brings Monet's use of colour at Giverney to mind. There is a wonderful pink border, filled with roses, clematis and blushing perennials, which, rather than clashing as they would if the pinks were used in ones and twos, fascinate the eye. There's a red border too, full of jolly crimson and carmine combinations: red salvia, dahlia 'Bishop of Llandaff', *Crocosmia* 'Lucifer' and *Rosa Cinensis* 'Bengal Crimson', and borders which shade through the spectrum, yellows merging with oranges and pinks running into purples. Long before it was fashionable, Rosemary Brown grew clematis and old roses like 'Wedding Day' which scramble through the cordylines - to encourage their natural habit.

A green lawn surrounded by fascinating shrubs like the ballerina skirted *Cornus alternifolia* provides a refreshing pause for the senses before the plunge into the rich, green jungle of growth in the rock garden of ferns, hellebores and such leafy exotics as datura, *Mellaluca gibbosa*, *Leycesteria crocothyrsos* and *Brachyglottis maurii* (used by the Maoris as toilet paper).

This is a garden full of changes of mood. A tour includes a pond surrounded by lush growth where there must be one of the few giant hogweeds grown on purpose amid drifts of white willowherb, a small arboretum which includes a snake bark *Acer grosseri van hersii* brought back as seed from China, and *Sorbus vilmorinii* known as the dead rat tree for its stinking blooms, with a magnificent border of old roses and clematis nearby.

There is a connoisseur's cocktail of plants to be savoured, including a handsome Madeiran cow parsley *melanoselinum* with shining leaves, pink flowers and striped stems, which is probably the only one in Ireland, the delectable penstemon 'Castle Forbes' from the garden at Mount Stewart, hellebore 'Graigue Conna' and bushes covered in the large golden blooms of *Hypericum* 'Rowallane'. There are also curiosities like the mule dianthus (a cross between a Sweet William and a pink, dating back to Henry VIII's day). Old roses - many grown from cuttings from Rosemary Brown's late mother's garden at Ballyorney – and species clematis are a speciality here with Rosemary's pride and joy, a huge *Rosa californica* 'Plena', the threepennybit rose, the apothecary rose, 'Perle d'Or', 'Phyllis Bide', 'Cecille Brunner' and clematis 'Madame Julia Corrivan', *durandii* and 'Perle d'Azur'.

The final treat in this very rewarding garden is a conservatory festooned in summer with a crimson passion flower, *Passiflora antioquiensis*, and angels' trumpets.

WATERS
AND THE WILD

'Come away, O human child,
To the waters and the wild'

T hese lines from Yeats fit the scenery of West Cork, Kerry and the
West perfectly. There is something almost other-worldly about a
landscape which improbably combines spectacularly rugged mountains
with lush shorelines and wood-fringed lakes.

It is the contrast between wildness and subtropical luxuriance which
makes the gardens of this area so stunning. To look out from among the
exotica that flourish on Ilnacullin Island to the stark ridges of the Caha
Mountains is like being in a perfumed oasis in the midst of wilderness.
Similarly there is almost a feeling of unreality about being able to span
two different worlds at Derreen. In the shelter of towering hemlock
trees groves of exotic tree ferns grow just a few hundred yards from the
rocky shore of Killmacillogue Harbour. The benign warming effect of
the Gulf Stream embracing the coast of Kerry and West Cork ensures
that early rhododendrons are creating a glorious pink and red display
when Moscow and Montreal - on roughly the same latitude - are still in
the grip of sub-zero winter.

The topography of the area makes the landscape mysterious. Long
fingers of land poke out into the sea, full of hidden bays and coves.
Ridges of hills and wild mountainy land screen one sheltered inlet from
the next so that the scenery changes constantly, switching between
barren hillside and luxuriant woods and water.

The remote bays of West Cork may seem a strange place to become
aware of Ireland's Europeanness. But Bantry House, with its French
Armada exhibition, is a vivid reminder of Ireland's links with mainland
Europe. The alliance of Irish Catholic interests with the French and
Spanish, together with the threat of a European invasion via Ireland -

with the aim of striking at England – has always been a major factor in Irish history.

But in gardens the Continental influence has been altogether favourable and can be seen at its most sublime in West Cork when the formality of Italian-inspired gardens on Ilnacullin and at Bantry House are set against Irish scenery at its most dramatic.

The Lakes of Killarney and the Ring of Kerry enjoy a high profile and have become a scenic must on every tourist's itinerary. But part of the joy of the mountains, the peninsulas and the long, sheltered inlets of the south west is finding unsung but equally beautiful places – the beguiling bay at Derrynane, sheltered by a cup of hills and by Abbey Island with Daniel O'Connell's slate-sided home at one end and a rich cockle strand at the other, the stony, secret beaches of the Kenmare peninsula where you can swim in blood-warm water with a distant view of the Ring of Kerry as a backdrop, the peaceful inlet at Creagh where the scent of honey and sea mix on the wind and sea gulls answer a peacock's call.

ROUND AND ABOUT

E veryone who knows the coastline has their own favourite spot but for first-time explorers it may help to know some of the most attractive corners of the country, the best villages to linger in and the most breathtaking drives. Kinsale is where gourmets think they have died and gone to heaven; a clutch of really top-class restaurants are concentrated in this small fishing village which is the home of a gourmet festival. There are good bracing walks over the cliffs and to the village of Summer Cove and to Charles' Fort, the star-shaped stronghold built after the Battle of Kinsale. Open daily, mid June-mid Sept. 10am-6.30pm, except Tues. 10am-5pm, Sat. & Sun. 2-5pm. Also open mid Sept.-mid April, 8am-4.30pm. The museum in Kinsale's seventeenth-century court house is worth a visit. Nearby, Ballinspittle became the epicentre of the outbreak of moving statues.

Timoleague is a pretty, unspoiled little village in the innermost recesses of Courtmacsherry Bay with a ruined thirteenth-century Franciscan friary founded by Donal Glas MacCarthy, and Timoleague

Castle Gardens nearby. There really has been a Continental invasion at Baltimore - a contemporary one. The French Glenans sailing school is based there and in summer Baltimore Bay is often full of foreign yachts. As a result this is a lively spot with a good selection of restaurants and busy pubs. Chez Youen - the patron is Breton - is great for seafood. Local people especially recommend Casey's Cabin on the Skibbereen side of Baltimore for seafood and barbecue dishes. Memorable stories revolve around trips for both the food and the voyage out to the Hare Island Restaurant in the middle of Roaring Water Bay (groups preferred), tel. 028-38102, May-October. Dermot Kennedy's sailing course is very civilised, lunch on shore and back for tea. Skibbereen has a good complement of browsable shops. There is a good fortune teller in the town, drop in to John Field's coffee shop for a cuppa and inquire.

The extraordinary lagoon, Lough Hyne, with its unique marine life and narrow channel to the sea where the roaring waters stand still for just a minute at the balance of the tide, is fifteen minutes away over hills and narrow winding lanes.

On the Schull peninsula there are some glorious beaches at Crookhaven and Barley Cove. Heron's Cove restaurant at Goleen Harbour caters for everything from morning coffee to dinner.

Castletownsend near Skibbereen was the home of Edith Somerville, who lived at Drishane House (1790) and wrote the *Irish RM* stories with Violet Martin. Look for Mary Anne's pub, ancient, low-beamed and friendly. Whitewashed O'Sullivan's pub looking out over lovely Killmacillogue Harbour on the Kerry side of the peninsula belongs to Ireland as it was. Kenmare makes a very good base, the main street is full of tempting shops, lively pubs and delicious smells of coffee and garlic from a good selection of medium-priced restaurants. Cleo at the Glengarriff end of the town stocks the most covetable stylish Irish-designed clothes in linens, wools and cottons.

Watch out for Manning's Emporium at Ballylickey, with all kinds of Irish speciality foods from farmhouse cheeses to cakes. If you are looking for the makings of a special picnic Adele's in Schull is a good bet: bread, salads, quiches and the most irresistible cakes are on sale here. The Durrus peninsula is a surprise setting for a Japanese restaurant. The Shiro Japanese dinner house is located in the former Bishop's Palace at

Ahakista. Blair's Cove restaurant has a mouthwatering display of starters, diners can sit out on the terrace in summer or in a stone barn when the weather is less kind.

The drive round Bantry Bay to Glengarriff and over the hills to Kenmare is spectacular and the drive over the mountains from Kenmare on the N71 to where the road drops through Killarney National Park even more so. The crystal waters of the Torc waterfall are just ten minutes walk from the car park, half-way down the descent.

The Ring of Kerry is like the curate's egg - good in parts. One of my favourite parts is round lovely Derrynane Bay, site of Derrynane House, home of Daniel O'Connell the Liberator; there is a pretty green garden and the house has much of its original furniture. The 2,500-year-old Iron Age Staigue Fort is nearby, half-way between Sneem - a pretty village with good pubs, food and an uncharacteristic green - and Caherdaniel.

This area was a favourite with Victorian tourists, and the award-winning Park Hotel at Kenmare retains that wonderful air of Edwardian comfort, the food - using local ingredients in a highly original way - being the best you will find anywhere, tel. 064-41200. For the adventurous there are trips out to see the Skelligs, dramatic rocky islands which were the site of an early Christian settlement and are still a bird sanctuary for gannets and puffins. Landings are limited, however. The western stretch of the Ring of Kerry between Caherciveen and Glenbeigh has beautiful views across to Dingle Bay and Mount Brandon with the Blaskets off the tip of Slea Head.

Inside the sheltering arms of Valentia harbour there is a subtropical island paradise where tall woods sweep down to the sea. A truly secret wild garden, Glanleam, was created by the Knight of Kerry a century and a half ago. Walks are bordered by luxuriant tree ferns, palms, bamboos and even bananas. Open daily 11am-5pm. Tea-rooms April-October. Admission £2.50. Tel. 066-76108.

PLACES TO STAY

Ballylickey House overlooks Bantry Bay, one huge factor in its favour. The former fishing lodge of Lord Kenmare surrounded by 10 acres of grounds, Ballylickey is also known for its cuisine. B & B £40.00 plus, dinner £21.00.

Near Skibbereen, Killeena, an attractive complex built in the Dutch colonial style where peacocks wander in the courtyard, has 4 self-catering apartments; first-floor lounges have studio windows with splendid views. The grounds slope down to the sheltered inlet at Creagh half-way between Skibbereen and Baltimore, tel. 028-21029.

Crookhaven Coastguard Cottages, the 90-year-old coastguard cottages on a peninsula overlooking Crookhaven, have been converted into self-catering cottages with superb views over the sea. The lovely strands of Barley Cove and Cocklebeach are close by, tel. 028-28122.

Muxnaw Lodge, a Gothic 1801 house overlooking the Kenmare estuary, is a friendly, family-run guesthouse. Many of Mrs Hanna Boland's guests come back year after year for the comfortable informality, and I like the way the family found something delicious for me when I arrived one evening long after dinner. B & B £17.00, dinner £14.00, tel. 064-41252.

On the Seven Heads peninsula, Sea Court, with views of the sea, is an eighteenth-century Georgian mansion surrounded by acres of parkland, open from June to August only, B & B £23.50, dinner from £16.50, tel. 023-40151.

A stately stay at Bantry House is now possible since one wing overlooking the formal gardens has been converted into special guest accommodation by Mr and Mrs Egerton Shelswell White. Concerts in the library at Bantry are a possibility. B & B £50-£55.00, dinner £20-£25.00, tel. 027-50047.

Right in the heart of the Ring of Kerry, Glendalough House, run by Mrs Josephine Roder, has views over Macgillicuddy's Reeks and Caragh Lake. Local fish and game are a speciality at this 120-year-old house, an ideal base for shooting, fishing or touring. B & B £30-£38.00, dinner £22.00, tel. 066-69156.

Nearby on the shores of Caragh Lake, Carrig House is run by Mrs Heide Windecker. French cooking is a speciality at her Georgian home and the organic vegetables come from her own garden. Open March-Oct. B & B from £28.00, dinner £19-£20.00, tel. 066-69104.

CREAGH

Skibbereen, County Cork

WILD GARDEN

A romantic setting on a wooded estuary.

A dozen years ago I accidentally came across the place which began my love affair with old gardens. On the road to Baltimore a gateway with a board advertising the grounds at Creagh was too much to resist. At the end of a long drive there was a mellow bow-ended house, and outside the front door someone had trustingly left a trug on the bench with a notice saying 'Please pay here'.

Grassy paths led off through luxuriant jungle where tree ferns and perfumed late-flowering rhododendrons added exotic touches. Every turn of the path showed something new - a ruined tower, a lake surrounded by lush greenery, a gate onto the seashore with a view of Inisbeg Island. There was a sense of discovering a secret world all by myself.

I went back recently, half afraid that the place would have changed and that the memory would be shattered. It was exactly as I remembered, even the notice seemed the same, except that the fee had gone up by 50p.

The garden is the creation of the late Peter and Gwendoline Harold-Barry. In 1945 they purchased Creagh from the Fuller family, who had already planted many of the specimen trees on what was once the land of Fineen O'Driscoll. The garden is designed so that every turn reveals some new vista. My favourite one is from the 'proposal bench' (a more romantic spot to pop the question would be hard to imagine), with a serpentine mill pond in the foreground and a view of the house across rich vegetation glimmering with white roses and Calla lilies. The creation of this prospect was inspired by a 'Douanier' Rousseau painting.

The revolutionary Irish gardener William Robinson rebelled against formal Victorian gardens, and the pleasure grounds at Creagh are a perfect example of his theory 'That we may have more of the beauty of hardy flowers by naturalising plants of the many regions of the earth in our fields, woods and copses and the outer parts of pleasure grounds'.

There are many things to be discovered at Creagh: a pepper-pot mill, the newly built Hens' Hilton which is the walled vegetable and fruit garden, the double-seater lavatory where Victorian gentlemen went to smoke companionably, a new collection of *Abutilon* (including the gorgeous 'Nabob' with peach petals and crimson sepals), real shamrocks, a rose walk, a huge old *Lomatia ferruginea* with lichen among its blooms. In this sheltered spot the camellias and rhododendrons begin blooming in January and the late rhododendrons continue into July.

All the walks have names; Didi's walk, named for a dachshund which used to race the car back to the house (now used by a pug who gets about on a trolley), the Ho Chi Minh jungle walk to be taken by children while their parents have a peaceful stroll up the drive, and the Fern walk.

Like many pleasing gardens with older owners, Creagh faced an uncertain future; however, the Gwendoline Harold-Barry Trust has now been set up and it is hoped that Creagh's tradition will continue.

Admission £2.50, children £1.00, open 1 March-31 Oct. 10am-6pm (other times by arrangement), tel. 028-22121, ideal for children. Partly accessible to wheelchairs. Directions: On the right a few miles outside Skibbereen on the road to Baltimore.

ILNACULLIN

Garnish Island, Glengarriff, County Cork

ISLAND GARDEN

As near as you can get to paradise, worth crossing the entire country to see.

If Mount Stewart is the most special garden in the North then Ilnacullin has to be a strong contender for the position in the 26 Counties. A whole combination of factors makes it memorable and - the word really is appropriate here - magical.

There is the exquisite island location, the short voyage past rocks covered with basking seals and then there is the juxtaposition of the elegant Italian garden with a glorious wild garden. Every few yards the layout offers a change of mood, a dramatic vista or an invitation to explore.

The very real threat of a French invasion - witness the story of the 1796 French Armada at Bantry House - is a strong element in the history of Bantry Bay. In the early nineteenth century the 37-acre island was bought by the War Office and a Martello tower and barracks were built there as a defence against Napoleon. In 1910 Annan Bryce bought the bare rocky island from the War Office and, with extraordinary imagination, set about developing its potential as a garden. Rocks were blasted, boatloads of soil were brought in and shelter belts of conifers planted. Mr Bryce commissioned the English architect Harold Peto, known for his Italianate designs, to plan a house and garden.

The house was never built, but the Italian garden with its Casita and pool remains the centrepiece of the whole garden, beautifully linked by a series of architectural devices to the wild garden. A second major phase in the planting of the garden took place during the time of Annan's son Rowland Bryce, advised by the great Scottish gardener and plantsman, Murdo MacKenzie. In 1953 Ilnacullin was given to the nation on the death of Rowland Bryce and is in the care of the Office of Public Works.

There are three main areas in the garden and a well prepared booklet gives a guide to the island and to some of the plants of particular interest. The Casita of golden Bath stone, curtained with wisteria, and the Italian garden with its pool and temple are breathtaking. Around the pool the points of the compass are marked by venerable bonsai trees; one, a *Larix*, is 300 years old. Clipped hedges and the architectural shapes of cypress and yew are a foil to the colours around the pool, showers of rosy *Leptospermum scoparium*, *Clematis durandii*, festoons of purple *Abutilon* 'Ashford Red', the scarlet and gold brushes of *Callistemon rigidus*.

The great vista across the aptly named Happy Valley runs the whole length of the island from the Grecian temple with its view of the Caha Mountains and avenue of Italian cypress to the Martello tower atop a wide flight of steps at the other end. In between are shrubs and trees from every corner of the globe. The broad grassy walk dips at the centre to a lily pond crossed by stepping-stones and the planting on either side of the walk allows choice rhododendrons and rare trees like the beautiful weeping *Dacrydium franklinii* from Tasmania and the miniature *Rhododendron yakushimanum* to be seen to full advantage.

Inland is an area known as the jungle where woodland cover provides a perfect habitat for a wonderful collection of rhododendrons and azaleas. The third great treat on the island is the walled garden with a magnificent double herbaceous border running the whole way down the centre. In midsummer the beds are packed with bloom – delphinium, phlox and asters among the old-fashioned border favourites.

It is a shame to see that some areas of the walled garden are now neglected; the giant *Cardiocrinum* lilies have vanished and the tender *Cupressus cashmeriana* has died in the Happy Valley. It may seem churlish to mention this but Ilnacullin is an important national treasure as magnificent in its own way as the Celtic gold in the National Museum or Russborough House, but much more fragile.

Admission £2.50, groups and OAP £1.75, children £1.00, family £6.00. Open March and Oct. Mon.-Sat. 10am-4.30pm, Sun. 1-5pm; April-Sept. Mon.-Sat. 10am-6.30pm, Sun. 1-7pm; July-Aug. Mon.-Sat. 9.30am-6.30pm, Sun. 11am-7pm. Tel. (027) 63040. Take the boat from Glengarriff (don't miss the last boat back). Last outgoing boat leaves 1 hour before closing. There are toilet facilities but no shop.

DERREEN

Lauragh, near Kenmare, County Kerry

In a grove of exotic tree ferns surrounded by soaring hemlock trees the warm air is filled with heady perfume and the hum of insects. Just a few yards away a path carpeted with pine needles leads to the seashore and a view of the bleak ridges of Keecragh Mountain across Killmacillogue Bay.

The juxtaposition of these two contrasting worlds, the wild Kerry scenery and the lushness of the subtropical garden, is part of what makes Derreen special. The garden is the result of a happy marriage between the warming effect of the Gulf Stream and the enthusiasm of the fifth Marquis of Lansdowne, who created the gardens there over a 60-year period. Since he was Viceroy of India and Governor General of Canada between 1883 and 1894, the Marquis was in a position to bring back many of the exciting new plants from both continents.

He oversaw the planting of more than 400 acres of woodland between the sea and the mountains, among them giant conifers: red cedars and hemlocks. Within their shelter he planted a large collection of rhododendron, azaleas and many tender trees and shrubs, the beautiful feathery swamp cypress *Taxodium distichium*, crinodendrons with their scarlet lanterns, hoherias, magnolias, myrtles, camellias, *Myrtus luma* and *Drimys winteri*.

The land was originally granted to Sir William Petty, physician to Cromwell's forces in Ireland in 1650, and his daughter married Lord Kerry later Lord Lansdowne. The demesne is still in family hands having passed from the fifth Lord Lansdowne to his granddaughter Lady Mersey. Now in the hands of her son, the Hon. David Bigham, it is open to the public. Head gardener Jacky Ward's father was also head gardener there before him and – another touch of tradition – the drinking water still comes from a spring with a wheel pump.

Neatly labelled paths lead past spectacular displays of rhododendrons in spring. Some of the walks have evocative names like King's Oozy (Edward VII came to visit and planted a tree in a squelchy spot). Others lead to vantage points:

the Knockatee seat looks towards the mountains across a forest of *Rhododendron arboreum*, which is a sea of deep pink blossom in spring. Near the boathouse there's a view of a plank bridge leading to an island and further away a flotilla of blue-painted boats at anchor in a sheltered inlet.

The huge trees and jungle-like growth, complete with thickets of bamboo and tree ferns (*Dicksonia antarctica*), give the feeling of having strayed into some primeval forest, especially where a vast *Cryptomeria japonica* has fallen over the path, creating a natural bridge. In the damp Kerry air mosses, lichens and ferns flourish and huge boulders and stone outcrops form a natural rock garden.

Planting still continues in the gardens and a pond with great possibilities has just been made near the Boathouse Walk. The gardens are at their most spectacular in spring when the rhododendrons and azaleas are at their best but they are well worth a visit during summer too. Since they are not very well known you may have the privilege of feeling that you have the place virtually to yourself.

The bay around Killmacillogue Harbour which gave the McFinnan Duffs a profitable living from smuggling and fishing in the eighteenth century is beautiful and quite unspoiled. The twisting coast road has a view of the mountains with the Ring of Kerry in one direction, and of pine trees growing by the water's edge in the other. At Teddy O'Sullivan's, beside the harbour, there used to be fresh salmon teas and just nearby there's a bathing place where the sun-hot rocks warm the sea to bath temperature in summer.

Admission £2.00 (pay in box provided), open daily 1 April-Sept. 10am-6pm, tel. 064-83103. There is a helpful guide to the gardens and at weekends teas are served at the gardener's cottage. There are picnic areas and toilet facilities. Directions: Off the Kenmare Castletownbere Road (follow the signs for O'Sullivan's pub from Kenmare).

BANTRY HOUSE

Bantry, County Cork

ORNAMENTAL GARDEN,
HISTORICAL INTEREST
A fine example of an Italianate
garden in Ireland.

On a sunny day Bantry House, looking over an azure sea and the islands of Bantry Bay, seems the most peaceful and idyllic spot. But this bay has been the scene of one of the most potentially explosive incidents in Irish history.

The sight of 16 French warships lying off Bantry Bay on a stormy Christmas Day in 1796 must have caused panic onshore. In the event the invasion in support of Wolfe Tone and the United Irishmen never happened; the ships and the rest of the French Armada dispersed due to bad weather. But the way the threat of the landing was handled by Richard White of Bantry House did a great deal to advance his family's fortunes and he was created Baron

Open daily except Christmas 9am-6pm. House and grounds, £4.00. The magnificent house, with its Aubusson and Gobelin tapestries and the dining room hung with portraits of George III and Queen Charlotte given by the grateful sovereign to the first Earl, is well worth a visit. There is a tea room, craft shop and a wing of the house has been converted to become bed and breakfast accommodation, B & B £47.00, tel. 027-50047 fax. 027-50795. There is also a French Armada exhibition in the grounds with many details of the 47-strong French fleet which might have changed the course of Irish history. Directions: On the outskirts of Bantry village.

and later Earl of Bantry in recognition of his loyalty.

His son Richard, later second Earl of Bantry, did the fashionable grand tour and became a dedicated visitor to Europe, travelling widely there for 20 summers. He amassed artefacts and sketch books full of studies of the great houses and gardens of Italy, France and Spain. These provided the inspiration for his extensive remodelling of the 1730 house and the gardens in the 1840s.

To provide a suitably splendid setting for his treasure-filled home, Richard White had the meadow in front of the house transformed into three terraced lawns, embellished with balustrades, urns and statuary. Behind the house parterres were laid out around a fountain surrounded with an iron pergola curtained with cascading wisteria and based on a rose temple at the Villa Pallavicino in Italy. The steep hillside behind the house became the site of a dramatic 'stairway to the sky', its flights of steps and terraces affording the most magnificent view of the bay and a bird's eye view of the Italian garden below. The design is thought to have been inspired by the Boboli Gardens in Florence.

The elaborate parterre to the west of the house is probably the earliest part of the garden. It may have been laid out by the Hutchinson family, the original owners who built the house around 1730, when French or Dutch-inspired formal gardens were still in vogue. Known as the Rose Garden, the box-edged beds are filled with a profusion of old-fashioned roses, 'Buff Beauty', 'Iceberg', *Rosa rugosa* among them, and colourful herbaceous plants. A series of circular beds, one guarded by a statue of the goddess Diana, to the south and east of the house, are planted in the Victorian manner with low decorative shrubs.

The present owners Mr and Mrs Egerton Shelswell White have been working, since 1986, on a long-term project to restore the gardens. The Italian garden, which had become overgrown, has been meticulously restored and replanted and there are plans to carry out work on the stairway to the sky.

DUNLOE CASTLE GARDENS

Dunloe, County Kerry

ARBORETUM

A most instructive garden of particular interest to dendrologists.

A succession of castles have stood guarding the pass through the spectacular Gap of Dunloe and the crossing points on the Rivers Loe and Luane. The last one was sacked by one of Cromwell's generals and left in ruins; only a portion of the keep remained. The shell of this keep is now a focal point in the gardens beside a large modern hotel.

The fine collection of trees and shrubs at Dunloe was begun by an American, Mr Howard Harrington, who purchased the estate in the 1920s. The arboretum is in an unlikely exposed site given only partial protection by the walls of an old garden, so Mr Harrington planted shelter belts before planting rare and tender shrubs - many imported from the Hillier Nurseries over a brief 10-year period. His work was continued by the German industrialist, Mr H. Leibherr, who bought the estate and built the hotel in the 1960s. The work was carried out with advice from the German dendrologist Dr Gerd Krussmann.

The backdrop of Macgillicuddy's Reeks and the Purple Mountain, the old walls and shady grass walks, all make this a delightful place to spend an hour or two. There is a fine collection of rhododendrons, camellias and azaleas and some rarely seen trees including *Lomatia ferruginea* with fernlike leaves and buff and scarlet flowers, the Chinese pond cypress *Glyptostrobus lineatus* and the Killarney strawberry tree. The contents of the garden have been meticulously catalogued by the great plantsman Roy Lancaster and are listed according to plan with descriptions and country of origin.

Admission free, catalogue priced £1.00 from the hotel. Open May-end Sept., groups by appointment, tel. 064-44111. Directions: Take the main R562 Killarney Killorglin Road and follow the signs for the Gap of Dunloe.

MUCKROSS

Killarney, County Kerry

FLOWER GARDEN

Beautiful setting for a popular spot.

As a visitor centre Muckross has proved a tremendous success and the car park fills up rapidly with buses and vehicles. Perhaps for that reason the garden lacks intimacy and while the grounds are pleasant, the overall effect is municipal.

The nineteenth-century house and grounds beside the Lakes of Killarney were given to the nation by the Herbert family in 1932. The setting is magnificent with distant views of the Purple Mountain beyond the wooded hills of Killarney National Park. Lawns shaded by Scots pines and dotted with clumps of *Rhododendron arboreum* slope down to the lakes. There is a stream garden bordered with damp-loving plants, a small garden laid out in the Victorian manner with bedding plants beside the house, and a natural rocky outcrop which makes a very successful setting for a shrubbery with winding paths.

Some of the most interesting shrubs are at the edge of the woodland area where there is a large collection of camellias, the lovely *Magnolia soulangeana* and the *Stuartia pseudocamellia* with its great show of yellow stamens. The colours are at their best in spring when the azaleas and rhododendrons are out and in September/October when acers and cherries add scarlet to the autumn tones.

There are lots of walks and trails through the grounds and there are always jarveys willing to bowl you along to the lake in a jaunting car. A new arboretum is being developed, tender trees including eucalyptus and acers do well in the mild climate, and perhaps the most famous tree of all is the indigenous strawberry tree *Arbutus unedo*. The Tudor-style manor now houses the Kerry Folklife Centre with an exhibition of folk craft.

Admission free, open daily 9am-5.30pm, tel. 064-31440. There are shops, tea rooms and audio visual aids. Directions: Just outside Killarney on the N71 Killarney Kenmare Road.

GLIN CASTLE GARDENS

Glin, County Limerick

GARDEN

A mellow garden surrounding a fairytale castle.

With its crenellated towers, gingerbread gate lodges and lovely position overlooking the Shannon estuary, Glin looks very much the fairytale castle. The surrounding grounds, designed to flatter its pre-eminence, are at their best in spring when hosts of daffodils dance on the hill behind the castle, when magnolias and cherries glow pink and white and later the scent of bluebells drifts across from the woods.

The garden is of a charmingly eccentric design. The original layout dates back to the time the house with its richly decorated new-classical interiors was built in the 1780s by Colonel John FitzGerald. The exterior was gothicised by the Colonel's son John Fraunceis who also added the folly lodges. By the end of the last century the garden had fallen into disrepair and was rescued by Lady Rachel Wyndham-Quin, grandmother of the present Knight of Glin. In the next generation Veronica Villiers, the 28th Knight's wife, carried out further restoration and planted many of the ornamental shrubs and formal hedges with their urns and busts.

A striking feature of the garden is the path running down the lawn to a sundial terrace flanked by two curlicues of yew hedge. At the end of this perspective a *Parrotia persica* provides glowing autumn colour and a decorative wall embellished with urns divides lawn from meadow. The walls of the castle are softened with climbing shrubs, *Ceanothus*, *Wisteria*, the creamy flowers of *R.* 'Felicité et Perpetué'.

The formal lawns give way to more naturalistic planting with a mixture of shrubs (myrtles, hydrangeas, magnolias and camellias) and to a frame of stately trees: blue cedar, *Pinus radiata*, limes, beeches and *Cornus capitata* with its summer show of creamy bracts. Rhododendrons provide a show beginning as early as Christmas and continuing into summer. In the woods sheets of bluebells are spread under ancient oak trees in spring.

Hidden from sight behind high grey walls a kitchen garden is still in full productive use. In the traditional way all manner of things are grown within its confines: asparagus, sea kale, sorrel and other vegetables, which are used in the castle kitchens. Flowers are grown for cutting, figs, wineberries and clematis climb the walls beside espaliered pears and apples, grapes still ripen in the glasshouse and the fowl have their own gothic henhouse. A rustic temple houses a seventeenth-century marble statue of Andromeda chained to a rock. Behind the kitchen garden is an area known as the violet ground where Lady Wyndham-Quin grew violets which were sent all the way to London to be sold.

Admission £3.00, groups by appointment. Open 1 May-30 June, 10am-12 noon and 2-4pm. Meals can be arranged in the castle, tel. Bob Duff 068-34112. Castle with wonderful collection of Irish furniture. Directions: Glin is nine miles/14.5 km from Foynes on the N69 Tarbert Road.

ARDCARRAIG

Bushy Park, Oranswell, County Galway

FLOWER AND WILD GARDEN
A unique series of secret water gardens to inspire novices and delight the plantsperson.

There are gardens worth travelling across continents, never mind countries, to see and this is one of them.

On an unpromising boggy hillside Lorna MacMahon has created a succession of truly enchanting water gardens. Twenty years ago the site was nothing but waste and scrubland. Armed with a crowbar, a bushman saw and love of plants and water, Mrs MacMahon has transformed four acres into a paradise which is especially inviting in spring, early summer and autumn.

The garden has a series of hidden compartments hewn out of wilderness. A path leads off beguilingly between a double herbaceous border to a green tunnel through a hazel coppice carpeted with ferns and bluebells. Beyond it is a rose and azalea garden where the perfume of the flowers is trapped by the surrounding woods. The constantly changing levels and terrain contribute to the sense of mystery; it's the kind of garden where I found myself exclaiming over and over again as one after another delight was revealed.

Steps lined with azaleas plunge down to a green water garden lit by candelabra primulas and brilliant green foliage plants, among them *Hosta albopicta* and the 'Veridistrata' bamboo. A streamside walk is the prelude to a dazzling bog garden where there is a magnificent display of primulas (the garden has a collection of over 40 varieties including *Primula vialii*). Astilbes, Kaempferi irises and drifts of magenta coloured *Primula poissonii* add to the kaleidoscope of colour. The jewel in the heart of the hillside is a Japanese garden, complete with a much travelled Yukumi dora (snow viewing lantern), a cascade and a miniature Mount Fuji, and complemented by choice acers and ferns. Rare shrubs and plants - some from Australasia – and a collection of camellias are hidden away in further clearings.

In a hollow in front of the house in complete contrast to the wilderness gardens there is a rock garden centred on a lily pool with a splendid collection of dwarf conifers and Alpines. These hidden gardens contain some wonderful treats for the plantsperson and Mrs MacMahon, a horticulturist who lectures far and wide to flower clubs, is extremely knowledgeable. A small sample of the treasures would include *Podocarpus salignus*, *Metasequoia glyptostroboides*, a variegated tulip tree *Liriodendron tulipfera*, a *Euonymus oungeanus* and a variegated *Cryptomeria* 'Sekkan-sugi'. The garden is all the more remarkable since Mrs MacMahon created and is maintaining it singlehandedly. Each one of her gardens within a garden is a wonderful source of ideas which could be adapted for modest plots.

Each year Lorna MacMahon creates a new area. The latest addition is a glorious herb garden, on the site of a former tennis court, which features both Shakespearean and biblical herbs and vegetables. There is a central knot bed planted in a wonderful scented purple, yellow and green scheme, with plants like golden marjoram and oregano, lavender and heartsease viola.

At the end there is a raised bed with a very Mediterranean air, where herbs are grown in sections – oxslips, thyme and violets from *A Midsummer Night's Dream*, rue, dill and hyssop from Luke XI, Matthew XXIII and John XIX respectively. In all, there are dozens of different varieties of medicinal and culinary plants in a lovely celebration of one of the most ancient forms of gardening.

A former vegetable garden has also taken on a new lease of life. It is

Admission £3.00, open strictly by appointment to groups, tel. 091-24336. Not suitable for wheelchairs or children. Directions: Take the Clifden Moycullen Road out of Galway, second turn on the left after Kelehan's pub (a quarter of a mile/.4 km before Madden's Nurseries), the house is ninth up on the left.

known as the Rankin garden, in honour of Lorna's aunts who gave her inspiration. This is a circular, sunken garden, with a great Cretan urn as the conversation piece and many unusual and tender plants. There are some lovely examples of recycling here, like the old mill wheel which forms the centre of the garden and the railway sleepers which have been split and used to create a pergola.

Boyce's Garden

Mount Trenchard, Foynes,
County Limerick

GARDEN

Colourful small garden with informal compartments.

This intimate one-acre garden, which provides a foil to its Celtic neighbour, is the kind that those with small gardens can relate to readily. Overlooking the Shannon Estuary, the garden created by Phyl and Dick Boyce over a dozen years is on a site once occupied by Lord Mount Eagle's workers' cottages. The original river cobblestones have been used to create paths which wind around the different features of the garden.

A loggia twined with passionflower provides the perfect spot to contemplate the fountain playing in the lily pool and the rock garden where unusual plants like the succulent aeonium grow. A sunken garden screened by shrubs and trees provides shelter for rhododendrons, camellias and spring bulbs in season, while a lawn surrounded by paths and raised beds leads to a pergola festooned with roses, clematis and honeysuckle. A small, walled vegetable and herb garden is tucked in beside the house and the various rock gardens are planted with alpines and saxifrages.

Some of the plants in the garden are unusual, others like the vibrant phloxes and rose *Astilbes* have been chosen for their striking colour. Mrs Phyl Boyce spends at least three hours a day in her prize-winning garden and is happy to share her accumulated knowledge with visitors.

Admission £2.50.

Open May-31 Sept. 10am-5pm, tel. 069-65302. Directions: 0.8 mile/1 km from Loughill, just off the N69 between Tarbet and Foynes.

BALLYNACOURTY

Ballysteen, County Limerick

GARDEN

A relaxed informal garden.

This is a garden which grew and, unlike Topsy, has kept on growing. When George and Michelina Stacpoole found their house on the Shannon Estuary nearly thirty years ago, it was almost derelict and surrounded by fields. The Stacpooles knew that there was some land with the house and were delighted to discover in time that they had nine acres of undulating pasture, with views across the broad reach of the estuary to County Clare and to the distant Cratloe Hills.

The limestone bones of County Limerick poked through the thin soil at intervals: a menace for machinery and a reminder that this was not the kind of terrain that could be smoothed into submission.

The first garden around the house was informal, with deep beds of shrubs and irregular shaped herbaceous borders full of the kind of obliging plants that look after themselves and don't require any attention: hellebores, *Pulmonaria*, hardy geraniums. A dip in one corner became a little sunken garden, with steps guarded by urns and sheltering a gothic seat.

Now, a whole network of informal gardens which invite pleasant exploration have grown out from around the central garden. There is a spring garden, where drifts of bulbs are planted under groups of trees and self-seeding plants like polyanthus and bluebells are colonising along the high sheltering hedges. There is a neat kitchen garden, where serried ranks of beds provide vegetables, soft fruit, herbs and flowers for the house. Towards the estuary, where the garden becomes wilder, the Stacpooles gave up the unequal struggle with the rocks and excavated them so that they have become a feature, like grey, sleeping sheep in the midst of grass shorn by the mower.

In the same pragmatic way, a boggy area has been encouraged to become a pond surrounded by damp-loving plants like *Gunnera* and a sheltered vantage point has been created where visitors can sit and admire the blue bulk of the hills far beyond the Shannon. Hardy shrubs, including a host of old-fashioned shrub roses, have been planted in sheltered corners.

When I went to visit, one April morning, the winding lanes leading to Ballynacourty were scattered with primroses and George was enthusing over one of his latest additions. This is the laburnum walk, underplanted with lavender, which provides a dramatic diagonal vista - curtained in gold racemes of flowers - ending with a classic statue simply known as 'Fred'. Bought in a moment of enthusiasm, Fred turned out to be more of a heavyweight than George had bargained for: a lorry and several strong men had to be hired to get him home safely.

There are several such intriguing focal points scattered around - from chimney pots to magnificent urns originally from Belvedere near Mullingar. George Stacpoole's profession as an antique dealer provides the opportunity for such finds and the garden offers the excuse for buying them. Around the diamond-shaped laburnum garden informal beds of shrubs and decorative trees promise a fine display in a few years' time.

A long, narrow strip of, as yet, untamed land links the various gardens. George can already see great possibilities - a long allée with a grass path shorn in the meadow, perhaps a central feature where a pyramidal bonfire is awaiting the torch and a high point that is just begging for a folly. One thing you can be quite certain of is that, between one visit to the garden and the next, something new will have been added to the tour of Ballynacourty.

Admission £3.00 to groups, by appointment at any time, tel. 061-396409, fax 061-396733. Contact George Stacpoole. Directions: fifteen and a half miles/25 km from Limerick, off the Foynes Road.

CLUAIN ÓG COILÍN

Kilcornan, County Limerick

CLASSICAL GARDEN

A new garden with a classical theme beside a Celtic park.

Necessity can be the mother of original gardening ideas. Casting around for an activity to complement his farm work, Bernard Downes saw the potential of agritourism and hit on the idea of developing a Celtic Park which would give visitors an insight into Ireland's ancient past.

Beside an original crannóg or lake settlement on his farm at Kilcornan in County Limerick, he built a replica of these neolithic, reed-thatched island huts as well as recreating a holy well, Ogham stone, dolmen, a cooking site, a stone circle, an early Christian church and other features.

A garden in the beautiful lakeside setting to provide peace, tranquillity and colour seemed the next logical step. Bernard and his wife Pat dreamed up a sunken garden where classical pillars are reflected in the water of a lily pond and surrounded by raised beds of colourful planting. Flights of steps lead up from the golden gravel surrounds to the ranks of pillars. The contrasting shapes and colours of conifers, broom, malva, hardy geraniums and busy lizzies provide plenty to please the eye.

With beguiling views of the surrounding countryside it's the kind of place that invites people to sit and relax. A path with natural limestone kerbing leads from the head of the pool to a rose garden

Admission to Celtic Park and Gardens £3.00. Open daily March-Nov., 9am-7pm. Teas. Tel. 061-394243. Directions: On the N69 at Kilcornan Church between Limerick and Foynes on the coast road to Tralee.

and pergola walk planted with over 1,000 roses including the National Trust rose, while a rockery area leads visitors across a bridge with views of Dromore Castle, once the home of Lord Limerick, to an ancient ring fort. A second bridge leads to an area featuring herbaceous beds and shrubs. The Celtic Garden is situated on land which was once apportioned to one of Cromwell's commanders, Sir Hardress Waller, and is one of the group of gardens on the N69 garden route.

THE LAKELANDS

F or most drivers the Midlands are little more than a blur as they race for Galway or Cork, or set their foot on the accelerator and their sights on Kerry or Connemara. The dismissal of the central counties is nothing new. Mr and Mrs Samuel Carter Hall in their otherwise discursive 1841-3 guide to Ireland dismissed Westmeath in two paragraphs and Longford with six. Yet these can be two of the most rewarding counties of central Ireland.

For years I subscribed to the common theory that Ireland is like a saucer with the interesting bits around the edge and a flat boring bit in the middle. It took a visit to Westmeath and the advice of a friend to change my mind. The visit took me to the O'Haras of Mornington House near Crooked Wood. And there just a few miles from the horrors of the M4 were little dragon-backed hills like something from a Japanese painting and the mysterious Lough Derravaragh where the Children of Lir swam as swans for 300 years. And in a countryside full of old landmarks and folktales there wasn't a single blighting bungalow in sight.

The friend has a theory that once you turn off the main roads of the Midlands you are back in eighteenth-century Ireland. Certainly the past there is less disturbed than it is around the coastal fringe. There are fewer petrol stations shouting visual abuse on the fringes of towns, fewer developmental blots on the landscape, more old shop fronts and pubs survive.

The scenery may be more low-key than around the coast but the pastures and woods, the unexpected lakes and hills like the Slieve Bloom Mountains, have a charm of their own. The landscape around river valleys - the Boyne, the Nore and the Blackwater - tends to be especially beautiful.

There are spectacular visual experiences to be had in central Ireland too, the incredible medieval skyline of Trim broken by the silhouettes of the great castle, the friaries and the church, the shimmering view of Lough Ennel from the terraces of Belvedere House, the fairytale castle of Tullynally revealed on its hilltop. I have stood on top of the Hill of Slane where St Patrick lighted his paschal fire and seen a huge pink winter sun dance over half a dozen counties.

There is also a splendid streak of eccentricity running through the Midlands which is part of its appeal. The past yields a wonderful store of examples. The Parsons family at Birr produced generations of benign inventors. It is quite extraordinary to think of the third Earl of Rosse in 1842 constructing, with the help of workmen, what was to become the largest telescope in the world for three quarters of a century. His son Charles invented the steam turbine. The much married Richard Lovell Edgeworth (father of the novelist Maria) was also an inventor and filled Edgeworthstown House with labour-saving devices including a pump which dispensed halfpence to beggars for each half-hour that they worked it.

Robert Rochfort, Baron Belfield, left the Jealous Wall as a monument to sibling rivalry (see page 102). He built the enormous sham ruin to blot out the view of Rochfort (afterwards Tudenham Park), his brother's nearby house. The architectural manifestations of sibling rivalry at Slane are the four identical classical houses which face each other at the crossroads. They were built for three Conyngham sisters so that they could live separately yet keep a watchful eye on each other's comings and goings. There were comings and goings of a different kind at Slane Castle. The remarkably straight road is said to have been built to speed George IV on his way to visit his mistress, Elizabeth Marchioness of Conyngham.

Perhaps a similar inspired streak of eccentricity has motivated Midlands gardeners. They face more of a challenge than their counterparts around the coast, with a harsher climate and the threat of winter frosts. The gardens of the lakelands tend to be wonderfully individual creations: each very different and often representing the most extraordinary achievement.

There are the fabulous bones of the Lutyens architectural garden at Heywood, the magnificent garden created over a 20-year period from pastureland at Trim by Jim Reynolds, a quarter-century of dedication by Cholmeley Harrison given to the restoration of the demesne at Emo Court, and the inspired riverside and formal gardens created by Anne

Countess of Rosse at Birr. And the great joy is that all of these gardens are within a pleasant day trip from Dublin.

ROUND AND ABOUT

The lakelands drive which starts from the pretty village of Tyrellspass, laid out by the Countess of Belvedere in the eighteenth century, is very attractive. The Village Inn there is a pleasant place for a break and it serves a running buffet. The route leads past Jonathan Swift's birthplace, round the Midlands lakes, Ennel, Owel and Derravaragh to Belvedere, and could include Tullynally and Carrigglas. Crookedwood House, tel. 044-72165, north west of Mullingar, is recommended by friends for dinner; seafood and local venison are among the specialities.

Butterstream at Trim makes a pleasant day's outing. The Japanese Gardens in the National Stud, the demesne at Emo, the newly created gardens at Gash and the Lutyens garden at Heywood couldn't be more different from each other but are conveniently close together. The castle at Trim, once one of the principal strongholds of the English Pale, is a fine example of medieval military architecture. Brogan's, an old-fashioned hotel in the centre of Trim, offers good traditional home cooking at reasonable prices; Mrs Brogan makes delicious meringues every day.

Near Drogheda, Newgrange is a must on most visitors' lists; with a megalithic burial chamber lit by the sun at the winter solstice, it is one of the most impressive prehistoric tombs in Europe. Further north on the N2 to Belfast, the romantic ruins of Mellifont Abbey (1142), and Alain Chawner's antiques in The Square, Collon, are worth a detour.

The Hill of Tara has a tremendous hold on the imagination and is associated with the goddess Mebh and the Kings of Tara. The monuments (six miles west of Navan) may not quite live up to expectation, but it is a wonderful place to get a feel of timelessness.

Less known, but providing its own fascinating story of the poet Francis Ledwidge who was killed in Flanders, is the Ledwidge Museum half a mile/.8 km from Slane on the road to Drogheda. Admission £1.00. The famous Hill of Slane is to the north of Slane. The

Conyngham Arms, Slane is a lively pub with excellent food, the steaks are particularly recommended.

A favourite stopping-off point on the main Dublin Galway Road, the N6, is Locke's Distillery at Kilbeggan, which combines the attraction of the restored distillery with a restaurant known as the Kitchen, offering ideal food for light meals - quiches, salads, tempting cakes; there are also antiques and crafts shops.

Another excellent pausing place on the main Cork Road is Morrissey's pub in the centre of Abbeyleix. Almost the last of a vanishing breed this gem - which last changed hands in 1887 and dates back to 1775 - offers pub food. Frank Murphy's antiques shop directly opposite is well worth looking into; I once found a set of beech chairs made by an estate carpenter there.

A detour to Tullamore to see Charleville Forest (1798), the setting for a spectacular fairytale castle by Francis Johnston, is worth while. Admission £2.00, open April and May, Sat.-Sun. 2-5pm; June-Sept., Wed.-Sun. 11am-5pm. In 1785 Tullamore had the uneasy distinction of being destroyed by a great balloon fire. Bridge House there is busy from morning till late with people popping in for coffees, day-long pub food and full restaurant meals. Even the sandwiches are more adventurous than the usual pub fare, with filled pitta bread, and beef and horse-radish on rye among the treats.

PLACES TO STAY

B eside Lough Derravaragh just north west of Mullingar, Mornington House, County Westmeath, makes an ideal weekend retreat or base for exploring central Ireland. The house has been in the Warwick O'Hara family for five generations and Anne O'Hara is a superb cook. Local rib of beef on the bone a speciality. Open March-Oct., tel. 044-72191.

Roundwood House, Mountrath, County Laois is both an architectural and a culinary treat. The house is Palladian and Rosemarie Kennan's cooking is a great favourite with weekenders. An ideal place to sit by the fire over a bottle of wine in congenial company, tel. 0502-32120.

There can't be a more welcoming sight than Allison Dowling bustling apron-clad out of the Georgian doorway of the Old Glebe House in Ballinakill. The best of home cooking can be found here with a very relaxing atmosphere. The house overlooks the Nore Valley and is just beside Heywood. Mrs Dowling is very knowledgeable about the area, tel. 0502-33368. Architectural enthusiasts might like the idea of staying in Gandon-designed accommodation. Carrigglas Manor, near Longford, has a number of self-catering apartments to let in the converted Gandon stables, tel. 043-45165, B & B £45-£55.00, dinner £22.50.

Lovely Annesbrook House, at Duleek, County Meath, with its dramatic portico, is an established favourite with people who like to stay in country houses. B & B £25-£30.00, dinner £16.00, tel. 041-23293.

Mearscourt is a large Georgian mansion just outside Mullingar at Rathconrath and is the home of Brendan and Eithne Pendred. The house looks out over parkland and country home cooking is a speciality. B & B £18-£20.00, dinner £17.00, tel. 044-55112. The gardens there are under restoration.

BUTTERSTREAM

Trim, County Meath

FLOWER GARDEN

The Sissinghurst of Ireland, this is a series of gardens within a garden to provide endless inspiration.

The secret of success in planning a garden, says Jim Reynolds, is structure: 'You can have the loveliest plants in the world but without a structure they won't amount to anything.' His own garden at Butterstream is a splendid exercise in that golden rule.

One entrance to the garden, which is planned as a series of rooms, begins appropriately with a doorway - a very grand one indeed - which was once the doorway of Lord Langford's town house in Trim. Beyond the doorway is a glimpse of a hallway with walls of smoothly clipped beech, green for half the year and bronze for the rest, where arches lead tantalisingly to the next compartment. The other entrance is via a pathway through luxuriant foliage plants or spring flowers according to season. With every few steps something new is revealed - a view down into a secluded green garden, a prospect along a stream planted with candelabra primulas and skunk cabbage, and the glimpse of a gothic bridge waiting to be crossed.

What precisely happens next is a secret, it would be churlish to explain the exact layout of the garden, rather like giving away the end of a thriller - the whole element of surprise would be spoiled.

Each room in the garden has a

completely different mood: there is a green area with pools of shade-loving leafy plants, a wonderful swirling effect created by massed hostas, and a romantic Pineapple House which would make a perfect setting for *A Midsummer Night's Dream*. Among the cool green tones, touches of colour have all the more impact, a drift of rosy *Astilbe chinensis*, a golden elm and the sprightly pink chestnut rose 'Roxburghi roxburghii'. There is a hot garden where, enclosed by walls of beech hedging, the reds of *Crocosmia* 'Lucifer' sizzle happily beside the scarlet 'Bishop of Llandaff' dahlia, and *Ligularia* 'the Rocket' blazes away near a golden *Robinia*.

Another of Jim's principles is that in gardens as in meals, the main courses should be interspersed with something to refresh the palate. In this way a quiet green walk beside the stream has a sorbet-like effect before the demands of a formal garden where the architectural shapes of clipped box contrast with the blooms of old shrub roses swathed in velvety *Clematis viticella*.

Among the glories of Butterstream in late July and August when many gardens pause for a breather, are the herbaceous borders. Twenty-five feet/7.6 m deep they provide a truly spectacular sea of colour which starts in a symphony of pinks and blues, changing, as August progresses, to purple and pink tones, and continuing into September with asters, lobelias, crocosmias and Japanese anemones. This area of the garden is laid out so that one progresses along an oval ribbon of green lawn between massed ranks of blooms. Many of the plants are varieties chosen for their particularly good colour, a

Admission £3.00, open daily 1 April-30 Sept. 11am-6pm, tel. 046-36017. Suitable for well-behaved children and wheelchairs (use the drive to the house to avoid steps). There are plants for sale (some are treasures, others will remind you of the garden), toilet facilities, car park, teas. Lunch or dinner for groups by arrangement (cuisine much recommended). Directions: On the outskirts of Trim, signposted from the town.

vivid magenta phlox, pink or purple mandara, deep crimson scabious. The sound of splashing water is a signal to investigate its source and when one does – discovering in the process a Medusa who is clearly quite terrified of the serpents in her hair – another enticing vista is revealed.

Twenty years ago, apart from a small garden attached to Jim's parents' house and a framework of trees, there were nothing but fields where the garden now stands. A visit to Sissinghurst with its series of beautifully conceived compartmentalised gardens lit a fuse of enthusiasm in Jim. Here were gardens on a scale he could relate to much more easily than sprawling wild gardens. The creation of Butterstream then proceeded by leaps and bounds, with a croquet lawn and rustic summer house here and a weeping laburnum pergola there. Then came the follies, a temple with Doric columns admiring its reflection in a lily pond, a new vista of a classic doorway (thanks this time to Lord Mornington), a small formal garden with topiary pyramids, and a splendid medieval edifice known as Reynolds's Rapunzel which affords dazzling views over sections of the

garden. The entire garden is managed with just two pairs of hands – Jim's and his assistant Susie's.

A garden which owes some of its inspiration to Sissinghurst wouldn't be complete without a white garden. And there is one, guarded by urns overflowing in summer with white petunias and planted with phloxes, feverfew, variegated miscanthus, the ghostly *Lysimachia ephemerum* and white honesty.

Never one to do things by halves, Jim has two new follies or, to be more accurate, two charming Georgian pavilions – one serves as a tea-room, the other for all manner of events from concerts to wedding receptions and, given the wonderful backdrop of the garden, it should make a memorable venue.

One of the intriguing things about Butterstream for those who make very worthwhile return visits is the way the garden provides an ever changing display throughout spring and summer. Another is the way that there is always some new project in the making, a dramatic avenue of limes disappearing off behind the open door of a folly, perhaps, or a brand-new vegetable and fruit plot with an avenue of sea kale and bay trees marching off to reclaim another piece of field.

GROVE GARDEN

Fordstown, Kells, County Meath

FLOWER GARDEN

A good place for an outing with small children.

The garden at Grove farm was made with families in mind. A barbecue area, a tree house and hut hidden away in a jungle and a pretty summer house for parents to relax in.

Farmer Pat Dillon began gardening as a hobby, clearing areas round the farm that has been in his family since about the time of the Battle of the Boyne. People often came to admire his colourful plantings of roses and annuals and so he decided to open the garden.

Five years on miracles have been achieved and the garden now offers a huge collection of clematis (there are nearly 400 varieties) which draws people from all over the world. Pat specialises in the *macropetala* and the late, large flowering cultivars. He has been experimenting with different ways of growing clematis – among them tubs topped with pyramid frames where clematis like 'White Swan' and 'Markhams Pink' are grown in combination – and a cutting garden for sweet peas and clematis, where each day some new velvety beauty like *C. viticella vinosa* 'Violaces', or *C. warszawska* 'Nike' opens for admiration. There is also a clematis walk where over seventy different varieties of clematis feature.

Roses are also a speciality here with a rose garden, centred around a sundial, with roses like 'Sweet Juliet' and a recently created shrub rose bed with old favourites 'Chapeau de Napoleon', 'William Lobb' and 'Gertrude Jekyll'.

The plan of the garden is informal, with one area flowing into another and much of the planting is cottage style with plants happily

Admission £3.00. Open June-Sept. 2-6pm. Suitable for wheelchairs. Teas and plants for sale, tel. 046-34276. Directions: Take the Athboy Road from Kells; five miles/8 km out look for signs to the garden on the right.

vying with each other: star gazer lilies, the 'E.C. Buxton' marguerite, deep red *Knautia* and drifts of *Penstemons* and delphiniums.

There is an inviting summer house flanked by a rose pergola and a blue, silver and pink bed edged with scented dwarf Hidcote lavender and *Dianthus* 'Doris'. Children can run riot through the green garden surrounded by mature trees, where the display begins with dozens of different daffodils and hellebores and runs through to spectacular delphiniums.

Pat spends up to 100 hours a week in his garden and it shows. He claims to have planted over three tons of daffodils and he is a knowledgeable plantsman and full of helpful tips. One hint - the idea of using wheat spray on roses to prevent mildew - has been adopted by French rose expert André Eve, who came to visit this young and constantly developing garden.

COOLCARRIGAN

Naas, County Kildare

GARDEN

A happy and imaginative restoration of a Victorian garden with many choice shrubs.

Coolcarrigan is an inward-looking garden relying on man-made features to provide interest in the flat pastures of Kildare at the edge of the Bog of Allen.

John Wilson Wright's great-great-grandfather built the handsome house in 1838 and planted sheltering belts of trees. His son created the main features of the Victorian garden, laying out winding paths, planting specimen trees and building a delightful glasshouse with a central door and flanking wings.

The long avenue leading to the house displays the legacy of John Wilson Wright's mother, who planted thousands upon thousands of spring flowers. Carpets of snowdrops, aconites and crocuses are followed by a golden wave of daffodils, Bird's Eye narcissi and Apennine anemones and finally by a tide of bluebells. Planted among them are dozens of varieties of rhododendron and azalea.

Crinoline-wide paths bordered with a fine collection of shrubs wind back and forth through the 10-acre grounds creating the illusion that the gardens are larger than they really are. From the front of the house a path leads past a small lake to a sylvan temple of clipped yew guarding a set of Doric columns. The column theme is repeated at the end of the axial path and double border, creating a dramatic vista. The paths wind on past a grove of camellias which provides a splendid display in spring despite the relatively harsh Midland climate. A series of open groves of choice shrubs planted in grass strewn with spring bulbs provide a pleasing effect and show each specimen off to advantage. Every few yards reveal some new surprise, a heady scent, a blaze of colour or an unusual shrub. The garden tails away into a wild area with woodland paths leading to the site of a now vanished bog garden. The most recent addition is an arboretum with over 100 different species of trees.

The mood of the lawns, Lutyensesque tiered terrace with many interesting plants and a fine herbaceous border facing the windows of the house, makes a formal contrast. Few gardens can boast a peach and nectarine house or an original greenhouse complete with ancient vines, a 100-year-old rose, melons and hot-house plants. Behind the house a pleasant walk leads to the family's church. Built in 1885 it incorporates features from the twelfth-century Temple Finghin at Clonmacnois and the stained glass windows by Kate O'Brien were inspired by the Book of Armagh.

When he inherited Coolcarrigan in 1972 John Wilson Wright and his wife Hilary faced the challenge of restoring a garden overgrown with evergreens. A happy chance brought them in contact with the great plantsman Sir Harold Hillier, who subsequently became a mentor visiting regularly and supervising the planting of over 2,500 shrubs and trees. The results are delightful, providing all the seclusion and variety which made Victorian gardens such a pleasing backdrop for dalliance.

Admission £3.00, April-Aug. by appointment only, tel. 045-863512/863524. The garden is suitable for wheelchairs and well-behaved children. Seen at its best in spring or autumn. Directions: From Dublin take the Lucan bypass and follow the Celbridge Clane Prosperous Road. Look out for Dagwell's pub two miles/3.2 km outside Prosperous where there is a signpost to Coolcarrigan.

JAPANESE GARDENS

Tully, County Kildare

HISTORICAL INTEREST
*Exquisite, small-scale garden, an
altogether different experience.*

There are Irish 'Japanesey
gardens' but the only true
Japanese garden in Ireland is beside
the National Stud at Kildare. When
the eccentric millionaire Colonel
William Hall Walker hit on the idea
of a Japanese garden to ornament his
very successful stud farm he decided
most properly that only Japanese
would know how to create an
authentic design. So it was that Eida
and Minoru, a father and son team,
came to lay out the garden regarded
as being among the finest examples
of its kind in Europe.

Like all such gardens this one is
symbolic and sets out to tell the
story of a man's journey through
life. On the way he meets his wife,
knows both ecstasy and despair and
has a few domestic tiffs. Almost as
fascinating as the unfamiliar
arrangements of Japanese shrubs,
trees and stones (the stones came all
the way from Japan), is trying to
figure out the meaning behind each
little tableau presented by the twists
and turns of the paths. The only
non-Japanese plants allowed were
Scots pines.

Admission adults £4.00, OAP
and students £3.00, children £2.00,
family ticket £10 (includes
admission to the National Stud),
open 12 Feb.-12 Nov., 9.30am-4pm,
Sundays 2-5.30pm, tel. 045-21251.
Not suitable for wheelchairs
or children. Garden centre and
tea room. Directions: On the main
road on the Dublin side of
Kildare town.

Water forms an essential feature with pools and streams crossed by bridges and mirroring foliage and rocks. The focal point of the garden is a tea house with a fine collection of bonsai trees nearby. One section of the garden is in the Karesansui style and is very emblematic with arrangements of sand and stone representing eternity.

The garden is at its most dramatic in autumn when the many different acers change to colours ranging from gold to brightest scarlet; among the most charming sights are *Acer palmatum* 'Senkaki' and 'Osakazuki'. Conifers - pines, cedars, *Cryptomeria* - and bamboos are well represented.

A water garden and a conservatory are also features of the garden, there are plants for sale including a selection of bonsai trees. The stud and the gardens were donated by the Colonel to the British Government in 1915. Curiously they continued to own it long after independence before handing it over to the Irish Government in rather tricky circumstances in 1943. Now it is part of the National Stud, where the state-owned stallions stand. Arkle's skeleton is on display in the Irish Horse Museum and it can be visited by special arrangement.

GASH GARDENS

Castletown, County Laois

FLOWER GARDEN

A plantsman's garden and inspiration to novice gardeners.

Old established gardens have a certain predictability about them, whereas new gardens offer an element of surprise and none more so than the Gash gardens.

In Keenan's dairy farm and roadside nursery there is nothing to suggest there might be an extraordinary garden hidden beyond double wooden gates. Yet in four acres of low-lying pasture where cows grazed just a decade ago Noel Keenan has created a plantsman's arcadia.

A lifelong gardening devotee, he began by creating a walk across his fields to the River Nore. A herbaceous border, an arboreal area, a stream garden and a formal garden of raised beds followed rapidly. Within this young garden are many choice plants which Noel Keenan

takes great delight in showing off to fellow enthusiasts; he remembers every name and will tell you where - on his holiday expeditions to gardens and nurseries - he came by them.

At the centre of the garden there is an eye-catching grotto known as the Moon House, with a cascade

Admission £2.50 adults only, open 1 May-end Sept. 2-5pm. Other times by arrangement, tel. 0502-32247. No children; not suitable for wheelchairs. Toilet facilities. Plants for sale. Directions: Take the Limerick Road from Mountrath to Castletown, keep left as you enter the village and follow signs for the garden half a mile/.8 km further on, on the left.

tumbling past its circular window into a lily pond. The planting has matured well so that raised beds – some filled with rare alpines – are softened by plants spilling over their edges and onto the gravel paths. The fall of the land invites a view of the garden stretching towards the river, and there are seats and a gazebo invitingly situated at vantage points.

A wooden bridge guarded by a clump of Trinity birches crosses a small stream, bordered with lush planting of *Gunnera*, *Ligularia* and hostas. Beyond it a river of lawn runs between handsome, mixed plantings of shrubs and perennials, where golden forms of shrubs and trees like yew and *Sambucus* draw the eye. There is a hidden walkway over a stream waiting to be discovered and a newly created laburnum pergola makes a dramatic entrance to the riverside walk.

Among my pleasing memories of the garden in early autumn were a *Cornus nuttallii* putting on bracts for the first time, a variegated sweet chestnut, *Polygala purpurea*, *Andromeda polifolia* 'Nikko', *Parahebe*, the French honeysuckle *Hedysarum coronarium*, *Fuchsia bacillaris* and the amusing *Osteospermum* 'Whirligig'.

This is also a very inspirational place for novice gardeners, showing how virgin field can be transformed into an intriguing garden in a remarkably short space of time. Noel Keenan propagates plants from his collection and there are lots of interesting plants at his nursery.

EMO COURT

Emo, County Laois

DEMESNE AND ARBORETUM
Sensitive replanting has enhanced this fine old estate.

The demesne at Emo is a green haven of peace just five minutes drive from the racetrack of the main Dublin Cork Road. The magnificent house designed in 1790 by James Gandon for the first Earl of Portarlington was originally approached via the imposing mile-long avenue of Wellingtonias, said to be the longest of its kind. Parkland, a formal garden with statuary and yew walks were part of the original layout of the estate, with the great house, its domed rotunda modelled on the Parthenon, as centrepiece.

When the last of the Portarlingtons left in 1920, Emo Court fell into decline. Its saviour has been Mr Cholmeley Harrison, who purchased the house and part of the estate in 1969. Over the last 22 years he has restored the house and has carried out extensive planting and restoration of the 50 acres of ornamental grounds.

Within the framework of nineteenth-century timber, a series of grassy walks has been laid out, each with a different theme: the Apiary Walk, the Beech Walk, Mad Margaret's Walk (named for a housemaid who hanged herself a century ago), planted with a collection of shade-loving plants. The Davidia Walk is named in honour of the handkerchief tree discovered by the French missionary Père David, and the 20-year-old tree should produce its breathtaking display of white bracts for the first time any year now.

The new planting has created a series of vistas which allows the great mansion to be admired from a distance and also opens up prospects from the house. There is an idyllic view from the drawing room down a broad grass ride to the Golden Gates. An extensive new arboretum with fascinating trees including *Abies delavayi* var. 'Forrestii' and *Sequoia sempervirens*, planted in flower-strewn meadows, stretches on either side of the ride.

The area between the 20-acre lake and the house has been planted with a collection of rhododendrons, pieris and azaleas and a fine new grove of camellias (far more hardy than people imagine) to provide a wonderful spring display. Pleasant grass paths wind back and forth, now revealing a view of the lake, now a small herbaceous garden hidden in the midst of woodland. Interesting shrubs include a Victorian favourite, *Kalmia latifolia*, with its pink bells and the snowdrop tree *Halesia carolina*. The planting is Robinsonian so that beautiful flowering shrubs look as though they had grown there naturally among drifts of bluebells and under a canopy of the green fire of young beech leaves. The woodland drive to the house has a picnic area and the gorgeous Gandon-designed church of St John the Evangelist at Coolbanagher nearby is also well worth a visit.

The demesne at Emo has now been donated to the nation and is in the charge of the Office of Public Works.

Admission (£3.50 including house), gardens open daily 10.30am-5.30pm, toilet facilities. Suitable for children and wheelchairs. Teas on summer Sundays. Best March-June and autumn. House open 2 April-18 Oct., Mon. only, 2-6pm, tel. 0502-26110. Directions: On the Dublin Cork Road between Monasterevin and Portlaoise, Emo is to the right on the R422 at New Inn Cross.

HEYWOOD

Ballinakill, County Laois

HISTORICAL INTEREST
Romantic eighteenth-century landscaping is combined with Lutyens's splendid formal garden.

'Paint as you plant and as you work design.' So runs the apposite final line of Pope's poem framed in jasmine and set in the wall of the pantiled pavilion at Heywood. In front of this summer house is the sunken garden and centrepiece of Edwin Lutyens's formal design for the irascible Colonel Poe. A pool and fountain is encircled by a series of elliptical beds and terraces, the whole sheltered by a circular wall pierced with *œil de bœuf* windows.

The garden is one of four designed by Lutyens in Ireland and has a spectacular setting on a hillside looking south east over a sweep of undulating country which takes in seven counties. His work is the jewel in the crown of a landscaped

garden created in the eighteenth century. The demesne is an enchanting example of gardening in the 'romantic poetic' tradition of the period.

Michael Trench continued the work begun by his father, the Rev. Frederick Trench, the first recorded owner of the property, building a new house, creating artificial lakes and enhancing the sylvan landscape with gothic features. The turreted gate lodge, a gothic ruin boasting a fifteenth-century window from the nearby Aghadboe friary, as well as a bridge and stone cross still stand, but the Temple of the Winds at the lower end of the lake was demolished.

Heywood was said to be the only house in Ireland named after a mother-in-law. The house passed to Colonel and Mrs Hutcheson Poe, descendant of the Trenches, and Colonel Poe commissioned the new garden by Lutyens in the early 1900s. There are four main elements to Lutyens's design: the sunken garden linked with a formal lawn atop ramparts by an alley of pleached limes backed by stone walls decorated with niches and classical urns, a series of herb gardens sheltered by wall-like yew hedges, and a terraced pergola overlooking the largest of the estate's ornamental lakes. On the autumn day when I was there the lake mirrored golden beech woods and a lone pair of swans patrolling its waters.

Although the wisteria and roses which once wreathed the pergola are gone, it is a magical place. The shadows cast by the top of the pergola make a pattern radiating from a statue of Bacchus which stands at the end of the terrace. The original planting of the garden was designed by Dr Gertrude Jekyll and there are plans to restore the planting, based on photographs from that period. The stonework and paving used in Lutyens's design, which closely resembles Liscannor stone, was quarried nearby.

In 1941 the house and estate were purchased by the Salesian order, the house was demolished and a modern school has been built nearby. The Brothers assumed the role of guardians of the garden, which was partially restored by AnCO trainees in the mid 1980s. Although in need of further work this fascinating garden retains its beautiful bones and has been taken into the care of the Office of Public Works which is carrying out restoration work.

Admission free, April-Sept.

11am-6pm daily, tel. 0502-33563.

Not suitable for wheelchairs.

Parking for coaches.

Directions: Just under

five miles/8 km south

east of Abbeyleix close to

Ballinakill look for the gothic

gateway on the right as you

approach the village.

BELVEDERE

Mullingar, County Westmeath

GARDEN AND DEMESNE

A garden with a beautiful setting and
some remnants of its former glory.

Robert Rochfort, Baron Belfield, carried sibling rivalry to extreme lengths. His remarkable monument is the Jealous Wall, the largest gothic sham ruin in Ireland, built to blot out the view of his brother George's opulent home at Tudenham Park. Worse still, he locked away his lovely young wife, suspected of having an affair with another brother, Arthur, to languish at the family seat of Gaulston until his death 30 years later.

Whatever Rochfort's sins, Belvedere, Richard Castle's bow-ended Palladian villa, has the most heavenly setting on the shores of Lough Ennel. It was embellished a century later with a series of ballustraded terraces in the Italian manner by the then owner Charles Marley, who also added the walled garden.

Jealousy aside, sham ruins were extremely fashionable features at the time when the 'wall', now looming dramatically amid groves of trees, was built in 1760. The garden has three main areas: the arboretum which slopes down to the lakeside, an enclosed garden with shrubs and trees, and the walled garden which once contained a fine plant collection built up by Marley's cousin Charles Howard-Bury and continued by his friend Rex Beaumont to whom he left the property. Lt. Colonel Howard-Bury travelled widely collecting plants and seeds from as far afield as central Asia. He was also the leader of the first attempt to climb Mount Everest in 1921.

The walled garden is laid out in an unusual manner: the central gateway affords a vista over an interior designed as a pleasure garden with lawns, rose beds, and herbaceous borders once considered to be among the finest in Ireland. Some survivors of the garden's heyday remain - old roses, hydrangeas, the white tufted flowers of *Fothergilla* and the thistly *Echinops*, but the borders now contain mixed plantings of shrubs and perennials.

There are some charming details: a wishing well and a waterlily pond. There is a pleasant walk down through the wild garden to the shore line. Wild flowers flourish among the shelter of fine trees and there is an old ice house and a gothic archway to add to the interest.

The gardens are now the property of Westmeath County Council. Part of the walled garden has been closed off to become a pets' corner. Some of the magic has been lost due to a municipal approach in the use of tarmac and concrete kerbings but no doubt things will improve. The house with its delicate rococo plasterwork is closed at present but could provide a wonderful setting for an exhibition of Irish furniture or other artefacts.

Admission £1.00, open daily May-Sept. noon-6pm, tel. 044-40861. Suitable for wheelchairs. Directions: Situated three and three quarter miles/ 6 km from Mullingar on the Tullamore Road.

103

CARRIGGLAS MANOR

Longford, County Longford

FLOWER GARDEN

A very successful young garden to delight flower and rose lovers.

As a law student Thomas Lefroy of Carrigglas Manor had a youthful fancy for Jane Austen and provided the inspiration for Mr Darcy in *Pride and Prejudice*. The fine Tudor gothic house was designed by Daniel Robertson, in 1837. The magnificent 1790 stables were designed by James Gandon for the Newcomens, the previous owners of the estate.

Perhaps the romantic associations lingered on to inspire a delightful linear water garden created by Tessa Lefroy. Its starting-point was a pond, scooped out in a day by a JCB and lined with local clay, and fed by a small stream. Water-loving plants,

a collection of David Austin's old-fashioned roses and traditional herbaceous flowers are the main features of the planting. The winding layout of paths and stream is designed to reveal vistas of flowers, foliage and water.

Colour is used in a Jekyllesque way with plants grouped together in yellows, blues or shades of pink, red and purple. At the top end of the garden are banks with a display of old pink roses ('Felicité Parmentier', 'Abraham Darby', 'Madame Isaac Pereire', and 'Reines des Violettes'). The eye is drawn to an area of golden planting (lupins, decorative grasses, lilies, *Alstroemeria*, *Roscoea beesiana*) and on to a ribbon of yellow and green where *Mimulus guttatus*, candelabra primulas, hostas and astilbes follow the course of the stream. Above the pond pinks and deep crimsons predominate in a large shrub and herbaceous bed with a showy *R.* 'Abraham Darby', *R. Moyesii* 'Geranium' and a 'Rosa Mundi' in the centre.

On the far side of the stream the path winds past beds of magnificent old roses and peonies to a small paved Italian garden guarded by stone lions and planted with aromatic herbs. And beside the entrance to the stables there is a pleasant terrace area, where visitors can sit and enjoy tea or coffee over-looking the pool.

Tessa's garden is now escaping its present confines - as gardens will - and extending beyond the drive, where two Victorian notions - a stem garden and a fernery - are taking shape. Ash trees provide a canopy for shade-loving plants and shrubs like rhododendrons and azaleas on a suitably 'gothic' mound, in what is already a natural garden. The idea behind a stem garden was to allow the admiration of some of the more architectural plants like bamboos. The next phase of the plan will involve the creation of a potager, a fruit wall and inviting paths leading back to the house.

Admission £2.50, children £1.50 to garden, costume museum and stableyard. House £1.50, open first weekend June to first weekend Sept. Thurs.-Mon. 1.30-5.30pm, Sun. and Aug. 2-6pm, tel. 043-45165. A visit to Carrigglas may include an entertaining tour of the house given by Tessa or Jeffry Lefroy, and visits to a costume museum, a Victorian gift shop and a tea room. Self-catering accommodation in the Gandon mews makes a good base. Directions: On the main Mullingar-Longford Road about three miles/4.8 km before Longford follow signs to the right for Carrigglas.

STROKESTOWN PARK

Strokestown, County Roscommon

GARDEN RE-CREATION

A reinterpretation of a walled Edwardian pleasure garden, still very young but growing lovelier by the year.

If there was a moment when I thought I had hit upon the nearest thing to earthly paradise it had to be in the midst of the great double herbaceous borders of the walled garden at Strokestown Park.

Huge satisfying drifts of plants, with half a dozen different varieties of delphinium interspersed with blue, yellow and green planting edged with a frothy green wave of *Alchemilla mollis*, change to reds and purples in the mid distance and pinks and mauves in the distance. It is the longest herbaceous border in Ireland and I don't think anything so ambitious can have been planted since the days when Mr MacGregor found Peter Rabbit in his lettuce patch.

The original garden had become a shell, with only a pond, neglected yews and a runaway box hedge as reminders of former glories. The original garden had been supplanted by an Edwardian one which had not been worked for over thirty years and had become derelict. The re-creation of the garden was one of the final aspects of the restoration plan for Strokestown: first the walls were repaired, lowered and capped, the ground thoroughly prepared and treated with weedkiller, plans were drawn up by garden experts Helen Dillon and Jim Reynolds and load upon load of manure was added to the borders.

The investment in preparation has paid off handsomely. A splendid vista - through a decorative gate and down the central path of the four-acre garden to the lily pool and backed by an architectural feature - greets visitors. Beech hedge compartments will, in time, give the garden a sense of mystery and surprise as visitors discover the maze garden, the philosopher's walk with twenty-six niches for statues and other details, and a winter/flower arranger's border. Period details like a grass tennis court and a croquet lawn have been retained.

The rose garden with its lozenge shaped beds around a sundial is already well established and filled with old favourites like scarlet 'Trumpeter', 'Polar Star' and 'Sexy Rexy'. Planting in the fernery at the lower damp end of the garden is taking shape and the new pergola on a raised terrace will be softened by climbers and offers a vantage point over the garden.

The work was carried out by FÁS workers and backed by EU and National Heritage funding in conjunction with gardener Catrina White, garden consultant Rachel Lambe and Strokestown director Luke Dodd. Incredibly, Catrina is the only gardener - there were fifteen working in the gardens in the 1920s - and manages the eighteen-foot deep borders with an annual weeding and a deep mulch of spent mushroom compost.

In the future there are plans to restore the 1.3-acre kitchen garden with its range of Georgian greenhouses and seventeenth-century tower, and develop details like the vista down an overgrown walk to the Kilglass Hills and the planting in the park.

The story of Strokestown is inextricably linked to Ireland's turbulent history. In the seventeenth century land which had belonged to the O'Conor Roe was confiscated and granted to Nicholas Mahon. The house was built for his grandson, Thomas Mahon, and the ornamental estate was created to complement its Palladian design.

The town of Strokestown with its gracious wide streets was also built by the Pakenhams and was an expression of confidence in what in the eighteenth century appeared to be a buoyant economic future.

By the mid nineteenth century, however, the picture was bleak. The population of Ireland had doubled in just sixty years. Cottage industries which gave tenants alternative sources of revenue had collapsed, holdings had been sub-divided and Irish tenants had become dependent on a mono-crop. The 1845-1850 potato famine was a disaster waiting to happen. When it did, Major Denis Mahon, landlord of what had been a model estate, attempted to clear his 8,000 tenants through eviction and assisted passage to Canada. He was assassinated.

The last of the Mahons, Mrs Olive Pakenham Mahon, sold the house to the Westward Group.

Thanks to their imagination the contents and family papers were saved so that the house and the Famine Museum developed in the stables now provide a haunting insight into a dark chapter of social history, while the garden - as gardens do - restores the spirit.

Admission £2.00 adult, £1.00 child. The garden, house and museum are open May-30 Sept. Tues.-Sun. 11am-5.30pm. Full restaurant facilities. Directions: Strokestown Park is at the eastern end of Strokestown, fourteen miles/22.5 km from Longford, on the Dublin-Sligo N5.

TULLYNALLY CASTLE

Castlepollard, County Westmeath

DEMESNE, HISTORICAL INTEREST

A most beguiling spot to spend an hour or two wandering.

The castle and pleasure grounds at Tullynally are a fascinating reminder of the whims of changing fashion. The building started its existence as a fortified house and has been the home of the Pakenham family since the seventeenth century. Transformed into a Georgian mansion and then enlarged by successive generations, it was changed back into a gothic revival castle to the design of Francis Johnston. The final transformation, carried out by Sir Richard Morrison for the third Earl of Longford in 1840, has made Tullynally today the largest castellated private house in Ireland.

The garden also underwent a metamorphosis. A 1736 description of the grounds refers to a magnificent garden in the Baroque manner with water falling in cascades through a series of huge basins and canals – one nearly a mile/1.6 km in length – amid formal plantings of trees. This elaborate design was swept away in the craze for romantic landscaping and, by 1760, naturalistic pleasure grounds – executed in a homespun way – had taken shape. A wonderful skeleton of this mid eighteenth-century garden remains beside the enchanting castle with its parkland setting.

These are the main attractions of Tullynally: a rich assortment of flowers should not be expected.

The gate to the right of the castle front leads to a Victorian terrace with magnificent views across the county towards Knockeyon; a pair of young wellingtonias have been planted here by the current Pakenham in residence, writer Thomas Pakenham, nephew of the sixth Earl of Longford, famous for his work at Dublin's Gate Theatre.

Walks wind from here through sylvan glades of fine specimen trees, including a cut-leaved beech and a tulip tree. Among the devices to entertain strollers are a small grotto with views towards Lough Derravaragh where the Children of Lir swam as swans, and the River Sham (an ornamental lake masquerading as a river).

The first of the walled gardens contains the remains of a Victorian flower garden. Old roses, jasmine and clematis cover the walls, there is a weeping pillar with water trickling down rustic stones to a small pond, a modest herbaceous border, a summer house (where the sixth Earl's mother-in-law used to exercise in wet weather with a pedometer to check her mileage) and informal planting of acers and flowering shrubs.

The kitchen garden – its entrance guarded by a pair of Coade stone sphinxes – is a ghost of its

Admission £3.00, May-Sept. 2-6pm daily. Groups at other times. Tours of the castle are sometimes available to groups by appointment, tel. 044-61159. Suitable for children but rather uphill work for wheelchairs. Directions: Follow the signs for the castle from the square in Castlepollard.

former glory. Only the Yew Walk with its stately Florence Court yews and intriguing patchwork hedge of yew, box and holly, a small rose walk and a couple of the Regency hothouses, with their scale-like curved glass panes, survive. Valerie and Thomas Pakenham are carrying out some restoration work and replanting the gardens with help from FAS. There are plans afoot to create new herbaceous borders and to do more in the flower garden.

Undeterred by thin limey soil over a layer of rock, Thomas Pakenham is creating a new area of arboretum with a collection of 43 acers, a variety of magnolias, and a group of oaks grown from acorns and showing interesting variations. There are adolescent specimen trees including a 17-year-old *Wellingtonia*, *Cryptomeria* and the handkerchief tree *Davidia involucrata*.

His latest project is an extension to the wild garden in the forest walk beyond the River Sham. A streamlet meanders beside the path, trickles into a pool bordered with damp-loving candelabra primulas, astilbes, skunk cabbage and yellow flags and meanders on again. The soil along this walk goes from limeyness so extreme that even Christmas trees turn yellow - to ground so acid it is nearly sterile.

In the more hospitable areas there are new plantings of rhododendrons, azaleas, metasequoias, silver maple and sorbus, while primroses and foxgloves are seeding among the trees.

The walk leads to a rustic shelter beside Swan Lake. Like Euridice in the Underworld, you must not look back until you reach the shelter and then, just as Francis Johnston intended, you will see the fairytale castle of Tullynally standing atop its hill. The energetic can continue on a circular walk through rhododendrons and woods and back across parkland.

An exciting new area is taking shape around pools created by diverting the stream. Known as the 'Chinese Clearing' or the 'Expedition Garden', this garden is the exclusive home of plants grown from seed brought back from Thomas Pakenham's recent expedition to the Yunan region of China. Just as the original plant discoverers once did, Thomas brought back seeds from unfamiliar species and - having 'wintered' the seeds in the fridge for a few weeks - propagated them successfully to create the makings of a very unique garden.

The approach to the castle is through magnificent parkland dotted with ancient oaks. The entrance to the pleasure grounds is through a hedge beyond the forecourt; sensible shoes are advisable as the grounds are extensive.

BIRR CASTLE DEMESNE

Birr, County Offaly

DEMESNE AND GARDEN
The fascinating estate of a family of outstanding scientists and gardeners.

With its fairytale setting beside the River Camcor the great estate at Birr has something for everyone. In contrast to the grandeur of the castle keep, the side entrance to the 62 hectares of pleasure grounds is low key. Situated at the end of a street in the town it gives onto a sweep of parkland with the lake shimmering in the distance. To the right, paths lead to a small formal garden - the creation of Anne, sixth Countess of Rosse - based on a seventeenth-century design with hornbeam *allées* and marvellously intricate box hedges. Squares of beautifully pruned apple trees surround pristine glasshouses. Beyond are the huge greenhouses and enclosed gardens - with the tallest box hedges anywhere - where scientific work is still carried out, and the garden staff includes a full-time propagator.

Outside what was the original kitchen garden, paths lead off into woodland where there are some of the many surprises hidden in the grounds: among them a fernery and a waterfall with a gravity-driven fountain jetting water high above wooden bridges. Deeper into the woods (Coill an Tobair) there is a shell-well.

To the left of the entrance there are paths to the imposing castle. First acquired by Sir Laurence Parsons in 1620, Birr was once known as Parsonstown. Parts of the castle are extremely old, dating back to 1620 and earlier; the building was enlarged and gothicised at the beginning of the last century.

An area of informal garden was created below the castle by the fifth Earl of Rosse with a series of terraces overlooking the river. Many rare shrubs and trees around the estate were grown from seed brought back by the various plant expeditions to China, Asia and the Americas sponsored by the sixth Earl. He was a particularly fine plantsman and he bred a wonderful hybrid tree peony named for the sixth Countess, Anne Rosse. A graceful suspension bridge - one of the earliest of its kind - gives private access to the river garden where some of the most spectacular specimens in the garden can be admired from afar: the rare *Carriera calycina*, *Magnolia dawsoniana* and *veitchii*, and a coffin juniper. Like the *Paeonia* 'Anne Rosse' the *Tilia henryana* has been painted by Wendy Walsh and will feature in her new publication *A Prospect of Irish Flowers*. A lilac walk and a lagoon garden are also among the features in this part of the grounds.

Further afield on the far side of the lake is an arboretum crossed by a cherry avenue and circled by a yew walk. If you are interested in trees there is an excellent guide, *Fifty Trees of Distinction*, partly based on the records kept at Birr. The *Magnolia delavayi* growing against the castle walls, for instance, was bought in 1912 for twelve and sixpence.

Right in the middle of the grounds is the display area for the enormous telescope created by William, third Earl of Rosse. It was originally mounted between crenellated arches and for three quarters of a century after it was invented in the 1840s, the leviathan was the world's largest telescope. The results of the third Earl's studies, including his extraordinary drawings of the nebulae stars, and the work of two subsequent generations of Parsons is now housed in the museum of astronomy at Birr. Brendan Parsons, the present Earl, still lives at Birr.

Admission Mar., Nov., Dec. £2.60, children £1.30; April-Oct. adults £3.20, children £1.60, groups (20 plus) £2.60. Tel. 0509-20056. Allow several hours and wear flat shoes as there is lots of ground to be covered. Suitable for children and for wheelchairs. Indoor exhibitions of some aspect of Birr's history, May-Sept. Light meals available at the coffee shop beside the tourist office across the road from the entrance. Excellent, reasonably priced plants propagated on the estate are on sale at the gate.

PORTRANE HOUSE

Portlaoise, County Laois

FLOWER GARDEN

A cheerful small garden to pop into if you are passing.

One of the essential pieces of equipment in Mrs Joan Tyrell's garden is a sheet used to pose brides on when wedding parties come to have their pictures taken in her attractive garden.

Mrs Tyrell has been gardening at the Tyrell family home for 40 years and new areas and choice new plants constantly appear in her one-acre garden. The latest creation is a rock garden filled with year-round colour, made from an unpromising stony bank. Irregular-shaped stones around the edge of the lawn hold a choice selection of plants and shrubs, all with interesting stories attached. A flourishing *Abutilon violetta*, a *Fremontodendron* and a pineapple tree *Cytisus battandieri* are proof that tender plants can be grown in the Midlands if the right site is found for them.

Among Mrs Tyrell's favourite plants are old shrub roses (including 'Gertrude Jekyll'), and shrubs *Cornus controversa* 'Variegata', *Viburnum* 'Mariesii' and *Acer negundo* 'Variegatum'. Portrane House, a former rectory and base for James Tyrell's veterinary practice, is a busy place where callers, including hedgehogs in distress, are welcome.

Admission free. Garden enthusiasts may drop in any time. Directions: Coming into Portlaoise from Dublin, turn left after the large Catholic church and you will see the Tyrells' plaque a few houses up on the right.

LOUGH RYNN

Mohill, County Leitrim

DEMESNE

*A good place to bring the family for
an outing.*

Lough Rynn was once the
property of the wicked third
Earl of Leitrim. He may have been a
very brilliant man with
revolutionary ideas on agriculture
and a passion for straight hedges, but
he has gone down in history as an
evicting landlord. He was
assassinated in 1878.

At the time the demesne was the
nerve centre for a vast 90,000-acre
estate in four counties. The earliest
part of the house is in the Tudor
revival style and dates back to 1832
and the later wing and the
stables were designed by Sir Thomas
Drew in 1878 for the fourth Earl
of Leitrim.

A very great deal of money has
been spent on turning the property
into a leisure centre. The jewel in
Lough Rynn's crown should be the
terraced walled gardens overlooking
the lake designed by Deane and
Woodward in 1859. But while the
waterside setting and the design of
the garden with its charming gothic
folly and lynch-gate are very fine,
the planting is disappointing. The
sheltering walls could provide ideal
conditions for all kinds of glorious
things to be grown.

The pleasure grounds are laid
out with wide walks leading to the
ruins of a sixteenth-century tower,
to a Bronze Age dolmen and to a
wishing seat. The fine collection of
specimen trees in the arboretum is
in good condition and all are
carefully labelled. The house itself is
empty and the estate office has
become a craft shop and restaurant.

Admission £3.50 per car. A
children's playground, boat rides
and a fast food restaurant are
among the attractions, tel. 078-
31427. Directions: Lough Rynn is
signposted from Mohill three
miles/4.8 km out on
the Drumlish Road.

BALLINLOUGH CASTLE

Clonmellon, County Westmeath

DEMESNE

An ornamental Edwardian walled garden under restoration in the setting of a magical seventeenth-century demesne.

A sense of anticipation as visitors breast a hill in the wooded avenue is richly rewarded by the sight of Ballinlough Castle perched on the edge of an incline overlooking a sparkling lake.

Like the perfect illustration in a book of fairytales there is something totally beguiling about this view of a curving arm of land, encircling the spring-fed lake and crowned by the castle. The site was probably chosen with defence in mind when the castle was originally built in the fifteenth century; but it must have satisfied eighteenth-century sensibilities which required splendid sites with views of water for impressive new country seats. Perhaps this is why the O'Reilly's castle was incorporated in the castellated 1730s house, which was enlarged and embellished in the 1790s.

The castle's beautiful setting was also enhanced during the rage for ornamental demesnes which swept Ireland. A canal was dug from the corner of the lake to simulate a river terminating in a rustic bridge and can be seen in the first 1813 Ordnance Survey map. Walks were laid out around the lake, woods and parkland planted with native timber and the walled garden and a charming stable block built by Sir Hugh O'Reilly in the mid 1700s.

Ballinlough Castle is almost unique in that it has been continuously inhabited by a Celtic Catholic family since it was built. The Nugents of Ballinlough were originally O'Reillys, Hugh O'Reilly having changed his name in order to inherit in 1812.

The landscaping was altered in the 1840s when a second lake was dug to give employment during the Great Famine and a curious mounded island was created. Built

The gardens will open fully at Easter 1997 on a regular daily basis. Full details are not yet available.

of turf, the island was accidentally set on fire during construction and has a crater in the centre to this day.

Phase one of the exciting restoration undertaken by Sir John and Lady Nugent at Ballinlough - the first to be carried out under the £4 million Great Gardens of Ireland Restoration Scheme and implemented by a team of FÁS workers - involves the reinstatement of the lakeside paths and the dredging of the famine lake. The summer house - where the housekeeper of fifty years standing, Betty, did her courting - affords an enchanting view from the Badger Bank across the lake to the castle, and a landing stage for rowing boats will be replaced.

The second phase has involved major alterations to the Edwardian ornamental garden within the three-and-a-half acre walled gardens. By the 1940s the area was being used as a stallion paddock and when I saw the garden in 1995 only the bare bones were there: the grass tennis court, sunken garden, a few trees and shrubs and the encompassing walls. The new plan will evoke the heyday of garden design when it was inspired by the influence of practitioners like Gertrude Jekyll and Edwin Lutyens.

Drawings for Jim Reynolds' new design show a central walk flanked by double herbaceous borders, traditional shade borders along the north wall, formal yew hedges, new planting around the sunken garden and existing grass tennis court, and strategically placed summer houses affording vistas of the garden. Two smaller walled areas will contain a rose garden and a scented garden with cottage style planting. Outside the walls there are plans for an ornamental vegetable garden, a nursery and propagation area screened by a beech hedge, a café and a shop overlooking lawns, and yew and magnolia walks.

The ornamental gardens lie in a sheltered area to the south of the castle and are linked to the lake by a charming informal area with woodland paths and a water garden with a rustic bridge and a stream bordered in candelabra primulas. From there, walks will lead around the lake to a vantage point backed by beds of scented azaleas, where the distant castle can be seen like a fairytale vision.

The story of Ballinlough Castle and demesne echoes the rise and fall in the fortunes of great Irish estates: expansion and building during the optimistic eighteenth century, the crises and decline of the nineteenth century and the uncertainty followed by new hope during the twentieth. By the end of the last century the original estate had been reduced from 6,000 acres to 500. If

Sir John's father Sir Hugh Nugent had not asked the 1931 Land Commission to retain the castle and gradually pieced back the land inside the demesne wall, Ballinlough would have been tumbled and its stone used for roads.

Now the tide has turned again. The Nugents wish the story of Ballinlough to continue and the restoration of the demesne and gardens was chosen as a way of sharing a rare and enchanting aspect of Irish heritage.

LODGE PARK
WALLED GARDEN

Straffan, County Kildare

WALLED GARDEN

Compartmentalised fruit and flower garden beside a steam museum.

The great fascination about walled gardens – inspired by Frances Hodgson Burnett's *Secret Garden* – is that you never know what lies inside these private worlds.

At Lodge Park there are some most rewarding surprises to be discovered in the two-acre garden surrounded by mellow brick walls: among them a crown-shaped rosarie, filled with intoxicating scents and sights.

There are also all the charming features that might be expected in an old-world garden: deep herbaceous borders filled with great drifts of colour, fruit blushing ripe on neatly espaliered trees and a sundial marking off the scented hours. In fact, though, the garden

at Lodge Park has recently been re-created and is full of intriguing details which could readily be adapted for average sized gardens.

The traditional feature of a main path offering a vista down the length of the garden has been retained. The formality of its box edging, punctuated with yew pyramids, offers a pleasing contrast to borders filled with a profusion of shrubs and architectural plants. The path gives access to a series of garden rooms, each with very different moods. There is a salad garden – its geometric design paved in brick, edged in chives and filled with a red and green pattern of lettuces – and a soft-fruit garden fenced with espaliered apple trees. A sweet pea pergola, its blooms shading through the spectrum, provides scented access to the vegetable garden proper with its beds of sea kale, courgettes and asparagus peas (delicious to look at and to eat).

The wrought iron rosarie is hidden away in a peaceful green orchard area. At the heart of the brick-paved arbour twin benches allow visitors to sit and admire the canopy of favourite old climbers like 'Rambling Rector' and 'Wedding Day', with smaller roses like The Fairy and Little Pet at their feet.

Mature beech hedges create room-like compartments in the garden and help to maintain the element of anticipation as to what might lie next. I lost my heart to a small white and silver garden, with a stone well-head as a centrepiece and informal planting punctuated with white agapanthus, miniature *Gypsophila*, *Nicotiana* and white petunias. Nearby, in another small garden, a velvety lawn separates a purple border from a peony border.

The garden at Lodge Park is a happy example of the way old gardens can be restored to a version of their former glory. In 1948 half the garden was used as a stud paddock. In the fifties, herbaceous borders and a vegetable garden were reinstated. The second restoration over the previous decade included ornamental vegetable gardens and the addition of ornamental shrubs and flowers in the overall composition designed by Anthony O'Grady (now head gardener at Penshurst Place) and Michael Thomas. Brendan Walsh, a self-taught iron worker was responsible for the execution of the rosarie, while John Moriarty, now a psychologist and author, breathed life into the trees.

Patrick Ardiff, the gardener, has continued the creativity in a garden originally inspired by the Du Pont family's garden at Longmoore. Restoration work is in progress on a handsome brick greenhouse (1834), fronted by a pool garden. And in the north facing border, the sheltering walls provide protection to plants which don't normally survive the inland frosts. There are lots of choice varieties to reward keen plantspeople - the variegated *Nora Leigh phlox*, chocolate scented *Cosmos atrosanguineus*, *Tulbaghia violacea*, a wonderfully dark miniature agapanthus and a lovely collection of violas including 'Irish Molly' and 'Jackanapes'.

Admission £3.00, Open June and July Fri.-Sun. 2-5pm; August Tues.-Fri. 2-3pm; or by appointment for groups, tel. 6288412. Directions: Just outside Straffan, turn off the N7 at Kill or off the N4 at Lucan or Maynooth.

Beside the tennis court, a particularly handsome herbaceous border provides a feast for the senses. Old-fashioned plants like hollyhocks, pale lemon sunflowers, yellow centurion and *Erigerons* provide a touch of nostalgia, while stately *Onopordums* and cardoons give an architectural element to the planting.

But this isn't a place purely for plantspeople. St Jude's - once the engineers' church at Inchicore - has been rebuilt in the grounds to house a superb collection of model locomotives and a great thundering collection of steam engines from distilleries and breweries, including the engine from a sludge dredger. The Steaming Kettle tea room, decorated with a collection of steam prints, offers sinful delights like iced coffee and chocolate cake and there is a gift shop stocked with the National Trust collection - the only one of its kind in the twenty-six counties.

HILTON PARK

Clones, County Monaghan

HISTORICAL INTEREST

A Victorian garden set in an ornamental eighteenth-century estate.

'The place is pretty, a very fine wood of all sorts of forest trees planted by Dr Madden just by the house surrounded by a fine river,' wrote Mrs Delaney of Hilton Park in 1748, fourteen years after Dr Samuel Madden bought the property which originally belonged to the MacMahon sept from descendants of Sir Robert Fort.

The indefatigable Mrs Delaney was a great supporter of the eighteenth-century wave of enthusiasm for garden visiting. Going to view 'improvements' - the landscaped parks and pleasure grounds designed to offset handsome, country mansions - was one of the favourite occupations of the day for the gentry. And Mrs Delaney's diaries provided a helpful reference in the fascinating task of unravelling the history of the garden undertaken recently by the present Maddens in residence, Johnny and Lucy.

Basically this lovely estate consists of an eighteenth-century recreational park, featuring a particularly fine oak wood and great stands of beech, chestnut, oak and pine grouped around lakes and parkland and a nineteenth-century ornamental garden.

The Maddens are now involved in an exciting restoration project. They have re-created the 1876 formal parterre under the dining-room window. Box, yew, holly and

Admission adults £3.00, OAP £2.00. May-Sept. Sundays and Bank Holidays 2-6pm. Groups (min. 6) by appointment. Tel. 047-56007. Directions: Three and a quarter miles/5 km from Clones on the Scotshouse Road.

Euonymus have been used for the design based on a Maltese cross originally laid out by Ninian Niven for Johnny Madden's great-grandfather, John Madden. Beyond it the nineteenth-century rose garden has been reinterpreted and is planted with old-fashioned favourites like shrub roses, delphiniums and phlox. The restoration, begun in 1993 and aided by EU Leader and European Architectural Heritage funds, will also include the re-creation of a much earlier herb garden.

The Maddens' garden detective work took them back to the seventeenth century when the estate was purchased from the MacMahons in 1624 by Sir William Temple Knight, Provost of Trinity College, Dublin, who built a house there. Maps and evidence in the grounds suggest that there may have been some kind of garden there from as early as 1690, before the present house (decorated in 1870) was built in 1735. There are still a great many mysteries to be solved - like the origins of the man-made canal which runs between the two lakes through an area known as the 'Lovers' Walk' and planted with hydrangeas and rhododendrons.

Hilton Park is a lovely object lesson in the way that gardens, people and history are inextricably entwined. Dr Samuel Madden belonged to the enlightened generation which founded the Royal Dublin Society. He was known as 'Premium Madden' because of the incentive payments he offered to improve Irish agriculture. In his 1735 treatise on 'Reflections and resolutions proper to the gentlemen of Ireland' he wrote about the need for 'added value' for Irish produce - a concept that is still urgently promoted today. In 1862/3 Premium Madden engaged the services of a Mr Frazer, landscape gardener, whom he described as having 'the most experienced and most valuable opinion in these matters'.

John Madden (1837-1902) belonged to that great generation of Victorian amateur enthusiasts. He travelled the world and was one of the first to bring back the seeds of Californian redwoods, sequoias, Douglas Fir and other specimen trees from the western seaboard of America and introduce them to Ireland at Hilton Park.

Despite the marginalisation of the estates generally, the Maddens' desire to survive has created another chapter at Hilton Park and in addition to the restoration scheme the kitchen garden has been rescued and is in use much as it was in previous centuries, thanks to vegetable producers who run it on biodynamic principles.

THE NORMANDY
OF IRELAND

Everyone has their own Nirvana, a blissful place of escape that waits in the corner of the mind or at the end of a road marked holiday. Ireland is full of such places held in the imagination. And for a great many people the scenery of West Cork, Kerry or Connemara is the promised land.

But the landscape that has a hold on my heart and head lies in the south east. It is a country defined not by counties but by gentle mountains: the Blackstairs, the Knockmealdowns, the Comeraghs, and wooded valleys cradling the Suir, the Blackwater, the Nore, the Barrow and the Slaney. It is an elusive territory, always changing, never fully revealing itself, so that I feel I have to keep going back to catch the essence of it.

The countryside is different, somehow, from the rest of Ireland, more opulent, less bleak. Easy access and rich land made the area a favourite target for successive waves of invasion, settlement and plantation. The Vikings gave their names to coastal settlements: Wexford, Waterford and Youghal. There is a strong Norman imprint and the south east has been called the Normandy of Ireland. The bones of history show through clearly; places like Kilkenny city, Clonmel and Fethard in County Tipperary have medieval layouts or defences still.

The riverside towns have a charm lacking in the typical linear developments of the Midlands. There are places like Graiguenamanagh on the Barrow, a spot like something out of a Thomas Hardy novel, or quaint Thomastown, its narrow streets running up and down the banks of the Nore and Inistioge, surely one of the prettiest small towns in Ireland. More of the land is cultivated - especially in Wexford - than in any other area of Ireland.

The lure of rich land meant historically that the area had a large share of monasteries, Jerpoint Abbey, Kells, Callan, Ferns, and great houses and estates: Coolattin, Curraghmore, Castletowncox and Lismore. Undeservedly the least discovered, the area is almost untouched by the bungalow blight which has hit Donegal and Connemara so hard. There are incredible gardens, with one of the finest collections of rhododendrons in the world at Mount Congreve, an exquisite prize-winning garden on the fringes of Wexford, and the magical Robinsonian gardens at Altamont where the most gorgeous drives wind between the gardens through constantly changing scenery; and there are some fascinating places to stay.

ROUND AND ABOUT

For a scenic drive to Altamont from Dublin go via Rathdrum, Aughrim, mourning the lost oaks as you pass Coolattin, admiring the estate village of Shillelagh created by Lord Fitzwilliam. Aughrim is a stronghold of nurseries with hardy shrubs at a fraction of Dublin prices. Arie Van der Wel's Cappagh Nursery has a particularly good selection of rhododendrons. Altamont is a satisfying trip in itself, Marlfield House, Mary Bowe's wonderful restaurant, is signposted from the bridge just as you come into Gorey from the Dublin side.

Enniscorthy is a satisfying place to poke about in, County Wexford Museum is housed in Enniscorthy Castle, once owned by Edmund Spenser (admission £1.00), and a little further up Castle Hill there is a rather tempting antiques shop. The Kiltrea Bridge Potteries, which produces the most wonderful flower pots and jardinières, is signposted from just outside Enniscorthy. The turn off the main road at Ferns will bring you to Bunclody, a pretty estate village with the unusual feature of a stream running down the wide main street.

The turning off the main Dublin Road just outside New Ross for Inistioge leads to a cluster of attractive villages including Thomastown. Take a mini-voyage across the mouth of the Barrow on the Ballyhack ferry. The Reginald, built into the ninth-century Viking wall on the main route through Waterford, is a good place to stop for anything from a coffee to a slap-up meal in original surroundings. Kilkenny is known as the Marble City; the streets were once paved with marble from the nearby quarries. It has a great deal to offer, from the magnificently restored Kilkenny Castle and gardens to the eighteenth-century St Canice's Cathedral. The Dunmore Caves are nearby, and for a meal in unusual surroundings try Kytlers Tavern situated in the basement of a house reputed to have been owned by a witch.

About three miles/4.8 km from Wexford town at Ferrycarrig is the Irish National Heritage Park beside the River Slaney which takes you through 9,000 years of Irish history. One much recommended village is Dunmore East with thatched houses and some excellent pubs.

There is a breathtaking drive through the Vee of the Knockmealdown Mountains to the water garden at Glenleigh. And in nearby Cahir the beautifully restored Swiss Cottage at Cahir Park is well worth a visit.

PLACES TO STAY

Cullintra House, Inistioge, County Kilkenny, is a 200-year-old farm at the foot of Mount Brandon which looks like a building from a Beatrix Potter book. This is a place where one should rise in leisurely fashion and linger late over Patricia Cantlon's excellent dinners. B & B £20-£23.00, dinner £16.00, tel. 051-23614.

At Aherne's, Youghal, an attractive new bedroom wing has been added to the pub and justly famous seafood restaurant. It is situated in the old port of Youghal.

Lorum Old Rectory, Bagenalstown, County Carlow, is a good base from which to explore the lovely Nore, Barrow and Blackwater valleys (tel. 0503-75282), as is Lisnavagh, Rathvilly, County Carlow, with its beautiful parkland setting (tel. 0503-61104). Ballinkeele House near Enniscorthy, County Wexford, was designed for the Maher family by Daniel Robertson in 1840 (tel. 053-38105).

MOUNT CONGREVE

Kilmeadan, County Waterford

DEMESNE AND WILD GARDEN

One of the wonders of Ireland.
Magnificent all year but intoxicating in
spring from February onwards.

A private garden of the sheer size
and splendour of Mount
Congreve must be virtually unique
not only in Ireland but in the world.
This is gardening on a scale rarely
seen since the eighteenth century,
but whereas the Georgians devoted
their energies to creating impressive
landscapes, Ambrose Congreve has
spent a lifetime amassing a
magnificent collection of flowering
shrubs and trees.

The estate is situated atop hills
overlooking a majestic bend in the
River Suir where beech and oak
woods provide a canopy of cover for
one of the largest collections of
rhododendrons in the world. Within
the 110-acre garden there are over
3,000 varieties of rhododendron,
600 types of camellia, 300 varieties
of magnolia and 250 types of
Japanese maple.

Mr Congreve began his collection

as a child, inspired by the Rothschilds' gardens at Exbury, and is said to have planted his first *Magnolia campbellii* at the age of 11. The gardens at Mount Congreve were designed and laid out according to his philosophy that shrubs should be planted not in ones or twos but in hundreds.

The results are stunning. With planting in massive sweeps of single species, the effect - especially in spring - is to produce spectacular bands of contrasting blossom. On the avenue running down from the house to the walled gardens, for instance, magnolias, rhododendrons, pieris and bluebells provide ascending layers of colour in blue, crimson, coral and white.

Paths running through the woods allow the blossom to be seen from different angles and one of the most stunning sights comes from looking down on a sea of *Magnolia soulangeana* or catching a glimpse of the river framed by the yellow blossoms and handsome dark green leaves of *R. macabeanum*.

Each turn and undulation reveals further breathtaking sights and smells - it would be worth a visit to the garden for the heady perfume wafting from a swath of the pink-flushed bells of *R.* 'Lady Alice Fitzwilliam' alone - or to see the huge fragrant trumpets of a collection of *R. loderi* lighting up

their surroundings; and for sheer dazzling colour it would be hard to beat the sizzling coral of Mr Congreve's favourite azalea, named appropriately 'Favourite', which borders a walk near a classical temple with a view downriver.

Every garden should have its surprise but Mount Congreve has a whole series of them. The most spectacular is the view of a brilliantly coloured Japanese pagoda suddenly revealed at the foot of 100-foot cliffs, centre-stage in a pool surrounded by lawn. Pass through the door of the classical loggia and there is another surprise, a small area

Guided tours only by appointment, tel. 051-84115. Most paths suitable for wheelchairs. Directions: Just off the main Cork Waterford Road five miles/8 km from Waterford. Look for the Arks sign on the left, follow the road taking the right fork and the main gate to Mount Congreve is on your left.

enclosing a pool, known as the Girl's Garden, and where the poetic name of one of the dwarf Japanese maples translates as 'snipes rising out of a bog'.

There is also a splendid water feature fed by cascades running over a dramatic rock face, and my favourite surprise: a secluded amphitheatre where an audience of pencil-slim cypress and a family of the small Japanese R. *yakushimanum*, named after the seven dwarfs, overlook a rock pool.

The plan makes full use of the views of the river and at the far end of the grounds a broad ride framed by magnolias is aligned with a view upriver. Nearby there is an Alpine area and a newly created bed with a mouthwatering collection of tree peonies. Thousands upon thousands of crocuses, *Muscari* (grape hyacinth) and *Chionodoxa* (glory of the snow) have been planted to give carpets of flowers even in the earliest days of the year.

Aside from the flowering shrub collections there is a huge amount to reward arboreal enthusiasts. Among them the foxglove tree *Paulownia tomentosa*, the handkerchief tree *Davidia involucrata*, *Nothofagus menziesii*, the Kentucky coffee tree *Exochorda macrantha*, mahogany-barked cherries, many fine conifers including *Picea orientalis* 'Aurea', a dawn redwood (*Metasequoia glyptostroboides*), tree ferns and one of the finest specimens of *Michelia doltsopa* in these islands. The collection is superbly maintained on an unimaginable scale. During the flowering season the rhododendrons and azaleas are sprayed once a fortnight and when their flowers have finished blooming, every single shrub is deadheaded.

Gardener director Herman Dool or his assistant Michael White give the most informative tours of the garden and are extremely enthusiastic about the relative merits of the thousands of species in their care. Among them are a number of Mount Congreve hybrids; one of the great aims of the propagation programme there is to produce an early yellow-flowered rhododendron. In the extensive nursery - open to trade only, alas - beyond the walled garden, many of the species from the garden are now being produced commercially.

This glorious garden will eventually be left to the nation with a trust for maintenance for the first 25 years.

CURRAGHMORE

Portlaw, County Waterford

DEMESNE

The appeal of this great estate lies in the combined impact of the imposing house, landscaped grounds and surrounding scenery.

For sheer grandeur and scale it would be hard to equal the great estate at Portlaw. Curraghmore House has a magnificent setting amid ancient oak woods with the River Clodagh flowing through the estate.

Pheasants stroll about on the mile and a half/2.4 km long drive through woods and parkland. The first sight of the house suddenly revealed by a bend in the drive comes as a dramatic surprise; with its huge formal forecourt flanked by stable ranges Curraghmore looks more like a French château than an Irish mansion. There is nothing like it in the country and the imposing central tower surmounted by St Hubert's stag - the symbol of the de

la Poer family - adds to the exotic air of the place.

The grounds laid out by the first Beresford Earl of Tyrone around 1750 provide a splendid example of an eighteenth-century romantic landscape, with the house as its centrepiece. Behind the house is the garden in the French manner designed by Louisa, third Lady Waterford. Its formal terraces, with balustrades and statuary, overlook a man-made lake. To the west a vista through the woods stretches off to infinity. Hidden in a shrubbery is the most enchanting shellhouse, created by Catherine Countess of Tyrone with 'her proper' hands in 1754. The decoration of the folly took her 261 days to complete and the intricate patterns of shells from all over the world still glow with colour above a statue of the Countess by John van Nost.

The specimen trees surrounding the gardens date from the mid nineteenth century when many species were first introduced to Ireland, and at Curraghmore sequoias, abies and cedars have grown to magnificent size. One of the sitka spruces - nearly 180 feet/ 55 km high - is thought to be the tallest in Ireland. Spanning the River Clodagh is a bridge reputed to have been built for King John's visit to Ireland in 1205.

To the north east of the house magnificent oaks planted to supply timber for the British fleet climb Tower Hill, which takes its name from the monument to the 12-year-old son of the first Marquis of Waterford, who was killed jumping his horse in 1785.

The unique appearance of Curraghmore House rouses the curiosity of visitors and its architectural history is complex. The central tower is part of a medieval castle of the Norman de la Poer family and is incorporated in the front part of the house, which was rebuilt in 1700 and subsequently enlarged and remodelled by James Power, third Earl of Tyrone. His daughter and heiress, Lady Catherine, married Sir Marcus Beresford, who became the first Earl of Tyrone of the second creation, and built the stable ranges in the 1750s.

Tours of the house are normally conducted by the Marquis of Waterford and last for up to one and a half hours.

The nearby village of Portlaw was designed in the nineteenth century by the Quaker Malcolmsons as a model village for their mill workers.

Admission £2.00, the grounds and shellhouse may be viewed between Easter and October, Thursday afternoons and public holidays only, 2-5pm. Beware of fearless pheasants and sleeping policemen (ramps) on the driveway. The house, with some of the finest eighteenth-century interiors designed by James Wyatt, is open by special appointment at £150 per group for parties of up to 20, and £7.50 per head thereafter, tel. 051-387102, fax. 051-387481.

Directions: Curraghmore is 14 miles/22.5 km from Waterford, eight miles/13 km from Kilmacthomas and five miles/ 8 km from Carrick-on-Suir. The turning for Portlaw is off the main Waterford Dungarvan Road and the entrance to the estate is to the east of Portlaw.

ALTAMONT

Tullow, County Carlow

FLOWER AND WILD GARDEN

A truly magical place combining both wild and formal gardens.

The grounds at Altamont have an almost dreamlike quality about them. Lawns slope down from the house to a lake reflecting splashes of golden azalea, and beyond the encircling woods there is a glimpse of Lugnaquilla Mountain, blue in the distance. On the glorious May day when I was there the picture was completed by a pair of swans and their day-old cygnets framed in the arch of a yew peacock.

A grand stone gateway, a beech avenue and the sight of the pink-washed house snuggled into its coat of wisteria are enticing preludes to the garden. The tour begins with the cathedral-like splendour of the nun's walk, so-called because nuns were thought to have lived in the earliest parts of the house, which date back to 1500. The walk is carpeted with a succession of flowers from daffodils to autumn cyclamen and lined with beeches planted by the St George family, who built the 1720s house.

A small formal garden with a pool and box-edged beds set in gravel makes a perfect link between the house and the broad walk that goes down to the lake. This area was created when Corina North courageously removed the traditional bank hiding the basement. One of the twin beds holds a fine collection of dwarf conifers - including a silver fir (*Abies nobilis prostrata*) - underplanted with spring bulbs and heathers. Nearby other shrubs make a golden and crimson composition. Peacocks, mop-headed Chinese silkies and guinea-fowl wander around the lawns keeping a wary eye out for the fox.

The broad walk bordered with old-fashioned shrub roses and guarded by 130-year-old clipped yews leads down to the lake and informal gardens. Many of the rhododendrons and azaleas round the lake were grown from seed by Mrs North's father Feild Lecky Watson, who was a subscriber to various expeditions. A tulip tree, a handkerchief tree aflutter with thousands of white bracts in May, and a swamp cypress stand sentinel beside the lake, which was dug out in the 1850s to provide work after the Famine.

From the lakeside a series of inviting walks lead in different directions. The recommended route is to turn left at the lake and follow the path to the ribbon arboretum created by Mrs North 20 years ago, where tender specimens - among them Chilean flame trees and snow gums - flourish and huge *Gunnera* plants add a primeval touch. The path doubles back to a bog garden, then wanders down to a truly enchanting glen where a stream chuckles among ice age boulders velvety with moss and ferns. The stream's destination is a broad reach of the Slaney River where the path goes upstream to the delightful cottage garden of Altamont Lodge.

Downstream there is a walk through bluebell woods, up 100 granite steps, across a field known poetically as the Sunset Field (where there are fantastic views of Mount Leinster and the Wicklow Hills), and eventually back to the lake.

I found it impossible to resist strategically placed seats at beguiling viewpoints around the estate and could hardly tear myself away from such a blissful spot. Corina North calls Altamont her 'magic garden'

and has set up a trust to run courses there in the hope that the gardens with their fine collection of plants and perfect setting, may be enjoyed by many generations to come.

The garden centre in the old walled garden has a very good collection of herbaceous and water-loving plants. Residential gardening and special interest courses are available and accommodation is in a converted seventeenth-century granary.

Admission £2.00, open every Sunday and Bank Holidays 2-6pm, at other times by appointment, tel. 0503-59128. Residential gardening courses. Suitable for family outings; the lakeside and formal garden are accessible for wheelchairs. Home-made teas using Altamont farm produce are available in a sheltered courtyard. Directions: A little over five and a half miles/9 km from Tullow on the Tullow Bunclody Road look for a turning north, follow signs and a classical stone gateway.

THE RAM HOUSE

Coolgreaney, County Wexford

FLOWER GARDEN

A pleasing small garden divided into intimate areas.

The view of the Ram House from across the humpback bridge in Coolgreaney village is picture-postcard pretty. The cottage-style garden beyond the wicket gate is bursting with flowers and offers plenty of inspiration for the smaller garden.

Godfrey and Lolo Stevens started with an unpromising two-acre site full of nettles with a weedy lawn. Gradually, separate areas were created and the sloping ground levelled into a series of terraces. Diminutive Lolo did much of the work herself and as informal beds began to take over more of the garden, the couple dispensed with the labour-intensive lawns, which took five hours to mow. These were replaced with neat gravelled paths which wind around the many features.

The upper area of the garden has raised rock beds planted with low shrubs, flowers and spring bulbs. And a Lutyensesque pergola covered with clematis and roses creates the transition to a small formal garden backed by a weeping willow. The lower end of the garden has been transformed into a water garden where a series of small pools surrounded by water-loving plants cascade down to a pond.

Attractive use is made of local materials: slate set in a starburst pattern among paving, old railway sleepers used as steps. The planting is simple and effective with plants like saxifrage, bugle, lamium and white honesty used as ground cover. The log seats under the curtains of willow and the path running atop the boundary bank hold great fascination for children. This is the kind of garden where new features are constantly being added and where there is blossom and colour from spring to autumn.

Admission £2.50, open Easter-end Aug. every Sunday, 3-6pm; 21 May-27 June (Wicklow Gardens Festival) each Sat. Sun. Mon; and all bank holidays, adult groups by appointment, tel. 0402-32006 and 37238. Tea and delicious cakes available. Suitable for children but not wheelchairs. Directions: Turn inland off the N11 between Arklow and Gorey at Inch post office. Follow the road to Coolgreaney, The Ram House is the first on the right after the bridge.

MILLBANKS

Rosbercon, New Ross, County Wexford

FLOWER GARDEN
A rewarding and cleverly designed small garden.

Picture a man, paint pot in hand, going out while the dew is still wet to draw a bold design of interlocking curves on a rough meadow. This was Desmond Kirwan's novel approach to landscaping and - painter that he is - he literally drew his plan on the ground. The result is a garden full of strong, soothing shapes and many foliage plants - balm to the soul.

Millbanks started out as a typical suburban garden with little more than a driveway and a strip of border running beside it. Twenty years later the one-acre plot on the hillside overlooking the River Barrow has been transformed. And perhaps because Desmond designs stage sets, the garden - an exercise in structure and form - offers plenty of drama.

The tour of the garden begins with a gentle joke. The transition from gravelled forecourt to lawn is marked by pairs of 'bullets', the stone balls which were traditionally dragged behind farm horses to break up clods. But these bullets turn out not to be stone at all but meticulously clipped santolina. A nun's walk under gothic arches shaded with clematis, honeysuckle and old-fashioned roses leads to one of the garden's surprises. A crinkle-crankle hedge opens to reveal an oval garden enclosed in walls of green with grass walks curving around a design as intricate as the inside of a seashell. The aim was to create a secret garden which gives a sense of seclusion and discovery.

This section of the garden is particularly beautiful in late afternoon when slanting sunlight illuminates a variegated acer, and columns of topiary throw dramatic shadows. The sculptured hedges and cone shapes which look like yew turn out to be Leyland cypress, clipped into submission and looking most unlike the trees in front of almost every bungalow that blights the countryside. Foliage plants - in every shade from bronze through to silver - have been used to create painterly compositions within the garden's evergreen framework. Everyday plants like *Lamium* or deadnettle, the shuttlecock fern *Dryopteris filix-mas*, false spikenard or *Smilacina racemosa*, interesting grasses and *Pachysandra terminalis* have been planted in blocks and clumps to great effect.

Acers and azaleas in the borders around the front lawn area and a pair of double white cherries give particularly good colour in spring and autumn. There are lots of inexpensive but effective ideas here for smaller gardens: the way creeping plants like bugle or thrift are used to soften edges, the naturalistic planting both in and around urns and stone troughs or the way attention is drawn to a rustic seat by a pair of golden box pyramids. The planning shows that wonderful effects can be achieved without the use of rare or expensive plants.

Admission £3.00, by appointment only, tel. 051-21461. Not suitable for children or wheelchairs. Directions: Leave New Ross on the Waterford Road immediately after the bridge. Look for the Albatross factory on the right and you will see a statue of St Joseph waiting at the corner to guide you. Turn right almost immediately up a narrow road between two houses and you will spot the garden overflowing its walls on the left at the brow of the hill.

KILMOKEA

Kilmokea, County Wexford

GARDEN

An entrancing garden with an inspiring layout and planting and a very fine collection of camellias.

Picture a host of camellias, each head-high glossy bush laden with pink, white or coral blossom and with a carpet of perfect fallen flowers beneath. Imagine a peacock spreading his iridescent fan in display to a giant rival in topiaried yew or cascades of water framed by scented azaleas. Kilmokea is a garden of earthly delights which comes very close to paradise.

Where once there were only trees, an orchard and an ivy-covered wall, the late David Price and his wife Joan have made an idyllic, compartmentalised garden around an old rectory and stone dovecote. Their first priority was to provide shelter and to give the garden 'bones'. Like a series of rooms divided by walls and clipped hedges, one area of the garden precedes another with statuary and topiary marking the entrances.

A formal gravelled forecourt leads to a long herbaceous border backed with choice Australasian specimens like *Hoheria* and *Drimys*

winteri and superb shrubs like *Viburnum tomentosum* and *Daphne mezereum*. Another small garden leads back to a decorative gate guarded by a huge *Magnolia stellata*, a blushing *Camellia* 'Elegant Beauty' and the fiery bells of a *Crinodendron*.

Inside the original walled garden the layout provides constantly changing perspectives and vistas. Along one wall a great sweep of herbaceous border full of old-fashioned plants is echoed by a curving grass walk which disappears enticingly between ramparts of clipped yew. More exquisite camellias and magnolias luxuriate in a sheltered corner of the garden and beyond them a mysterious arch of cinammon-barked myrtle shows the way to a small temple overlooking a lily pool and formal rose garden. In the pool a bronze figure pours a never-ending trickle of water over goldfish and other carp.

In one section of the garden raised beds provide wonderful contrasts in foliage and shape, in another a *Prunus nigra* hedge creates a crimson foil for a pale yellow Yukon flowering cherry. A gate in the wall opens on a more informal area with azaleas, a magnificent

Magnolia soulangeana 'Lennei' with huge mauve blossoms, a Chilean flame tree *Embothrium coccineum* and a pool surrounded by golden-leaved skunk cabbage.

Their enthusiasm carried the Prices across the road to create a wild garden in what was once a very boggy field. There they uncovered traces of the previous occupants of this ancient place of habitation. The Vikings sailed up the River Barrow and founded a large fortified settlement on what was once an island. Early Christians followed and the site of their church and graveyard is thought to date back to the seventh century. Within the Viking earthwork there are also the remains of a unique fortified Anglo-Norman village.

Where once there was a primeval bog, a large pond can be seen, which is drawn from a natural spring that now feeds a series of pools and cascades running through woodland. Under the sheltered canopy of trees tender camellias, rhododendrons, acers and azaleas flourish in this linear garden. And in spring the glimpses of gorse-edged fields and estuary beyond its sanctuary accentuate the impact of this improbably exotic display of blossom. The many varieties of camellia begin flowering in February and continue until May. Each twist and turn of the streamside path reveals some new delight: a spread of candelabra primulas, a patch of lily of the valley, a bed of tree peonies, an obelisk stage prop from the Wexford Opera Festival or the incandescent pale pink of *Rhododendron loderi* 'Venus'.

There are many unusual plants and shrubs at Kilmokea lovingly collected from cuttings and the gardens of friends. As Mrs Price says, 'We never come home with our sponge-bags empty.' Within its seven acres Kilmokea offers tremendous variety and a great deal to please the plantsperson.

Admission £3.00; for groups, by arrangement only, 10.30am-12.30pm and 2-6pm, tel. 051-388109. Especially lovely in spring. Suitable for wheelchairs. Directions: Follow the signs for Campile and the John F. Kennedy Arboretum from New Ross along the Barrow and take the turn off for the Great Island for one and a half miles/2.4 km.

HEATHERSET

Rocklands, County Wexford

FLOWER GARDEN

An exquisite small garden to inspire serious plantspeople and novice gardeners alike.

This is a perfect Fabergé egg of a garden full of small, enchanting detail. Views of sea glimpsed between Mediterranean pines, woodland and a dramatic outcrop of rock garlanded with gorse provide a backdrop to an area little bigger than the average suburban garden, where Mary and Jim White have created an extraordinarily rewarding garden.

As intricate as a Baroque fugue, the planting works on many levels simultaneously. Each specimen has been meticulously chosen, not only for its own special qualities but for the way it relates to its immediate neighbours and fits into the whole composition.

The garden is made up of a series of themes centred on particularly enviable plants. At the back of the house an *Acer* 'Osakazuki' and the tiny candle-like cones of *Abies koreana* form part of a small-scale composition with a 'Canary Bird' rose in the background. Other compositions centre on a *Parrotia persica* which

Admission £3.00, open only by appointment to groups of 4 plus, tel. 053-23026. Not suitable for children or wheelchairs. Directions: At the bridge coming into Wexford from Dublin follow the signs for Rosslare. After one mile/1.6 km you will see the Cow and Gate Factory on your left and a rocky outcrop on your right. Turn right just before the Texaco garage, and Heatherset, several houses up, is on the right.

turns brilliant gold and red in autumn and a Judas tree. Judas Iscariot - who must have been very short - hanged himself from the purple-flowered shrub, according to legend.

In front of the house the steep site has been terraced and a seating area paved with Liscannor slate and edged with ericas overlooks the garden. In April/May the heady scent of *Rhododendron* 'Lady Alice Fitzwilliam' and the delicate tracery of young acacia add to the enchantment. Below in the raised beds surrounding the lawn conical shapes of conifers and a clipped *Carpinus betulus* 'Fastigiata' (Hornbeam) give an almost sculptural feel to the garden.

Although it is small-scale it still produces hidden delights: a diminutive pool and waterfall curtained with a tumble of white *Cytisus albus*, a miniature Japanese water garden with stone troughs and dwarf acers. Everywhere you look there are covetable plants each chosen with the eye of a perfectionist. Mary White says she sometimes finds herself wishing for a plant that doesn't exist to fill a particular spot.

The garden has won a great many prizes including the Bord Fáilte Best Garden in Ireland award and has been three times a prize-winner of the National Gardens Association competition. There is year-round interest here and it is a particularly lovely place in the western light of a summer evening.

BERKELEY FOREST

New Ross, County Wexford

FLOWER GARDEN

A small, delightfully original Italianate garden with a green and blue theme.

Amid the scent of herbs and the sound of tinkling water the most magical thing in this blue and green garden is to watch the valley below Mount Brandon turn azure in the lazy afternoon light to match the heavenly blue of gentians and delphiniums.

The walled garden at Berkeley Forest has passed through three incarnations. When the house was built by Colonel Deane in 1780 and named in honour of his uncle by marriage, Bishop Berkeley, the garden was laid out in the formal French manner. Plans from the period show a star-shaped design of hedges and beds. Unusually the garden is close to the house, one wall forming part of the courtyard. Like the kitchens of the period,

Admission £3.00, children £1.00 for garden and costume display, open May-Sept., tours 11.30am, 3pm and 5pm, Thurs., Fri., Sat., Sun., or by appointment, tel. 051-21361. An intriguing collection of eighteenth- and nineteenth-century costume and toys is also on display at Berkeley Forest to make this a very worthwhile visit. Not suitable for wheelchairs, fine for children.

Directions: On the main Enniscorthy New Ross Road, 16 miles/25.7 km from Enniscorthy and four miles/6.4 km from New Ross, look for a large ochre-coloured house a quarter of a mile/.4 km from the road and turn left and left again.

walled gardens were kept well out of sight of the gentry.

The Victorians turned the enclosure into a kitchen garden with espaliered fruit on every wall. Typically the south-facing wall was lined with brick to hold heat and help the fruit to ripen.

Count Gunnar Bernstorff and his wife, painter Anne Griffin, created an Italianate garden in one quarter of the enclosure. Their first step was to make a framework for the garden using the falling ground to create a series of terraces. Stonework rescued from an ecclesiastic ruin and the architectural shapes of cypress trees and box topiary provide strong features.

At the entrance to the garden is a small fernery, a feature much beloved of Victorians who collected unusual fern varieties on country walks. Gunnar Bernstorff's collection of bonsai trees - including native species like chestnut, blackthorn and rowan - finds shelter beside the garden door.

Plants were chosen for easy maintenance and year-round interest with shrubs like *Cistus* and *Potentilla* and leafy plants like *Acanthus* and *Hosta*. The eye is led here and there to a topiary peacock making up to a dark cypress, a trefoil window overlooking a pond and a ball of silvery variegated *Euonymus* which punctuates the herbaceous border. The garden moves upwards in stages and an axial path leads to a terrace backed by a crescent of the bluest hydrangeas. Above this is the focal point of the garden: a fairytale thatched summer house overlooking a small knot garden of azure blue flowers, gentians, delphiniums and *Lithospermum*. To one side an intensely blue *Ceanothus* echoes the sky reflected in a brick-edged pond where swallows skim the water.

JOHNSTOWN CASTLE

Murrintown, County Wexford

DEMESNE

A fine example of Robertson's work where landscape is married to architecture.

The silvery fairytale castle at Johnstown fits perfectly into its setting of lawns, lake and ornamental towers. This pleasing integration of landscape and house is hardly surprising since both were designed by Daniel Robertson, architect of the gardens at Powerscourt.

The castle looks across the lake to an Italian-style garden with terraces and balustrades where the central feature is a dramatic cascade falling into the lake. The imposing castellated gateways to the estate, the tower which rises from the lake and the conservatory are all part of the grand gothic design, courtiers to the queenly castle. It was built in 1840 for Hamilton Knox Grogan Morgan around an earlier tower house belonging to the Esmonde family. The name Johnstown derives from the visit of King John to Ireland in the very early thirteenth century. When the ubiquitous Mr and Mrs Samuel Carter Hall passed by on their travels in 1840 they pronounced that 'when finished the mansion will rank among the most elegant and magnificent in the kingdom'.

The pleasure grounds surrounding the castle probably look better now than they did in their Victorian heyday when the lawns were laid out for field sports and acres of laurel were planted to provide cover for pheasants. Many of the original specimen trees remain, a *Cryptomeria japonica* beside the lake, resting its elbows in the water, a very old monkey puzzle and a *Cupressus macrocarpa*.

There is a very pleasant walk beside the stream which feeds the cascade. The water glides over a specially cut channel through woods sheltering tender shrubs and trees: magnolias, rhododendrons, *Cornus kousa*, azaleas and the aspen-leaved beech. The nearby tower is not a folly but the real thing: an ancient Rathlannon castle. Other features of the grounds include a statue walk and a large rhododendron arboretum near the house.

With the exception of spring-flowering shrubs and trees, Johnstown is primarily a green garden, a wonderfully soothing place for a stroll. In the four-acre walled garden laid out in 1844 the double herbaceous border which runs along the central path has been restored. The original glasshouses have been taken down and replaced with a modern plant house which contains a collection of tender potted plants and scented jasmines. The estate farmyard contains an agricultural museum with a display of antique implements and rural transport.

The estate and castle were handed over to the Irish State by the then owners, the FitzGerald family, in 1945 and the property is now a centre for Teagasc, the agricultural research body.

Admission free, open all year 9.30am-6pm, tel. 053-42888. Best in spring when the rhododendrons are out. Suitable for children and wheelchairs. Directions: Take the Rosslare Road out of Wexford, Johnstown is signposted from the first turn on the right.

SHORTALSTOWN

Shortalstown, County Wexford

FLOWER GARDEN
*A well-planned garden with
year-round interest.*

Shortalstown is one of those gardens blessed with good bone structure thanks to the inheritance of previous generations. There have been Millers - descendants of the Sealy family - at Shortalstown since Cromwell's time, and the pretty nineteenth-century farmhouse incorporates part of an earlier building. When Brian Miller's grandmother came from England 75 years ago as a bride, she decided to make a garden in front of the house where none had existed before. A sweeping drive and oval forecourt, specimen trees, a sheltered area protected by a brick wall and beech hedge, a terrace topped by a tennis lawn, a shaded garden and herbaceous beds were the main features.

Admission £2.50, open by appointment only, tel. 053-58836. Suitable for wheelchairs; afternoon teas. Directions: Take the Wexford Ring Road and follow the signs for Johnstown Castle. Pass the main gate of the castle, continue to Murrintown, turn left at the village keeping the school on your left, turn left at the next two forks and Shortalstown is the next entrance on the left. Johnstown Castle is just nearby; if you are continuing towards Waterford, the L159 via the Passage East ferry makes an interesting route.

The skills of two further generations of Millers - Marjorie and daughter-in-law Helen - have contributed to the creation of a very pleasing garden with many interesting plants. The sheltered area allows tender shrubs like the honeybush *Melianthus major*, *Leptospermum* and *Loquat* to be grown. When I visited in spring, a peach tree, hung with small jars of honey to encourage bees, was blooming against the walls. A beech *allée* leads from this area to a wicket gate and beside it shade-loving plants - trillium, hostas, Apennine anemones and hellebores - grow happily under a collection of trees and shrubs which include medlar, *Drimys winteri* and *Embothrium*. A recent addition is a specially lined damp bed and an Alpine bed has been created at the foot of a towering eucalyptus.

A fine herbaceous border packed with old-fashioned plants - peonies, phlox, campanula, lobelia, *Erythronium* or dog-tooth violets, primulas - follows the curve of the drive and is backed by a very successful shrub border. One side provides height and interest behind the herbaceous area, the other a bank of choice rhododendrons and azaleas facing the tennis lawn. In a sheltered area beside the house *Abutilon* grows outdoors beside a bed of species of *Crinium*. Stone troughs and a rockery facing the house hold special treasures. A border for cool-loving plants runs along the hedge of griselinia, which screens a flourishing vegetable garden where Mrs Miller senior's greenhouse, full of propagating plants, is a cheerful reminder that gardening is something you never have to give up.

JOHN F. KENNEDY ARBORETUM

New Ross, County Wexford

ARBORETUM
Of great interest to tree enthusiasts,
otherwise a good place for a
family outing.

The arboretum sits on the southern shoulder of Slieve Coillte, a breezy spot with views across undulating hills to the coast. A modern creation, the arboretum was laid out in the 1960s with trees planted in the scientific manner, in plots. The park, run by the Irish Forestry Board (Coillte Teoranta), is first and foremost a research institution and its appearance reflects this.

There are over 4,500 different species in an area of over 300 acres. The overall impression is of trees planted in blocks with wide grassy vistas in between. The park is traversed by pedestrian walks so that the access is excellent for wheelchairs and there is a broad two-mile/3.2 km walk, which begins and ends at the reception centre, of a functional '60s design. The interpretative section and maps provide a guide to the way the arboretum works. Visitors can get a good idea of the layout from a vantage-point near the top of Slieve Coillte or from the car park.

I have encountered tree enthusiasts who spend hours happily engrossed in studying the many characteristics of different groups of trees. And for beginners, the labelling system should be very helpful in determining the subtleties of distinguishing a *Picea* from a *Pinus*.

There is a pleasant walk through an old wood, filled with bluebells in spring, to a small lake. In autumn the collection of acers gives tremendous colour and there is a spring display of *Prunus* and *Rhododendron*. Other enjoyable areas include dwarf conifer plants in a rock garden which simulates Alpine valleys, and the collection of bluey silver *Eucalyptus*, their leaves constantly dancing on the windy site. Come prepared for long walks.

Admission £2.00, OAP groups £1.50, children £1.00, families £5.00, minibus £5.00, open all year 10am-6.30pm, tel. 051-88171. Picnic areas, café, toilet facilities, suitable for wheelchairs and children. Directions: Off the N25 Wexford Waterford Road just south of New Ross and the R733 Road to Campile. Clearly signed from the main road.

MOUNT JULIET

Thomastown, County Kilkenny

FLOWER GARDEN AND DEMESNE
*Three different gardens within a
magnificent demesne.*

The first sight of Mount Juliet surpassed all my expectations. While many great Irish houses are sheltered from sight the eighteenth-century mansion stands proudly on a hillside above the River Nore looking out over undulating parkland and paddocks where brood mares and foals graze on grass so green it is almost blue.

The richly decorated house, built for the first Earl of Carrick, and the home of the McCalmont family for most of this century, is now a country club. The magnificent 1,500-acre walled demesne is still intact and part of the grounds have become a Jack Nicklaus designed championship golf course.

Many people remember the fine gardens at Mount Juliet from the McCalmonts' time; they remain relatively unchanged with the exception of the fruit and vegetable garden and are still being cared for by head gardener Paddy Daly, who has worked at Mount Juliet since he was a lad. There are three main features: the rose garden and walled ornamental garden some distance from the front of the house and an informal rockery and water garden near the drive.

The most spectacular sight of all - in the walled garden - is the dramatic vista of the double blue herbaceous borders designed by Mrs McCalmont seen through a moon window in the garden wall. In June and July the blue spires of dozens of different delphiniums in shades from pale lilac to deep sapphire stretch away in a double arc interspersed with old herbaceous favourites like phlox, penstemon, eupatorium and artemisia. The moon window is one of a pair: an intriguing architectural device originally designed to frame a vista through borders and urns looking towards its fellow.

Also within this section of the old walled garden are the fruit houses and vineries which hopefully will be retained. In some, apricots, nectarines and figs still ripen in season. Former head gardener Paddy Morrisey's bell which used to summon the gardeners to work at 7.30am is still hidden in a corner. A walled rose garden dating from Lord Carrick's time has been replanted with hybrid teas and old-fashioned roses - a showy scarlet 'Satchmo' and the cream and red of 'Double Delight' are particularly fetching.

The informal stream and rockery area on the approach to the house was created with advice from Mrs Sally Flood (who proved the point that gardening promotes longevity by living to be 100). Azaleas, rhododendrons, acers and *Gunnera* are used together with many interesting water-loving plants in an attractive planting scheme.

The seven acres of fruit and vegetable gardens once worked by a dozen men have gone now but part of the walls and a few of the fruit trees form a feature of the golf course. One hopes that the remaining parts of the gardens will be restored to their full glory as the development of Mount Juliet nears completion.

The story of the demesne, originally owned by the Waton family, stretches back 600 years, a cricket team and a band are still part of the tradition of the estate and the kennels of the Kilkenny Hunt are also in the grounds.

Admission on request, tel. 056-24455. Good access for wheelchairs. Ask about the grave of Santa Claus. Tradition has it that the remains of St Nicholas were brought from Turkey and buried in the old cemetery near Belmore House. There is a charming restaurant in the basement of the club where non-residents are welcome. Directions: Follow the signs for Mount Juliet from Thomastown.

ARDSALLAGH

Fethard, County Tipperary

FLOWER GARDEN

An excellently designed garden with a wealth of interest for the plantsperson.

The best of gardens have 'good bones' and the garden made by Betty Farquhar at Ardsallagh House combines a wonderful sense of design with splendid planting.

Enclosed spaces have been used to create a series of secret gardens, which one enters with a sense of surprise and delight. A walled courtyard paved with Liscannor stone provides shelter for exotic climbers and tender shrubs (among them the mimosa *Acacia pravissima* and the orange and yellow trumpeted *Bomarea caldasii*), and leads to the solarium lawn guarded by high formal hedges of Lawson cypress. I defy anyone to resist the temptation to discover what lies behind a lime tree standing in the middle of steps to a narrow entrance in the hedge.

Beyond is a sunken garden with a lily pool surrounded by double tiers of raised beds for Alpines and other small plants. Gnarled pairs of standard *Viburnum carlesii* planted beside the steps down to the pool have a sculptural air. And among the plants growing in sheltered corners are *Celmisia semicordata*, the fragrant evergreen *Daphne retusa* and Chatham Island forget-me-not *Myosotidium hortensia*.

On the other side of the stableyard, paths wind through a

Admission £2.00, open only to groups and by appointment only, April-May, tel. 052-31492.

Directions: On the Fethard to Cashel Road (follow the signs for the transport museum if coming from Fethard), continue for several miles and look for a pink house on the south side of the road.

shrub and woodland area so full of interesting plants that I progressed at a snail's pace to take in delights like willow gentian and a vigorous abutilon covered in clouds of white blossom. A gothic wrought iron gateway into the old walled garden frames a glorious perspective down a stone pathway, flanked by raised herbaceous borders planted in a vivid colour scheme of reds, yellows and pinks and ending in another gateway. On either side lawns are shaded by specimen trees and old apple trees, while deep herbaceous borders full of treasures - my eye was particularly caught by a *Meconopsis sheldonii* - run around the walls.

CAMAS PARK

Cashel, County Tipperary

FLOWER GARDEN

An attractively planned young garden already showing plenty of interest.

One of the most encouraging things for any aspiring gardener is to see a new garden looking really well established after just a few years. And Camas Park has just such a garden.

Trish Hyde started from scratch, dealing with an awkward sloping site by creating a number of different levels and pleasing contours. The result is a delightful garden with a strong sense of structure and good contrasts.

An old stone wall, virtually hidden behind a thicket of ash, was cleared, heightened and now forms the backdrop for a burgeoning herbaceous border and curving lawns. A gothic archway in the wall, discovered behind the undergrowth and enhanced with steps and a wrought-iron gate, provides the focal point for this area.

Beyond the gate is an unexpected and enchanting terraced enclosure; paved in old stone slabs and cobbles it demonstrates how a very attractive garden can be created without any grass. Pergolas covered with double wisteria, stone troughs with collections of Alpines, a pair of Irish yews and box hedging provide

Admission £3.00. Groups by appointment only; as this is a very busy household it may not always be possible to arrange a visit, tel. 062-61516. Directions: At the southern end of Cashel town at the T junction at the bottom of the square, turn right, continue for a couple of miles. Camas Park is on the left and the name is on the gate.

the structural element. And around the walls trellises and raised beds hold tender plants and climbing shrubs like *Robinia kelseyi*, *Bupleurum fructicosum*, *Cytisus battandieri*, *Passiflora caerulea* and *Schizophragma integrifolium* as well as the lemon verbena *Aloysia triphylla*, all of which benefit from this warm sheltered area.

Outside the drawing room window a formal beech hedge encircling a sundial is a simple but very effective feature. The same formal approach to planting is used at the entrance of the garden, with a small laurel lawn planted under young whitebeams and the white blooms of the fragrant rose 'Blanc Double de Coubert' echoing the snowy stems of the Himalayan birch *Betula jacquemontii*. Beyond a sunken lawn with an alcove covered with the pink 'Aloha' rose, grass slopes down to a wild water garden still in the early stages of development.

GLENLEIGH GARDENS

Clogheen, County Tipperary

FLOWER GARDEN
One of the loveliest gardens in the south-east - informal with a beautiful streamside setting.

With the dramatic Vee of the Comeragh Mountains in the background, a brook running around the boundary and rich black peaty soil, Glenleigh is three times blessed. Aside from its lovely natural setting it is a perfect place for rhododendrons and damp-loving plants.

A 12-acre informal garden sheltered by mature pines and oaks has been created around water features. A streamlet bordered with bevies of candelabra primulas and a profusion of lush plants wanders down from a pond which reflects azaleas and cherry blossom in season. Above the pond is a bog garden with Kaempferi irises, *Gunnera* and log stepping stones and a rather rare

swamp cypress *Taxodium distichium* 'Pendens', while beside it a moss lawn is in the making.

On the banks of the stream there is a wild garden where white and apricot foxgloves, frothy pink perennial geraniums, ferns, lily of

Admission £3.00, open by appointment 1 April-30 Sept., tel. 052-65251. Feasible for wheelchairs. Directions: Clogheen is on the road between Clonmel and Mitchelstown (beware for there are two Clogheens, the second one a few miles away in County Waterford). The most spectacular route is from Lismore through the Vee. Glenleigh is on the left just as you come into the village on the Lismore Road.

the valley and choice shrubs – including the Tasmanian Waratah, *Telopea truncata* – grow among a carpet of wood sorrel and moss. Edgar and Gypsy Calder Potts love unusual trees: Montezuma pine, the dancing cut-leaved beech *Fagus heterophylla*, swamp cypress *Taxodium distichium*, the dawn redwood *Metasequoia glyptostroboides* and many other fascinating specimens have been planted to maximum effect in the sweeping lawns.

Among some of the more eye-catching plants in the garden are erythroniums, the tender climber *Mutisia decurrens*, American blueberries grown in the walled garden with peacocks for company

and pin oaks grown from acorns. Near the river there is a particularly showy *Rhododendron* 'Royal Purple' and a pretty pale lilac hybridised candelabra primula is spreading by the stream.

In a buttercup meadow beside the drive is a rare manna ash, which bears flowery loaf-like white blossom in late May. The Calder Potts' garden is beautifully planned, presenting a series of inviting grassy vistas among irregular beds of shrubs and trees. All the more unusual plants are thoughtfully labelled and many have been grown from seeds or cuttings. Spring and early summer are the best times to visit these beautiful gardens.

LISNAVAGH GARDENS

Rathvilly, County Carlow

FLOWER GARDEN

An excellently designed garden with a wealth of interest for the plantsperson.

Not many houses in Ireland can claim to have been cut in half like Lisnavagh, a grey-stone, gothic revival mansion set in parkland, with panoramic vistas of Mount Leinster, and the Wicklow and Blackstairs Mountains. Faced with ruinous taxes, the fourth Lord Rathdonnell demolished the front half of the house in 1953, leaving a very substantial rump surrounded by a garden designed in the 1850s by Daniel Robertson, best known as creator of the formal gardens at Powerscourt.

Today the ten acres of pleasure grounds, with their beautiful prospects, still retain many of the original trees and features, and peacocks stroll around the acres of lawns. The first treat is a pair of low, mossy, stone walls, which channel the curving drive between shrubberies. There are lots of different areas to explore in the grounds, each with its own special atmosphere. Within the existing framework of specimen trees and mature shrubs, areas of the garden have been redesigned and replanted over a fifteen year period by Lady Jessica Rathdonnell.

Beside the house a huge raised L-shaped border, built of matching grey stone, provides a sheltered haven for a profusion of herbaceous plants. Here a secret pathway paved with old kitchen flags leads through the heart of the bed, allowing closer acquaintance with great fountains of delphiniums and old roses, yellow Turk's cap lilies and yellow *Alliums* in season and dozens of different varieties of bulbs - especially daffodils - in spring. A curving azalea walk unearthed recently by Jessica leads through giant shrubs of *Drimys winteri*, ginkgoes, *Eucryphia*, camellias and the fragrant *Rhododendron luteum* to a magical cruciform yew walk. The branches of these Florence Court yews meet to form an arch, framing a vista of an arboretum and distant Mount Leinster. There are some particularly spectacular candelabra primroses colonising the walk.

One of the pleasures of a garden like this is the sense of discovery. At one point a honeysuckle arch and wicket gate leads to a peaceful green area with Kifsgate roses scrambling through trees. Beyond it there is a secret garden hidden behind the high walls of the old kitchen garden.

Here a former melon or pine pit (used for growing fruit below ground level) has been converted into a handsome swimming pool which looks as though it might have been by Lutyens but, in fact, was ingeniously created by recycling old stonework. Within the sheltering walls, a lush water garden flourishes with great whorls of hostas, architectural *Rodgersia* and *Gunnera*, variegated bamboos and other damp loving plants. In contrast there is also a rock garden packed with alpines, *Cistus*, phormiums, *Potentilla* and treasures such as *Celmisia* and *Meconopsis*. The south and east facing walls are ideal for tender plants like *Cytisus battandieri*, *Clematis seiboldii* and among the unusual shrubs are a *Clerodendron* and bladder tree.

Lisnavagh also offers hospitality as one of the Hidden Ireland Houses and is a good base from which to explore the lovely countryside around Mount Leinster.

Admission £2.00 adults, £1.50 children. Open mid May-end Aug. Sun. 2-6pm. Groups by appointment, tel. 0503-61104. Especially lovely in April, May and June. Directions: Lisnavagh is signposted from the Rathvilly-Hacketstown Road.

KILFANE GLEN AND WATERFALL

Thomastown, County Kilkenny

FLOWER GARDEN

An eighteenth-century demesne in the romantic manner.

The story of Nicholas and Susan Mosse's rediscovery of this historical gardening gem is an extraordinary one. A decade ago they moved to Kilfane House - a former gamekeeper's lodge - to distance themselves from Nicholas' pottery business at Bennetsbridge and began clearing the rampant laurel and rhododendron, uncovering eighteenth-century rides through the surrounding woodland in the process.

This jungle clearance revealed a ravine with a charming glade around a series of pools and cascades at its heart - as gothic in aspect as any eighteenth-century romanticist could wish. Nearby were the ruins of a mysterious little house. Faced with impenetrable walls of shrubbery, the Mosses thought they had discovered all until architect Jeremy Williams - a man who knows every stick and stone of Ireland - found an early map of the area which revealed further secrets. It showed not only that the building in the glen had been a thatched cottage *orné*, but that there had been a hermit's grotto and a dramatic waterfall cascading over the lip of the ravine nearby. The true nature of the waterfall came to light during Hurricane Charlie as torrents of water poured over the cliff, brought there, the Mosses discovered, by a man-made canal and diverted from a river a mile away.

The philosophy behind eighteenth-century gardening was very different from our own. Landscape designers sought to create demesnes where nature at her most sublime would inspire with harmonious prospects of water and trees. Nature was given a generous helping hand and pleasure parks were enhanced with follies, sham ruins and temples to excite admiration, encourage courtship and provide splendid locations for sybaritic picnics.

These ideals have been beautifully re-created at Kilfane. Walks through woodland paths become a voyage of discovery, leading through glades of bluebells and anemones and culminating in the revelation of the enchanting glade. Crossed by a rustic bridge, the river tumbles from pool to pool framed by mossy rocks. Beside it, the cottage *orné* with its dalliance parlour has been restored in perfect detail, straw-thatched by Jim Lenehan and furnished with hazel and vine furniture made by gardener Pat Butler. The cottage - with its perfect prospect of the glen and the waterfall - offers a tea-room at present and may become the perfect site for twentieth-century dalliance: available for rent as a honeymoon cottage. The path clinging to the cliffside on the far side of the glen was hand cleared at considerable risk to life and limb by Nicholas, and there are plans to restore the hermit's grotto and steps leading to the head of the waterfall with the help of a grant from the Heritage Council.

The woodland paths in the upper part of the demesne have become the sites for interesting sculptures. Near the house, which was originally part of the Power family estate, a series of charming gardens has been created by Susan Mosse in collusion with gardening guru Jim Reynolds.

There is a pool garden with a dining pergola made from stonework from Kilkenny station and a moon garden - a circular garden with silver and white planting. Nearby, at the entrance to the garden, there is a frog pond surrounded by lilies and foxgloves. The whole lovely scheme of things is still being developed, with new planting and clearance happening year by year and it provides a most endearing example of the way eighteenth-century ideals can be married with twentieth-century enthusiasm.

Admission £3.00, open 1 May-30 Sept. Tues.-Sun. 2-6pm, tel. 056-24558. You can also phone in advance to arrange a picnic basket filled with goodies and served on Nicholas Mosse pottery. Directions: almost two miles/3 km off the Dublin-Waterford Road, two and a quarter miles/3.5 km above Thomastown.

THE RHODODENDRON ROAD

To separate Donegal from its neighbouring counties of Derry, Tyrone and Fermanagh doesn't make sense when one considers their shared history, their physical location and the way people there criss-cross the artificial border. The gardens of the north west have acid soil and the high rainfall and mild climate which make them ideal for rhododendrons. The rhododendron road stretches up into Donegal through wild country and into the peninsulas reaching out into the Atlantic, and it also stretches down through Derry and into the peaceful lakeland of Fermanagh. The contrasting scenery of Donegal and Fermanagh is ideal for a two-centre holiday.

Donegal is almost like an island, a place set apart by the penstroke of partition. Historically part of Ulster, it has been severed from its markets – just as Derry has been severed from its natural hinterland – and left attached to the other 25 counties by the narrowest neck of land. Like any island it breeds eccentricities which are part of its charm.

There's something immensely appealing about the county. Maybe it is the intimacy of a landscape which changes with every twist of the road. The hills and lakes Derek Hill paints so well are easy to relate to and of a manageable scale. The coastline is tremendously varied. There are the private golden coves of the Rosguill peninsula, lined with granite pebbles smoothed to perfect egg shapes; there are the long inlets near Ardara where warm water creeps in over cockle beds; and there are the stark rocky headlands tumbling into Atlantic breakers on the headlands near Glencolumbkille.

Alone of all the counties on the west coast, Donegal has a good crop of gardens, most of them concentrated in the north east of the county. Just why this should be so is intriguing; one could speculate that since gardens tend to go in clumps, the presence of one great garden like Glenveagh acts as a catalyst. It may be that gardening is in the blood, many of the people in Donegal come of different stock from the original native Irish. In the plantation of Ulster following 1609, 40,000 Scots came to west Ulster. And some of the gardens of Donegal are the creation of outsiders like Henry McIlhenny who were drawn by the beauty and the remoteness of the place and made the county their home.

Just an hour and a half away the landscape changes completely to the sleepy lakeland of Fermanagh. The combination of trees and water makes for soothing scenery and the place is a paradise for anglers and for cruising holidays. Water was the main means of travel in Celtic times and because it was accessible, the area is rich in prehistoric and early Christian history. Devenish with its twelfth-century monastery and richly decorated high cross also acted as the main gateway to the north west. The security offered by Lough Erne's numerous islands (official island tallies vary wildly from 40 to 150) attracted monastic settlements.

The area is dotted with seventeenth-century towers and strong houses - Monea, Devenish, Castle Caldwell. The landscape is criss-crossed by rivers and their attendant valleys - Swanlinbar, Ballinamallard, Colebrook and Termon. A prospect of water was always a must for the builders of the great country houses and Fermanagh has more than its fair share of stately homes.

Amabel and Kieran Clarke at Ard na Mona are promoting the idea of a north western garden tour, a kind of rhododendron road. And their extraordinary rhododendron forest on the shores of Lough Eske makes a wonderful start to a tour.

ROUND AND ABOUT

Everyone who knows the county has their own favourite part of Donegal. I have a soft spot for the area around Donegal town but my first love is the west side of Lough Swilly and the Rosguill peninsula.

Donegal with its diamond-shaped square and friendly pubs makes a good base. Recently restored Donegal Castle - Sir Basil Brooke's fortified Jacobean manor built around the fifteenth-century O'Donnell stronghold - is just off the Diamond. The ruins of the fifteenth-century friary where the *Annals of the Four Masters* - an account of Celtic history - were written is just nearby and there is a monument to the Four

Masters in the centre of the Diamond. The antiques shop there is worth a prowl and another favourite port of call is Magee's for tweeds and Hanna's for indestructible fishing hats. Modern Harvey's Point Hotel has a pleasant bar and restaurant and the complex overlooks Lough Eske near Donegal town, tel. 073-22208. Castlemurray House at St John's Point, Bruckless, specialises in French cooking and is a welcome addition in an area where restaurants are thin on the ground, tel. 073-37022.

The coast drive from Killybegs to Glencolumbkille provides some magnificent scenery. Glencolumbkille has a folk village (admission £1.50, open Easter-Sept.) and takes its name from the saint in whose honour a pilgrimage is carried out around ancient sites in the parish on 9 June. The drive from Donegal town around Lough Eske through woods and hills, with the Blue Stacks dominating the horizon, is lovely. Further south on the border near Ballyshannon there is the Beleek Pottery Centre, home of the historic cream pottery, where there is a museum, visitor centre and restaurant, open March-Sept.

Heading for north east Donegal there is the spectacular coast drive on the N56 around the coast or alternatively the quick route via Donegal town to Ballybofey and Letterkenny. Ramelton is a colourful plantation town on the Lennon estuary with a selection of wine bars and restaurants; the Old Meeting House there, now open, is one of the earliest Presbyterian buildings in Ireland and was the spiritual cradle of the Rev. Francis Makemie, founder of the Presbyterian Church in the US. At Rathmullan and Portsalon miles-long beaches with pinkish sand and idyllic views of the Inishowen peninsula are wonderfully inviting and the drive around the coast road has a splendid descent down to Ballymastocker bay. Rathmullan House with its award-winning garden is a delightful place for dinner, tel. 074-58188.

The circuit of the Rosguill Peninsula makes a very pleasant drive with a stop to find the most beautiful beach or to visit McNutt's of Downings for glorious rainbow-coloured tweeds. Doe Castle, just near Creeslough, is an impressive sixteenth-century castle built by the MacSweeney family on a promontory jutting out into Clonmass Bay.

In north Donegal there is an imaginative new attraction in the World Knitting Centre at Buncrana on the Inishowen peninsula, which tells the story of traditional knitting and tales behind all those stitches. The great stone fortress Grianán Aileach on a hilltop overlooking Lough Swilly near Speenoge on the N13 Letterkenny Derry Road is a dramatic series of circular stone terraces dating back to the dawn of Christianity or earlier. A 300-year-old flax and grain mill at Newmills on the R250 Letterkenny Glenties Road has been restored by the Office of Public Works and provides an interesting insight into early technology.

On the way south there are two worthwhile National Trust properties: charming Springhill, near Moneymore, County Derry, built in 1680 (attractions include a well-documented ghost and a costume museum), open Easter, weekends April, May, Sept. and daily June-Aug., 2-6pm, admission £1.90. The Wellbrook Beetling Mill near Cookstown, County Tyrone dates from 1765.

The Fermanagh countryside with its soothing lakescapes and monastic ruins makes a contrast to the wild beauty of Donegal. Enniskillen, between upper and lower Lough Erne, offers lots of intriguing possibilities.

Enniskillen Castle, built by the Maguires 400 years ago to guard the strategic pass through the Erne Valley, now houses two museums, one for the county and one for the famous Inniskilling regiment. Don't forget to ask what is on at the lakeside Ardhowen Theatre. Two small pilgrimages to a pair of Erne's many islands are a must, one to Devenish for the ruins of the Augustinian abbey, St Molaise's house and the perfect twelfth-century round tower; the other to White Island via ferry from Castle Archdale to see the enigmatic stone figures from the early Christian period. The Cedars restaurant at Castle Archdale is a good place to recharge the batteries, tel. (08) 013656-21493.

Franco's restaurant, Queen Elizabeth Road, Enniskillen is full of atmosphere and has good Italian food, tel. (08) 01365-3324424.

Castle Coole, said to be the finest classical mansion in Ireland, with an exterior by Richard Johnston and interior by James Wyatt jnr for the Earl of Belmore, is superbly furnished and presents an interesting contrast to Florence Court. Open weekends April, May, Sept. and daily June-Aug., 2-6pm, admission £2.30.

Ulster foods are a speciality at the Hollander restaurant, 5 Main Street Irvinestown, tel. (08) 013656-21231.

The Claddagh River has carved out a series of underground chambers and galleries known as the Marble Arch Caves under the hills near Florence Court, and a visit there includes a boat trip across an underground lake hung with cathedral-like stalactites.

Belturbet, an attractive market town on the River Erne at the southern end of Lough Erne, has a good curiosity shop near the bridge; if it is closed a notice tells you where to find the owner.

PLACES TO STAY

A rd na Mona on the shores of Lough Eske, near Donegal town, has been delightfully restored by Amabel and Kieran Clarke, and staying there is like being a member of a country house party. Guests eat together at the big dining table with Amabel's delicious home cooking on offer. Kieran might be persuaded to play the piano after dinner. B & B £30.00 per person sharing, dinner £16.00, tel. 073-22650.

The Manse in Ramelton contains a house within a house, a planter's cottage which was incorporated into the later Georgian house. The bathroom has a wonderful antediluvian shower, and the house, which has been Mrs Scott's family home for 30 years, is full of character; guests often end up in the kitchen chatting with Mrs Scott. B & B £20.00, tel. 074-51047.

Also in Ramelton, Ardeen is a pleasant Victorian house in a secluded garden with a tennis court. The house, run by Mrs Anne Campbell, is furnished with antiques and makes a good base for visiting Glenveagh and gardens in the area. B & B £16-£17.50, open Easter-Oct, tel. 074-51243.

With a setting on a bay 12 miles/19.3 km from Donegal town, Bruckless House, run by Mr and Mrs C.J. Evans, is an eighteenth-century country house with an old cobbled farmyard. Home cooking includes locally caught fish and mussels and oysters farmed in Bruckless Bay. B & B from £20.00, dinner from £15.00, tel. 073-37071.

In the Fermanagh lakelands Killyreagh, run by Lord and Lady Anthony Hamilton, has views of the Florence Court hills and is near the National Trust properties of Florence Court and Castle Coole. The nineteenth-century house has been renovated and boasts a four-poster in one of its bedrooms. B & B £30-£50.00, dinner £20.00, tel. (08) 01365-87221.

The picture of pink-washed Jamestown House alone would be enough to make you want to stay there. The 1760 house at

Magheracross, Ballinamallard, with a croquet lawn and clematis rambling round the door is run by Arthur and Helen Stuart; local game and fish feature in the excellent cuisine, tel. (08) 01365-81209.

ARD NA MONA

Lough Eske, County Donegal

WILD GARDEN

A spectacular jungle of rhododendrons and conifers in a forgotten paradise.

To go to Ard na Mona is to travel to another world. There is nothing else like it in Ireland - it is closer perhaps to the glory of the rhododendron forests of the Himalayas when their treasures were discovered by the first plant collectors over a century ago.

A lost paradise lay hidden behind forestry and thickets of wild *Rhododendron ponticum* for years. Local people told stories about a colourful Japanese garden and there was an even more colourful tale of a previous owner Mrs Hazel West. Over six feet/1.8 m tall she wore a pork pie hat, smoked with a cigarette holder and drove around in a Rolls Royce. A popular, colourful character, she left money towards the building of the Orange Lodge at nearby Donegal town.

The Wray family lived at Ard na Mona until 1870 and planted a magnificent collection of conifers on their 500-acre estate on the picturesque shores of Lough Eske. Sir Arthur and Georgiana Wallace developed the garden further, planting a huge collection of rhododendrons in the shelter of the trees.

Some of these specimens, mainly Hooker introductions - including *R. arboreum*, *falconeri* and *sinogrande* variations - are now up to 60 feet/18.3 m tall, creating a primeval jungle on the sheltered hillside above the lough. Their canopies of huge leaves, topped by blossom over gothic arches of cinnamon and russet branches are a memorable sight. Many of the rhododendrons have seeded themselves and enormous youngsters are legging up beside their parents. It is truly a wild garden and some of the finest sights come as a reward for scrambling through undergrowth and mossy glades.

Amabel and Kieran Clarke, the present owners, stumbled on the demesne while searching for a house, and bought the property from the Department of Forestry.

The estate with its 45 acres of rhododendrons has now been designated a Heritage garden, and with the help of a grant from the National Heritage Council the gardens are being catalogued and restoration work is beginning.

Clearance involves green sculpture on a grand scale and the original glades and paths among imposing conifers and shrubs are being carved out so that the treasures of the garden can be seen for the first time. Curious standing stones have also been uncovered and it seems that the locals were right, this was a Japanese garden, not in the stylised contemporary manner but in the Victorian manner. Strange things happen in this corner of Donegal; the night I was there a midnight moss raider was discovered in the grounds. A century and a half ago Mrs Wray had a narrow escape when a bomb was lobbed through a window of the house.

If you like gothic sights, ask about the ruins of Eske Castle two miles/3.2 km south, and Georgiana Wallace's grave (epitaph: She hath done what she could) which looks back to her garden from the little Church of Ireland churchyard on the far side of the lake.

Admission £3.00, open by appointment only, tel. 073-22650. Not for the frail, sturdy boots essential. Directions: Take the N56 Ardara Road out of Donegal town and almost immediately turn right for Lough Eske. Follow signs for Lough Eske, and Ard na Mona is about five miles/8 km along the road around the Lough, on the right-hand side. The delightfully restored 1790 house at Ard na Mona is now open for guests for B & B and dinner.

St Columb's

GARDEN

A pretty lakeside garden to linger in while visiting the Glebe Gallery and Derek Hill's former home.

The painter Derek Hill fell in love with Donegal and moved there in 1954 when he bought the former rectory in the remote parish of Churchill. St Columb's overlooks Lough Gartan, the birthplace of St Colmcille, and the garden there slopes down to the water's edge.

Derek feels that gardens should reflect the landscape that they are in. He doesn't believe in trying to grow plants which will not thrive naturally and – as a painter – holds that the laws of harmony, contrast and proportion should apply in a garden. Given an exposed hilly site, icy winds that whip across the lakes in winter, thin soil changing to bog near the lake, St Columb's isn't an easy site for plants.

Hedges of *R. ponticum* and *Cupressus* were planted for shelter and within it the grounds were planted informally in keeping with the wild surrounding scenery. Birches - *jacquemontii*, *utilis* and *ermanii* - were chosen for the contrast of their silver against grey skies, and white roses, Kiftsgate and 'Beauty of Edzell', were grown through apple trees for the same reason. Large-leaved plants *Gunnera*, *Rodgersia* and *Lysichiton* provide height in the bog garden without interrupting the view, and hostas, astrantia and primulas also thrive in this area. A trellis pyramid makes a focal point between house and lake and supports 'Albertine' roses and white *Clematis* 'Alba'.

The spiky forms of *Phormium* are another way of providing contrast and the purple-leaved sycamores and the ornamental rhubarb *Rheum* 'Bowles' variety are planted where the sun catches and enhances their colour. Creepers, their colours contrasting against the glowing walls of the house which are painted the colour of a Venetian fishing boat, sail and trail around a bust of Apollo. Scented plants - *Mahonia japonica* and honeysuckle – grow near the door and an *Abutilon vitifolium* defies the winds.

Derek Hill laid out the grounds with continued help from James Russell, who also helped to design the wonderful gardens of Derek's neighbour, Henry McIlhenny at Glenveagh. The planting at St Columb's is designed to enhance the landscape, and formality is limited to a small area around the house with a gravelled forecourt, terraced herbaceous beds and a stone terrace overlooking the river. The planting is simple and effective: old shrub roses, huge clumps of hostas, *Alchemilla mollis*, a vivid blue cranesbill geranium, veratrum, acanthus, *Lobelia tupa* and Corsican hellebores.

Shortly after Henry McIlhenny gave Glenveagh Castle and estate to the nation, Derek Hill decided to donate St Columb's to the people of Ireland. His delightful house, complete with furniture, is open to the public and the Glebe Gallery has been built to house a collection of his paintings. The gallery is thought to be on the site of a fifteenth-century O'Donnell fort attacked and destroyed by Cichester in 1608. There are the remains of a prehistoric rath in the garden.

Admission £2.00, open daily except Fridays, 11am-6pm, Sundays 1-6.30pm, tel. 074-37071. Suitable for wheelchairs and children; teas available. Parking and toilet facilities. Directions: About a mile and a quarter / 2 km outside Churchill on the Losset Road.

171

GLENVEAGH

Churchill, County Donegal

ORNAMENTAL GARDEN

A garden outstanding in terms of design and plantsmanship in a breathtaking setting.

Glenveagh is the great garden of Donegal, much visited but unspoiled since it can be reached only by shuttle bus from the Visitor Centre at the edge of the 25,000-acre National Park.

The setting is starkly dramatic with the peat-black waters of Lough Veagh lying between the bare hulks of Doolish and Farscollop Mountains. Despite the unpromising surroundings this is a wonderfully rewarding garden with a number of contrasting elements.

My particular favourite is the walled *potager* where flowers and vegetables are grown together in the traditional manner and hedged with clipped box. There is a magnificent double herbaceous border running through the centre of the garden, and the borders against the walls are packed with covetable plants. Although it looks like a Victorian garden, this area was created in the '50s. There is an extremely photogenic thatched gardener's cottage in one corner and in complete contrast a very grand gothic orangery designed by Philippe Julian beside the house.

The lower garden, with lawns surrounded by masses of foliage, plants and shrubs, is a green and peaceful place. Huge plantings of *Rodgersia*, hostas, ferns and astilbes make rivers of green leaves and there are many fine rhododendrons, some thought to have been introduced from Ard na Mona; among them are trumpet-flowered *R. cinnabarinum* and a huge *R. falconeri*. Tree ferns, rare shrubs like *Michelia doltsopa* and the Chusan palm also grow in this sheltered area.

On the far side of the castle are some delightful surprises: a small Italian statuary garden, a flagged terrace known as the Belgian walk lined with huge tubs of azaleas, and a shrub and rhododendron walk leading to a vantage-point overlooking lake and mountains. The mountain garden with its

dramatic flight of steps beyond the walled garden is sadly closed.

The gardens at Glenveagh were first developed by Mrs Cornelia Adair, widow of John Adair who bought Glenveagh as a sporting estate, evicted all the tenants between 1857 and 1859 and built the granite baronial castle around 1870. Adair died without living in the castle and his widow made it her home for part of the year. The second phase of development of the gardens was during Henry McIlhenny's time; he purchased the castle in 1937. The gardens were neglected, and, with a break during the war years when he served in the navy, he set about restoring the garden and introduced many rare and tender plants.

He simply adored flowers and used to spend hours doing the floral arrangements for Glenveagh, where he entertained lavishly. The *potager*, Italian garden and Swiss walk lined with splendid rhododendrons, as well as the vista garden south of the castle, were added in Mr McIlhenny's time with the guidance of landscape architects James Russell and Lanning Roper. Mr McIlhenny also added the great flight of 67 steps to the mountainside.

He liked to plant for effect and added many more rhododendrons, tree ferns and palms. Lilies were his particular love, especially the white and gold *L. auratum platyphyllum*. In 1980 the castle and gardens were donated to the nation by Mr McIlhenny.

Admission £2.00, OAP £1.50.

Open Easter to October 10am-6.30pm, tel. 074-37088. Restaurant and services at visitor centre. There are a number of walks, including the Derrylahan Nature Trail, through the National Park. The castle, furnished by Mr McIlhenny, is open to the public, with guided tours, £2.00. Directions: Glenveagh is about eight miles/12.8 km from Churchill on the R251.

GREENFORT

Portsalon, County Donegal

FLOWER GARDEN

A fabulous setting and strong design make this an enchanting place.

Two breathtaking vistas dominate the garden at Greenfort: one of a temple framed in roses. The other is of Ballymastocker Bay with Dunree Head rearing up across the water and a green garden winding mysteriously towards the sea.

When the late Lionel Perry designed the garden he already had one essential ingredient: shelter provided by a wind-stunted sycamore wood and the original garden walls. He also had a wonderful eye and created a strong framework - a little reminiscent of Lutyens - for selective planting.

A flight of steps guarded by a pair of stone eagles makes a dramatic entrance to the temple garden. Mr Perry chose to emphasise the narrow uphill perspective, placing the temple at the end, with two long beds filled with old shrub roses running towards it. Peonies and climbing roses are planted along the walls with the grey white of *Olearia* and *Cistus* and the prolific pink 'Aloha' rose and the pale pink

of 'New Dawn' making a very pleasing combination.

The vegetable garden, where climbing roses fountain through the apple trees, produces particularly lush raspberries. An escallonia hedge has been used to create a secret garden sheltering tree peonies, hoherias and other tender shrubs. In the green garden Mr Perry resisted the temptation to plant only rhododendrons, choosing choice shrubs, azaleas, hoherias, *Cornus kousa* and *C. alternifolia* to frame the lawn which winds off tantalisingly towards the sea. Gravelled courtyards with raised stone beds and woodland walks leading to the sea complete the picture.

Private garden, admission £3.00, open to groups by appointment only, tel. 074-59123/59134. Directions: One mile/1.6 km before Portsalon on the Kerrykeel Portsalon Road.

TULLY CASTLE

Church Hill, County Fermanagh

FLOWER GARDEN

A reconstruction of a Renaissance garden with plants and fruit grown at that period.

Renaissance-style gardens were introduced to Ireland at the end of the sixteenth century. Not surprisingly, only traces of them survive. They represent a mixture of ideas drawn originally from worship and the need to demonstrate mastery of nature.

The Department of the Environment hit on the delightful idea of creating a Renaissance-type garden beside the ruin of Tully Castle, which was sacked in the 1641 Rebellion, when the Irish rose to reclaim their land. The rebellion was strongest in Ulster where it was led by Sir Phelim O'Neill and between 10,000-15,000 Protestants were slaughtered.

The garden, sheltered by a wattle fence, is a reminder of more peaceful aspirations and shows the way in which the enclosed garden introduced in the Middle Ages had become more elaborate. Beds framed in hedges were laid out in a formal grid and planted with decorative plants and medicinal or culinary herbs. The range of species was much smaller than now, but included fruit or nut bearing trees, lilies, roses, marigolds, pinks, iris, lavender and daffodils. While the garden at Tully is not intended as an accurate representation, it does give a flavour of the period with the herbs, fruit and flowers grown in combination.

Open all year round, Tues.-Sat. 10am-7pm (2-4pm in winter). There is an entrance charge. Tel: (08) 01232-235000. Directions: Off the A46, three miles/4.8 km north of Derrygonnelly.

MULROY

Carrigart, County Donegal

WILD GARDEN

A fine collection of rhododendrons in a wild garden.

This secluded estate on the shores of Mulroy Bay has an impressive collection of rhododendrons in its grounds. It also provides an interesting insight into the link between gardens and politics. The existence of the house in this rather remote corner of Donegal is intricately tied up with military history, a subject of which the Hon. Hedley Strutt, the present owner, is a student.

For centuries Ireland was regarded by the French as a possible stepping-stone for the invasion of Scotland. Sir Frederick Hamilton, who was responsible for the plantation of Ulster, was put in charge of masterminding defences against the French. He chose Donegal as the crucial mid-point between the Antrim crossing and Limerick, where the French might land, and set up his HQ at Rosapenna near Carrigart and built defensive watch towers around the coast. Communication by semaphore between towers was a key part of the plan.

Hamilton picked Colonel Clements, one of the best officers in Cromwell's army, to hold County Leitrim, which was the pass between the Shannon and the Atlantic. Hamilton married off his granddaughter to him, founding the dynasty that was to become the Earls of Leitrim. The family have had property at Mulroy for 320 years.

In the nineteenth century the Donegal estate was inherited by a naval officer, later the fourth Earl of Leitrim, who proved that Mulroy Bay was navigable. He built a pier at Mulroy, bringing 1,000-ton ships, establishing a flourishing potato trade to Glasgow and bringing prosperity to the area. His wife, Lady Winifred Cooke, brought up on one of the best-run estates in Norfolk, established the demesne at Mulroy as a demonstration centre to teach modern agriculture to the 800 tenants.

The pier can still be seen at the end of the azalea-lined quay path, and across Mulroy Bay the straight hedges introduced by the third Earl of Leitrim, whose struggles against the Famine were not appreciated, run neatly over the headland. The gardens were largely the creation of

Hedley's late uncle, the fifth and last Earl of Leitrim, and his widow.

There are three main areas in the grounds – a formal garden in front of the house with German roses (planted by the Estonian gardener who started his career with the last Czar of Russia and who disapproved of leggy English roses), a walled garden with some remnants of former glory, and the wild gardens with their wonderful collection of rhododendrons.

In the shelter of woodland the grounds are defined by a series of walks, and in between them smaller paths wind around magnificent shrubs. This layout allows strollers to admire the quite staggering range of rhododendrons there. The large-leaved varieties are planted not in ones and twos but in some places in whole stately avenues, the new foliage making a midsummer display to follow late spring flowers.

The fascination of this garden is to see a huge variety of shrubs ranging from a rhododendron so tiny it looks like an erica to brilliantly coloured hybrids in a luxuriant jungle, spiced with the scent of the sea.

Many tender shrubs – the Chilean flame tree (*Embothrium*), *Drimys winteri*, huge eucryphias, magnolias, collections of acers –

flourish in sheltered woodland. The rhododendrons and azaleas make an incredible display of colour beside shady walks, especially in late April and May.

And among the extensive collection of rhododendrons (catalogued by the Estonian) are *R.* 'Countess of Haddington', a hybrid with rose-flushed trumpet flowers, *R. diaprepes fortuneii*, with large scented white flowers, 'Blue Diamond' with rich blue flowers, the dwarf Alpine *R. ferrugineum* 'Rose Crimson' shrub with pink bells, *R. manipurense* with large white trusses of flowers, the tiny *R. saluenensi* 'Prostrata', showy scarlet *R.* 'Matador', *R.* 'Keleticum' with deep purplish flowers, *R. lutescens* 'Centrifolium' with its bronze leaves and green-spotted yellow flowers.

Admission price discretionary, open only to special interest groups by appointment, tel. 074-55107. Suitable for wheelchairs. Directions: The estate is on the right of the road just before the town of Carrigart.

BROOK HALL

Derry

ARBORETUM

A fine arboretum with many rare and interesting trees and shrubs.

With its Regency architecture and graceful canopies, Brook Hall wouldn't look out of place in the peaceful English countryside near Bath, but its setting on the River Foyle is steeped in some of Ireland's most turbulent history. The infamous boom set up by the Jacobites to prevent supplies reaching Derry and broken by the Williamites was sited nearby. Both French and Jacobite cannons have been dug up from the river bank at the foot of the garden.

Nowadays large ships glide up and down river unimpeded, and the hilly banks afford a view of the undulating patchwork of fields stretching across County Derry.

The sheltered riverside at Brook Hall is also the site for a magnificent arboretum. The estate was originally laid out in 1780 but the arboretum is a recent creation largely planted by the late Frank Gilliland over a 30-year period starting in the 1920s. In 1958 his cousin, David Gilliland, inherited the property and he and his wife, writer Jennifer Johnston, have since restored and augmented the splendid collection so that today it is a dendrologist's paradise, though flowers should not be expected outside the rhododendron season.

Beautifully maintained trees and shrubs are planted individually or in small groups in 30 acres of lawns sloping down to the Foyle. The arboretum contains one of the first metasequoias to come to Ireland via Kew and has particularly fine collections of abies, rhododendrons, cypress and pines. There are nearly 900 specimens and all have been ingeniously numbered with cattle tags; there is an accompanying catalogue listed both according to numbers and by species.

For a novice garden enthusiast the arboretum is a delightful way to make the acquaintance of the habits and character of the more unusual trees. Among the specimens which particularly caught my fancy were *Podocarpus salignus* with its drooping willow-like leaves, the graceful weeping *Picea breweriana*, *Betula alba* and *Acer griseum* both with curious peeling bark, the calico bush *Kalmia latifolia* with its cup and saucer bells, the aptly named *Liquidambar*, the weeping blue cedar *Cedrus atlantica* 'Pendula' and *Abies koreana* with its violet cones. Many of the plants originated from the Hillier Nurseries and the arboretum is still being developed.

Admission fee at owners' discretion, open to groups by appointment only, tel. (08) 01504-351297. Directions: Take the A2 out of Derry for Culmore and Carrowkeel; after the second roundabout look out for a large pair of anchors at a gateway on the right.

DRENAGH

Limavady, County Derry

HISTORICAL INTEREST
Intriguing garden features and imposing house amid sweeping lawns set in a large wild garden.

Imagine a secret enclosure, filled with the glimmer of white flowers and silver foliage, with a curious circular window framing a lake-like vista of lush growth and stately trees. This is the effect of the Moon garden, a perfect hidden place perched on the edge of an escarpment overlooking a fine nineteenth-century arboretum.

The history of Drenagh stretches back over 300 years. The estate, acquired by William McCausland from the Speaker, William Conolly, around 1680, shows evidence of the changing tastes of successive periods. The gothic gate lodge at the entrance to the grounds provides a clue to the existence of an earlier house built by Robert McCausland around 1730; surrounded by orchards it was known as Fruithill.

When heiress Marianne Tyndall married Marcus McCausland in the early nineteenth century she wanted

Admission £2.00, open to groups by appointment, tel. (08) 015047-22649. Guided tours of the grounds by appointment. Not suitable for wheelchairs, lots of space for children. Streeve Hill on the estate has recently opened as a guesthouse specialising in garden tours. Directions: Come out of Limavady on the Coleraine Road. After one mile/1.6 km look for the estate wall and turn left at the gate lodge.

a more impressive residence and eventually the present house designed by Charles Lanyon was completed in 1837. It was one of his earliest country houses and is Georgian in style in contrast to his subsequent work in the Victorian idiom. Lawns with balustrades and an Italian garden were laid out at this period. The design made dramatic use of the escarpment on the site, with a terrace surmounting an alcove and a water feature in a manner reminiscent of the Villa d'Este. Beyond this, an informal pleasure ground and arboretum were laid out.

The next significant additions to the gardens were made in the 1960s, during Lady Margaret McCausland's time, by the Canadian landscape artist Frances Rhoades. An English garden, in pink, blue and silver with a rose and clematis arbour; the Orbit, a shrub garden with a mill wheel as the pivotal feature, a water garden and a circular azalea garden beside the Italian garden were her creations. The Moon garden, with its oriental-style loggias, was created from part of an existing building where bee boles, used to house bee skeps, are an intriguing feature and the circular steps leading down from the Moon window are flanked by weeping medlars.

The garden has been gradually restored and replanted by June and Peter Welsh who have moved to Streeve Hill on the estate. Their son, Connolly, is at present guardian of the garden at Drenagh. A host of appropriate plants has been found for the white garden (agapanthus, Canna lilies, *Romneya coulteri*, white primulas, olearias, potentillas, astilbes); tender trees and shrubs have been planted: eucalyptus, photinias, tulip trees and many others. New shrubs have been propagated from the rhododendron hybrids in the area known as the Glen, and the banks of the stream cleared from invasive skunk cabbage *Lysichiton* and planted with candelabra primulas and hostas.

DRUMADRAVEY HOUSE

Irvinestown, County Fermanagh

FLOWER GARDEN

A beautifully conceived garden with a wonderful collection of plants.

A handsome border of smiling plants, standing to attention like a guard of honour, is the most rewarding sight. And at Drumadravey Acheson Aiken has the kind of herbaceous display guaranteed to stop plantspeople in their tracks.

His delightful garden at the seventeenth-century former dower house of nearby Castle Archdale is sheltered by immaculate beech hedges. The garden is designed as a series of compartments with hedges and pillars linked by chains that make the framework for a collection of over 1,500 different plants.

The plan provides a series of treats: the first is a vista of the spectacular herbaceous border. Forming a tapestry of colour, each and every one of the plants is choice and covetable. Some are unusual colour variants - white *Thalictrum* and yellow catmint *Nepeta govaniana*. Others are relatively rare: *Veratrum californicum*, the burning bush (*Dictamnus albus*), *Lobelia tupa*, white willow gentians. Still others are

Admission free, donations to charity welcome, open strictly by appointment for groups, tel. (08) 013656-21257. Not suitable for wheelchairs or children. Directions: From the fountain in the main street in Irvinestown take the road to the right past the church and police station. Follow the Lisnarick Road for exactly two and a half miles/4 km, the gate with stone wall is on the right.

especially pleasing cultivars: *Alstroemeria* 'Princess Lily', the bronze *Crocosmia solafatire*, biscuit-flowered *Macleaya cordata*, and *Ligularia hessii*.

A former linen yard has been transformed beyond recognition into a Japanese Garden of Contemplation, complete with a Buddha and a lantern among dwarf acers and the parallel symbols of harmony set in the gravel.

At the heart of the plan is a sundial garden where clematis trails in swags around the frame of pillars and chains. The effect is of drifts of colour and interesting contrasts, a pale salmon potentilla against deep crimson cotinus, vibrant blue clematis trailing through a golden shrub.

An L-shaped garden, green and peaceful in summer and full of flowering bulbs in spring provides a change of mood. Hostas and peonies are particular favourites in this garden and there are over 20 varieties of the former and a collection of 30 different peonies.

The kitchen garden with rows of chard, leeks, asparagus and luscious raspberries shows just what a pleasurable sight a vegetable can be. A veritable Ritz for bees (not described here as it would spoil the surprise) is another of the garden's secrets. The final treat is a conifer garden with a collection of dwarf specimens, their contrasting forms and colours setting each other off to perfection.

FLORENCE COURT

Enniskillen, County Fermanagh

DEMESNE

A beautiful location with plenty for all the family to see and do.

The handsome pinnacle-topped yew which takes its name from the seat of the Viscounts of Enniskillen has made the name Florence Court familiar. The original yew, discovered in 1767 by the head gardener, Mr Willis, can still be seen in a clearing in the woods. Considered a freak at first *Taxus baccata* 'Fastigiata' can be propagated only from cuttings so all the thousands of Florence Court yews are descended from this tree.

Commanding views of the Cuilcagh Mountains and of Lough Erne, the Florence Court house takes its name from Florence Wrey, a Cornish heiress, who married Sir John Cole in 1707. The house was built by succeeding generations of the Cole family. Sir John's grandson William, first Viscount Enniskillen,

commissioned Davis Ducart to add the Palladian arcades and pavilions to the house in 1767.

The estate was laid out in the romantic late eighteenth-century manner with woods, a 'lawn' of parkland in front of the house and groups of trees, while a long sweep of drive leads up to the house. William King, a follower of Capability Brown, worked at Florence Court for a time in the 1780s.

To the south of the house, pleasure grounds were laid out in the early nineteenth century by the landscape gardener John Sutherland for the third Earl of Enniskillen with plantations of beech, oak and sycamore. The water-driven saw mill, powered by a paddle wheel, and the hydraulic ram used to pump water to the house have been restored recently and the ice house has also been renovated. There are plans to restore the little thatched tea house which was once a feature of the pleasure grounds. Thousands of daffodils have been planted in this area and in late spring huge arboreal rhododendrons make a fantastic display.

The four-acre walled gardens

(some distance away to the north of the house and reached by a romantic bridge over a river with meadowsweet and willow trailing on its banks) were originally laid out as a combined vegetable and ornamental garden. These are also under restoration by the National Trust, which was given the house and part of the estate by the fifth Earl of Enniskillen in 1953.

The rose garden has been remade with formal paths and box hedges and replanted with old shrub roses. The walls of the garden are covered with luxuriant creepers, while an ancient wisteria and a pergola flanked by herbaceous borders are also features of the garden.

Beyond the 300 acres of demesne under the care of the National Trust there are lots of interesting walks along trails through the Florence Court Forest Park. Sensible footwear is a must. The Rose Cottage, the former gardener's cottage in the walled garden and part of the staff quarters are currently being restored as self-catering accommodation. The house with its

elaborate rococo plasterwork is open April to September. The Marble Arch Caves are nearby.

Admission £1.50 per car (estate charge), grounds and garden open all year except Christmas Day. Suitable for children, mostly accessible to wheelchairs, shop, teas, toilet facilities. Check for interesting events. Admission to house £2.40, group rate £1.90. House open April, May, Sept. weekends 1-6pm; June-Aug. daily except Tuesday, 1-6pm, tel. (08) 01365-82249. Directions: eight miles/12.9 km south west of Enniskillen via the A4 and A32 Swanlinbar Road.

THE WEE NORTH

L egend has it that Lough Neagh and the Isle of Man were formed by
Finn McCool lifting a lump of land out of the middle of Ulster and
throwing it into the Irish Sea. And for the fanciful the theory that giants
had a hand in the landscape makes sense of the large-scale dramas that
occur in an otherwise demure countryside.

The typical landscape of the northern counties is very different from
the South. Drumlin country: seas of little hills with roads winding
around them and neat farms on their shoulders. Their small-scale
repetitiveness gives the major features like the Mourne Mountains,
islanded Strangford Lough, the cliffs and glens of Antrim, Slieve Croob,
the lakes of Fermanagh and the fiord of Narrow Water all the
more impact.

Evidence of the past shows through in a fabric made by layers of
history. The first settlers came to Ulster attracted by the presence of flint
in the middle Stone Age. The most dramatic reminders of the
prehistoric age are megalithic monuments including dolmens or portal
tombs. St Patrick has a strong association with the North. He is said to
have built his first church at Downpatrick and he established an
ecclesiastical primacy at Armagh which exists to this day. A monument
put up in 1900 at Downpatrick Cathedral supposedly marks the site of
his grave. The Normans left their imprint too, with castles and abbeys:
notably the great keep at Carrickfergus, the stronghold of Dundrum and
the twelfth-century Cistercian abbeys at Inch and Grey Abbey.

The plantation of Ulster has left its distinctive mark on the landscape
in the layout of towns with their central diamonds, and the patterns of
settlement and farming. Following the Battle of Kinsale in 1603 and the
subsequent Flight of the Earls, tens of thousands of English and Scots
were settled on four million acres of confiscated lands.

Many of Ulster's best gardens are around the coast and, from a touring point of view, they appear to fall naturally into distinct groups: the gardens clustered around the Mourne country and the Ards peninsula where the warm breath of the Gulf Stream makes it possible to grow all kinds of tender plants, the gardens of the north west with the wonderful rhododendron gardens of Donegal and Derry together with Fermanagh lakeland, and the gardens of Antrim.

Happily, good gardens tend to coincide with the most scenically interesting parts of the North. Having grown up in County Down I am probably biased in favour of the Down coast and the Mountains of Mourne. My childhood memories are strung together with a necklace of special places. They were destinations for picnics, treats and holidays: the bluebell woods of Saintfield Demesne and Rowallane in spring, the beaches of the Lecale peninsula in high summer, the Silent Valley and the Spelga Pass in the Mournes when the heather and the harebells were out.

The cliffs and glens of Antrim make a perfect contrast to the drumlin country of Down. The bracing air and uncompromising landscape make for hardiness and gardeners have to cope with a harsher climate. The rugged coastline provides some truly spectacular sights: Dunluce Castle, the great fortress of the chiefs of Antrim on a crag jutting into the Atlantic, and the Giant's Causeway, said to have been Finn McCool's stepping-stones to Scotland.

One of the most beguiling things about the North for those who aren't familiar with the territory is how short the distances are. It is just 19 miles/30.6 km from the meadows and glades of Rowallane to the serenity of Castle Ward House on Strangford Lough. From there it is no more than 15 miles/24 km via the picturesque ferry to the glories of Mount Stewart in one direction and in the other about 20 miles/32 km to the mountain scenery and forests of Castlewellan.

Inevitably the Six Counties has differences which set it apart from the South, given over 70 years of partition. There are better roads, superior signposting (all of it in miles whereas the South favours Euro kilometres), the kind of things that you notice when you are driving around. The gardens are differently organised too, many of the important estates and houses coming under the wing of the National Trust (the southern equivalent An Taisce is purely a conservation body and doesn't have the money to own property). Others like Castlewellan and Tollymore are run by the Forest Service of the Department of Agriculture.

Northern gardeners are very organised. Many of those with good gardens (large and small) open them once a year for charity. Under the excellent Ulster Gardens Scheme others hold open days in aid of the National Trust (details of the programme are available from the National Trust headquarters at Rowallane tel. (08) 0238-510131). There is a very high standard of gardening and many wonderful private gardens, and more are now open by appointment under the Ulster Gardens Scheme.

ROUND AND ABOUT

One of the best views of the Mourne Mountains is from the great strand at Tyrella with Slieve Donard rearing up majestically amid the 15-peaked range. The prettiest stretch around the Mourne coast runs along the fiord-like scenery from Narrow Water, through Rostrevor and out to Greencastle and Cranfield point. The road from Kilkeel to Newcastle suffers from bungalow blight and it is well worth turning inland to see the Silent Valley or the Spelga Pass. From here there are drives through hills and forests down to Tollymore and Castlewellan forest parks.

The Lecale peninsula is a peaceful world apart, cut off from the rest of Down by the Quoile and Dundrum Bay, with the medieval fishing village of Ardglass on its flank. The hills behind Dromara, dominated by Slieve Croob with dramatic Legananny dolmen nearby, present another unspoiled stretch of country. The area between Banbridge and Rathfriland, where the father of the Brontë sisters had his roots, is known as the Brontë homeland. The area round the Quoile and Downpatrick is St Patrick's country. The saint landed at Ringbane on Strangford Lough and preached his first sermon at Saul. Strangford village with its view across the narrow mouth of Strangford Lough is charming and a good place to dine or stroll before catching the frequent ferry across to the Ards peninsula, which reaches a long narrow arm around Strangford Lough and its lovely islands.

PLACES TO SEE

County Down. The imposing Tudor revival mansion at Narrow Water Castle, where there is a sculpture gallery, has been praised by William Robinson for its display of daffodils. Ardglass is a pretty fishing village with Jordan's Castle, a fifteenth-century tower house. Greencastle and Comber are good places for browsing and there are tempting antique shops. Beside the Quoile just north of Downpatrick there are the romantic ruins of Inch Abbey and to the west of the town there are the ancient Struell Wells, blessed by St Patrick. Delamont Country Park on the Downpatrick Comber Road, open daily 9am-10pm in summer (6pm winter), features a medieval rath, a heronry and fine views and walks. The Ulster Folk Museum at Cultra provides an intriguing insight into the rural lifestyle of previous generations.

Belfast. Richard Turner's glasshouse with the Victorian delights of the Fern House in the Botanic Park, Stranmillis, is worth a visit. Sir Thomas and Lady Dixon Park, Upper Malone Road, has a rose garden featuring new roses planted in the high municipal style.

Armagh. Ardress, a seventeenth-century house set amid the orchard country of County Armagh seven miles/11.3 km west of Portadown, has a fine collection of furniture and a drawing room with plasterwork by Michael Stapleton. There is a pleasant garden with a little formal rose garden and a herbaceous border.

Nearby the Argory, four miles/6.4 km from Moy on the Derrycaw Road, was built around 1820 on a fine site overlooking the Blackwater River. Inside, it is as though time had stopped, the drawing room is as it would have been in the last century, the house has its own gas plant, there is a curious cabinet barrel-organ, and the dining room table is laid as though for the return of the Bond family who owned it.

Antrim. Some of the loveliest scenery in Antrim is around the Glens off the A2 coast road: Glengariff, Glenarm and Glendun. A detour to Shane's Castle on Lough Neagh makes a good family outing; attractions include an antique railway system, which runs through a nature reserve, a deer park, bird watching and the ruins of the sixteenth-century castle. Open Sundays April, May, June, Sept.; and daily except Mon. July-Aug., 12noon-6.30pm. Lord and Lady O'Neill's beautiful garden is open once a year in July. Beyond Ballycastle there's a spine-chilling walk above the waves on the Carrick-a-rede rope bridge, open daily

May-September. The Giant's Causeway between Ballycastle and Portrush has a well-appointed visitor centre open all year. At nearby Bushmills just off the A2 there are weekday tours of the famous Bushmills whiskey distillery. Just three miles/4.8 km west is the spectacular Norman fortress of Dunluce. In spring it's worth crossing into County Derry to see the Guy Wilson Daffodil Garden at the University of Ulster, Coleraine (one mile/1.6 km out on the road to Coleraine), where there are over 1,000 daffodil cultivars.

In the wake of peace in the Six Counties aspects of garden tourism are growing hearteningly. In some cases attractions which had been closed during the Troubles are now open again. One lovely example is Derrymore House, near Newry, at Bessbrook, County Armagh. The thatched manor in cottage *orné* style was designed by John Sutherland, has a walled garden and is open Saturday afternoons, July and August, 2pm-5.30pm.

Other intriguing glimpses into social history are provided by: the Physick Garden at Grey Abbey, County Down, based on the medicinal plants grown for a monastery infirmary, open April-September, Tuesday-Saturday 10am-7pm, Sunday 2-7pm; the pit house for raising pineapples in the walled garden at Leslie Hill, Ballymoney, where Mrs Delany was once a guest, open summer, weekend afternoons and weekdays July-August; and Gosford Park, Markethill, County Armagh, where there is an 1820s arboretum and small garden which has many associations with Mrs Delany's friend Dean Swift (open daily). Just beside the debouchement of one of the most exciting pieces of cross border development - the Shannon Erne waterway link - Crom demesne near Newtownbutler, County Fermanagh, is a lovely example of the work of nineteenth-century landscape designer William Gilpin (open daily April-September). Carnfunnock Country Park at Larne, County Antrim, has interesting contemporary planting in the old walled garden and a hornbeam maze planted in the shape of Northern Ireland.

PLACES TO STAY/EAT

A t Tyrella House the sweep of private beach dominated by the view of the Mournes and a voluptuously overgrown Japanese garden hidden in the shelter of a wood make the most extraordinary contrast. The garden, complete with temple, wishing chair, rustic bridges and viewing house, on stilts, was constructed from rocks brought by rail and fetched from the station four miles/6.4 km away. David and Sally Corbett opened their beautifully furnished Georgian home to guests in 1992. Ideally situated for visiting both the Mournes and the Ards, the Corbetts can also arrange tours of private gardens in the area for their guests. Cross-country riding and hunting are also possibilities and the Corbetts serve the best of local produce including lobster, pheasant and venison in season. Tyrella House, Downpatrick, County Down. Double room with bathroom £37.50 per person, dinner £20.00, tel. (08) 01396-851422.

Forestbrook in the Fairy Glen above Rostrevor, run by Elizabeth Henshaw, is a listed building in a secluded spot. Furniture is simple and the atmosphere relaxed. B & B £15.00, tel. (08) 016937-38105.

The Garden House was once the home of the head gardener at Narrow Water Castle, Warrenpoint. Accommodation is in a Scandinavian-style wing overlooking a garden with views of the mountains. Run by Mrs Joan Campbell, B & B £15.00, tel. (08) 016937-73273.

Elderflower marmalade is a speciality at Sylvan Hill House, Dromore, a listed eighteenth-century building. Mrs J. Coburn is a gourmet cook, B & B £15.00, dinner £12.50, tel. (08) 01846-692321.

The Cottage lives up to its name: low, whitewashed with a pretty back garden, conservatory and antique furniture. Just outside Dundonald on the Belfast Comber Road, it is run by Elizabeth Muldoon, tel. (08) 01247-878189.

Havine is an award-winning eighteenth-century farmhouse with sloping eaves, on the Downpatrick Road from Clough. It is run by Mrs Myrtle Mulcahy, tel. (08) 01396-85242.

The Lobster Pot in Strangford has seafood - locally caught seafood to die for - huge plump prawns, scallops, crab and lobster. There is a cosy bar where you can wait for your order.

In the last decade Belfast has become yuppified with wine bars and a wide range of restaurants. Among the most successful is Roscoff's in Shaftesbury Square with original cooking at affordable prices.

To the east of Coleraine, Camas House (1685), 27 Curragh Road, Coleraine, is on a country road overlooking the Bann. Mrs Josephine King serves breakfast treats like home-made muesli, compote of autumn fruit and mango juice. B & B from £20.00, tel. (08) 01265-42982, open all year.

Despite its address, Greenhill House at 24 Greenhills Road is a Georgian country house where James and Elizabeth Hegarty serve local specialities like Ulster beef, and there is home baking. Open March-Oct., B & B from £20.00, dinner from £12.00, tel. (08) 01265-868241.

At Ballylough near Bushmills, the Traills, whose garden is featured (see page 222), have opened their delightful country home to guests, tel. (08) 012657-31219.

Nearby the Auberge de Seneirl serves elegant French cuisine where sorbets feature between starters and main course. Open for dinner, tel. (08) 012657-41536.

At the seaside resort of Portrush the Ramore restaurant on the harbour is an unexpected haven with a wine bar and restaurant, designer fast food and interesting fare, tel. (08) 01265-824313.

Among the Glens the Londonderry Arms at Carnlough - an ancient inn on the harbour - specialises in local seafood, tel. (08) 01574-85255.

THE ULSTER
GARDENS SCHEME

It is not so much that Northern gardens are different - more the gardeners themselves. Northerners are more organised. They open their gardens once or twice a year for charity on pre-arranged dates and, until recently, there were very few gardens in the Six Counties open on the informal, *ad hoc* basis of their southern counterparts.

Whether it is due to southern cross-fertilisation, the benefits of peace or the great growth of interest in visiting gardens (or a combination of all of these), the happy result has been that many more gardens are now open by appointment. Under the Ulster Gardens Scheme over a score of gardens are now open to visitors who ring in advance. There is a £2.00 standard rate of admission and the money raised is used to fund National Trust Gardens. The scheme is in addition to the existing calendar of fixed openings under the National Garden Scheme and the series of garden walks (details available from the National Trust, Rowallane, Saintfield, Ballynahinch, County Down, BT24 7LH).

The gardens open by appointment are as follows:

2 Old Glangorm Road, Ballymena, County Antrim: A mature town garden featuring a water garden, herbaceous borders and scree beds in a setting of lawns, trees and shrubs. Between Ballymena and Portglenone on the A42 at the junction of the old and new Glangorm Road. May-September. Tel. (08) 01266-41459 (Mrs Glynn).

Windrush, Station Road, Antrim: Informal two-acre garden featuring a peat garden, a vegetable garden, rhododendrons, azaleas, bulbs, hellebores. In the centre of Antrim opposite the Massarene Hospital. Groups of 10 plus. Tel. (08) 01849-462250 (Mrs Eppy Schierbeek).

Carrigbeag, 1 Cloughey Road, Portaferry, County Down: New and developing garden, with ponds and water-loving plants. Off the Portaferry-Kircubbin Road. May-August. Tel. (08) 012477-28777 (Mrs Wallace).

9 Portaferry Road, Greyabbey, County Down: Seaside garden on the shores of Strangford Lough, full of individual sections and interest. May-September. Tel. (08) 012477-88251 (Mrs Betty Brittain).

Walworth, Ballykelly, County

Derry: Old world, walled garden with water features and mixed planting. Opposite the Droppin Well Pub in Ballykelly. May-August. Tel. (08) 015047-62671 (Mrs Brown).

The Cottage, 43A Malone Park, Malone Road, Belfast: Town garden with intriguing plants and sculptures. June-September. Tel. (08) 01232-669734 (Mrs McGladdery).

30 Castlehill Park, Castlehill Road, Stormont, Belfast: A plantswoman's garden with pool and rock garden. Off the Upper Newtownards Road. May-September. Tel. (08) 01232-763665 (Mrs Christie).

13 Cairnburn Gardens, Cairnburn Road, Belfast: Town garden packed with unusual plants. May-September. Tel. (08) 01232-763575 (Mrs Merrick).

1 Newforge Grange, Newforge Lane, Belfast: Town garden, full of rare shrubs and herbaceous plants. Off top end of the Malone Road. May-September. Tel. (08) 01232-665640 (Lady Bates).

35 Cloverhill Park, Belfast: Suburban garden with rare shrubs and trees and a glen. Near the back gates of Stormont, off Massey Avenue. By appointment. May-September. Tel. (08) 01232-763882 (Mrs Chapman).

Redcot, 35 King's Road, Belfast: A fernery, wild garden and 100-foot long herbaceous border are part of the attractions of this 2.5-acre town garden. Going out of Belfast to the Upper Newtownards Road, turn right into Knock Road, then second right. By appointment. May-September. Tel. (08) 01232-796614.

91 Dromore Road, Ballynahinch, County Down: A half-acre cottage garden packed with interesting plants and two ponds. Turn right for Dromore, 1.5 miles from Ballynahinch. The garden is on the right after 1.25 miles. By appointment. May-August. Tel. (08) 01238-562462 (Mr McDowell).

Loughview Farm, 35 Lisbarnett Road, Lisbane, County Down: Sculptures and arbours add to the interest of this two-acre organic garden with mixed planting and a wildlife pond. Take the Lisbarnett Road from the middle of Lisbane village and turn right 0.75 miles on into a concrete lane. By appointment. May-September. Tel. (08) 01238-5414566 (Mrs Johnson).

28 Killyfaddy Road, Magherafelt, County Derry: Mixed planting and year-round interest in a one-acre garden. Take the Moneymore Road from the centre of Magherafelt, then second left. Open all year by appointment. Tel. (08) 01648-32180 (Mrs Buchanan).

Abbey House, 40 Abbey Street, Armagh: A collection of camellias and a white wisteria feature in this cottage-style garden. Beside the Church of Ireland Cathedral. By appointment. May-September. Tel. (08) 01861-522128 (Major Johnston).

117 Killeague Road, Blackhill, Coleraine, County Derry: A cottage-style garden, designed as a series of rooms. To the right, 7 miles out on the Coleraine Garva Road. By appointment. May-August. Tel. (08) 01265-868356 (Mrs Kennedy).

23 Mountsandel Road, Coleraine, County Derry: A riverside setting makes this 2.5-acre garden - with mixed planting and old-fashioned roses - special. On the south side of the city opposite the hospital. By appointment. May-September. Tel. (08) 01265-42112 (Prof Macfadyn).

Blackhill House, Crevolea Road, Coleraine, County Derry: At its peak in the rhododendron season and in July, this old garden site offers a wide range of conditions for plants from alpines to water-loving varieties. On the main Coleraine Garva Road, take the fifth named road and then turn first right. By appointment all year. Tel. (08) 01265-868377 (Mrs McIntyre).

Ballygawley House, 2 Broan Road, Garva, County Derry: One acre of mixed planting with a new bog garden. On the Coleraine Garva Road turn right at the Moneycarne Road. House is 2 miles on, on the right. By appointment. May-June. Tel. (08) 01265-868205 (Mrs Kerr).

MOUNT STEWART

Newtownards, County Down

FLOWER AND WILD GARDEN,
HISTORICAL INTEREST

A superlative series of gardens within a garden, exceeds every expectation.

Mount Stewart is, without a doubt, the premier garden of the North. And like all the best gardens it is largely the creation of one inspired individual, in this case Edith, seventh Marchioness of Londonderry, known to her powerful political friends as Circe the Sorceress.

It is a garden memorable for its richness of design, its wealth of plants, its fun (where else would you find the red hand of Ulster made from flowers, cheek by jowl with the Irish harp), its symbolism, and its brilliant use of colour.

Lady Edith was a remarkable woman: a society hostess, *femme fatale*, suffragist, founder of the Women's League and a wonderful gardener. When she came to Mount Stewart in the 1920s she set about transforming the house and grounds which she described as the 'dampest, darkest, saddest place'. Within a very short space of time Lady Londonderry had completely re-landscaped and replanted a huge section of the grounds, supervising the creation of a series of formal gardens around the house, their symmetry forming a link between its architecture and the woods, glades and water of the informal areas.

The sunken garden to the north west of the house, financed with the winnings of the St Leger, has a brilliant yellow, orange and blue scheme, with delphiniums, lilies, phlox and a dusky purple clematis trailing over tree heath and among the rose pergolas on the surrounding terraces. It is based on a design by Gertrude Jekyll.

This area leads on to a small compartmental garden featuring the red hand of Ulster picked out in begonias amid the gravel, and a topiary harp. Huge urns, clipped yew hedges and the deep purple *Acer palmatum* 'Atropurpureum' endorse the architectural feel of this area.

The Italian garden, inspired

partly by the Florentine Villa Gambaria and the Villa Farnese, and partly by the gardens at Dunrobin in Scotland where Edith spent her childhood, has another glorious planting scheme - of reds, yellows and oranges. Each bed has variations on the theme, with surrounding hedges in co-ordinating red, yellow or green. Deep purply *Cotinus* is an unlikely but successful addition to the planting. The stonework was all carried out by local craftsmen and the monkey pillars were designed by Lady Londonderry.

The Spanish garden, with its pool, loggia and cool green planting, is laid out in a pattern which reflects the ceiling in the Temple of the Winds. It takes its name from the Spanish tiles in the loggia. The row of airy green arches curving round either side of the garden is made - wonder of wonders - of clipped cypress, a lovely use for a tree which has become such a blot on the Irish landscape.

White gardens can be a bit of a cliché and are hard to carry off. But the white, silver and blue of the Mairi garden - named for the Londonderrys' youngest daughter, Lady Mairi Bury, who used to sit in her pram there - is a triumph. Among the silver and green foliage, blue and lavender flowers are planted in drifts, a sweet *Viola cornuta lilacina*, giant *Agapanthus*, a

Admission to house, garden and temple, £3.30, children £1.65, groups £2.60, garden open April-Aug. 1-6pm daily except Tuesdays; in Sept. and Oct. weekends only. House open May-Aug. 1-6pm daily except Tuesdays; in April, Sept., Oct. 1-6pm weekends only, tel. (08) 012477-88387. Largely accessible to wheelchairs; well-behaved children welcome. Restaurant for light meals in the Ark Club tea room with wall paintings of Circe the Sorceress, Charley the Cheetah, etc., shop, toilet facilities. Directions: On the east shore of Strangford Lough five miles/8 km south east of Newtownards on the A20 Belfast Portaferry Road.

lovely lilac *Phlox* called 'Prospero', *Thalictrum*, *Perovskia* 'Blue Spire'. In the centre of this circular garden is a fountain surrounded with cockle shells echoing the refrain of the nursery rhyme 'Mary Mary quite contrary'. The silver bells are there too in the shape of various campanulas and the pretty maids in the guise of *Saxifraga granulata* 'Plena'.

The Dodo terrace illustrates Lady Londonderry's whimsical symbolism. The members of the powerful circle known as the Ark Club, which she founded in 1915, met in Londonderry House and were given the names of various creatures; Winston Churchill was known as Winston the Warlock, Harold Macmillan was known as Harold the Hummingbird, her husband 'Charley' was known as Charley the Cheetah (appropriately, since he was very fleet in pursuit of the fair sex). The stone creatures on the terrace are in honour of members of the Ark.

In the subtropical climate of the Ards, warmed by the Gulf Stream with Strangford Lough on one side of the four-mile/6.4 km-wide peninsula and the sea on the other, it was possible to grow all manner of tender plants, *Mimosa pomegranates*, camphor trees, acacias, lapagerias and eucalyptus. Lady Londonderry subscribed to many of the plant expeditions and there are some particularly interesting rare shrubs planted on The Hill, an area below Tír na n'Óg (Land of the Ever Young) which is the family's private burial ground.

Part of the charm of the garden lies in the different atmosphere of each section, the vistas of trees and water around the Lake Walk, the spring display of the rhododendron wood, and the enclosed green areas of the lily wood with drifts of woodland plants and ferns, as well as the Peace and Memorial Gardens. Some of the major features of the garden were created by previous generations: the lake was made in the 1840s in the time of the third Marquis of Londonderry, shelter belts and the large specimen trees were planted in the nineteenth century and the gum trees which line the Fountain Walk were grown from seed by Theresa Lady Londonderry in 1894.

The nearby Temple of the Winds – an exquisite small banqueting house – made for the first Marquis of Londonderry in the 1780s to the design of James 'Athenian' Stuart – has idyllic views across Strangford Lough. In the distance is a local landmark, Scrabo Tower, the monument to the third Earl by Charles Lanyon.

Another factor in the almost instant success of the gardens was Lady Londonderry's ability to choose the best possible advisers - Sir John Ross, who had a wonderful garden at Rostrevor House, beside the Mourne Mountains, and Sir John Maxwell of Monrieth, where there was another fine garden.

It would be easy to say - as some envious neighbours did - that her gardens were 'manured with money'. But that is to underestimate Lady Londonderry's achievement; she became an expert plantswoman, devoted a great deal of time to the garden and kept meticulous records of everything. The gardens were given by Lady Londonderry to the National Trust in 1957 and Mount Stewart was donated by Lady Mairi Bury in 1977.

During the 1930s notables were flown in from London to Newtownards Airport which the family had specially built for the purpose. Ramsay MacDonald, W.B. Yeats, Osbert Sitwell, Sean O'Casey, Prince Juan of Spain and Harold and Vita Nicolson were regular guests. They would spend weekends at Mount Stewart enjoying lavish hospitality and relaxing in the gardens which continue to give just as much pleasure to the thousands who visit them today. They are at their absolute peak in summer, but marvellous in spring and autumn too.

CASTLE WARD

Strangford, County Down

DEMESNE, HISTORICAL INTEREST

A fine estate providing an insight into garden history.

Castle Ward is situated in the loveliest part of Strangford Lough, looking across the narrow mouth of the lough to wooded hills surrounding the colourful village of Portaferry.

The fascinating house with its classical front and gothic back facing towards the lough - the result of an architectural disagreement between Bernard Ward (later Baron Bangor) and his wife, Lady Anne - is the centrepiece of a great demesne. Its setting amid undulating parkland and cloud-like groups of trees is in perfect accord with the eighteenth-century romantic style. The extensive pleasure grounds to the west of the mansion illustrate certain aspects of gardening history.

The layout of the estate poses some intriguing questions. Why was the house, begun in 1762, situated so far from the ornamental lake and walled garden? And why is there a new lime avenue apparently leading nowhere?

The answer lies in the changing taste of different periods. Bernard's father, Judge Michael Ward, MP for Down, built a Queen Anne house and to complement it two formal canals (1728). One, known as Temple Water, survives together with an old yew walk as an important piece of garden history. The other has vanished but a double avenue of limes was recently planted to mark where it once lay. The house no longer exists but the classical temple atop the hill built as a summer house for Lady Anne Ward in 1750 is still a landmark. By the time Bernard Ward inherited the estate, fashions in architecture and landscaping had changed and he sited his new house nearly half a mile away.

The Victorian garden near the house reflects nineteenth-century taste with terraces, beds planted with annuals, palm trees and Florence Court yews. Originally known as the Windsor garden, it had once 61 such beds with an army of gardeners to maintain them. The old walled garden, built for fruit and vegetables around 1830, now houses a wildfowl collection.

History stretches back further still to Audley's Castle built in the fifteenth century and to the defensive tower house built by the Ward family when they came to Strangford in 1610. The estate is also a good example of the micro-economies of extensive properties, with lead mines, saw mills, several piers, a large farm yard and a corn mill, each with a contribution to make.

Admission £3.50 per car, estate open all year round, dawn to dusk; house open April, Oct., weekends 1-6pm; May-Sept. daily except Thursdays, 1-6pm, tel. (08) 0139686-204. Wonderful for children, parts suitable for wheelchairs, special access for disabled drivers. Shop, restaurants, Strangford Lough Barn interpretative centre. Check calendar for interesting events including craft fairs. Directions: seven miles/11.3 km north east of Downpatrick, and one and a half miles/2.4 km west of Strangford village on the A25.

ROWALLANE

Saintfield, County Down

WILD AND FLOWER GARDEN
A fabulous rhododendron and azalea
display in a natural rock and woodland
garden plus a lovely old walled garden.

Rowallane is one of those places which appeal both to plantspeople and to those who like to wander in a beautiful setting. The extensive gardens are best known for their spectacular spring displays of rhododendrons and azaleas, which are planted among woods and natural rock gardens. But there is plenty to see at other times of the year and the handsome walled garden with its collection of penstemons and old roses is a joy in summer.

The gardens were begun by the eccentric cleric the Rev. John Moore, who added the walled garden and stables to the estate. He occasionally preached to his flock from the dais in the pleasure ground; he also began planting the garden and created the extraordinary stone cairns on the avenue.

But the Rowallane gardens are mainly the creation of his nephew Hugh Armitage Moore, who inherited the property in 1903.

Despite the unpromising acid soil which lies in a thin layer over rocky outcrops he created a wonderful wild garden working with the natural terrain. The rhododendrons begin as early as December with *R. nobleanum* and end in July with *R. auriculatum* 'Polar Bear'. But the display reaches a climax in mid May when, together with azaleas, they form great banks of blending colour, shading from yellow to cream and orange through whites and pinks to red, purple and the blue of *R*. 'Blue Diamond'.

The 52-acre wild garden has a whole series of distinct areas linked by grassy paths and old stone walls, each with a different atmosphere. The vivid autumn shades of many varieties of acers and spring displays of daffodils add their share of colour. All of the place names have a meaning: the Hospital was originally where sick calves were grazed, and there is a throne-shaped outcrop in the area known as Bishop's Rock.

There are many other lovely shrubs and trees scattered through the gardens, all clearly labelled, among them the false camellia *Stuartia pseudocamellia*, a lovely dark

Acer rubescens with red-stemmed leaves and the sorrel tree *Oxydendrum arboreum*.

The planting in the walled garden is eclectic: Mr Moore simply put plants where they seemed happiest and Mike Snowden, the National Trust's head gardener at Rowallane, has continued the garden in the same spirit. Just inside the walled garden there is a fetching planting scheme of blue and silver plants. There are over 50 varieties of penstemons in the garden, which form part of the national collection, and great displays of primulas, meconopsis, colchicums (autumn crocus) and magnolias in season. Don't miss the early summer show of the enormous handkerchief tree and wisteria in the outer walled garden.

Restoration work is ongoing. The rock garden in a massive outcrop has recently been replanted with dwarf shrubs, Alpines, heathers and primulas, among them the lovely pink *P.* 'Rowallane Rose' which originated in the garden. The gardeners are also attempting to propagate from the ageing rhododendrons which are now up to 70 years old so that there will be continuity in any replanting. There are several other Rowallane varieties including a St John's wort (*Hypericum* 'Rowallane'), a *Viburnum plicatum tomentosum*,

quince and *Chaenomeles superba* 'Rowallane'.

A landmark much beloved of summer romancers, the bandstand from Newcastle has found a new home in the pleasure grounds, where many wild flowers, including wild orchids, grow in the natural meadowland. The National Trust acquired the gardens in 1955 and Rowallane House is now the organisation's regional head office.

Admission £2.50, children £1.25, groups £1.60, free to NT members, open April-end Oct. Mon.-Fri. 10.30am-6pm, Sat.-Sun. 2-6pm, tel. (08) 01238-510131. Partially suitable for wheelchairs, ideal for children, special disabled access, walks for the visually impaired. Shop, teas, toilet facilities. Ask for programme for details of wild flower walks, plants, sales, etc. Directions: Just outside Saintfield on the right-hand side, on the A7 Belfast Downpatrick Road.

BALLYWALTER PARK

Newtownards, County Down

DEMESNE, HISTORICAL INTEREST
A well-maintained estate where the grass and trees create a haven.

Peaceful pleasure grounds with magnificent trees and glades sheltering a fine collection of rhododendrons make a perfect foil to the Italianate palazzo designed in 1846 by Charles Lanyon for the merchant prince and Mayor of Belfast, Andrew Mulholland.

Ballywalter Park - built around an earlier Georgian house known as Springvale, owned by the Matthews family - reflected the status of Andrew Mulholland. He made his fortune in linen spinning, introducing with his brother the first power mill in Belfast in 1830; by the mid century the family's York Street Mill was one of the biggest in the world.

The magnificent Lanyon conservatory with a glass dome supported by Corinthian columns,

added to the house in 1856, was a further monument to Mulholland's success. His son John, created Baron Dunleath, would have been a multi-millionaire in today's terms.

Times change, however, and when the late Lord Dunleath inherited Ballywalter Park in 1956, people were inclined to feel sorry for him, chained, as they saw it, to a Victorian white elephant. Fortunately for Ballywalter Park and for Lord Dunleath, John Betjeman came to tea and waxed ecstatic over the glories of the house and conservatory. In a few decades, he predicted, the place would become a mecca for architectural enthusiasts.

Today Ballywalter is recognised as a splendid example of Lanyon's work in the Italianate manner. The sumptuous interior of the house is balanced by the soothing prospect of gently undulating lawns and plantings of ornamental trees and shrubs.

The framework of the original garden can be seen in the beeches and oaks planted by Major Matthews around 1800 but its formal layout was changed in the mid eighteenth century when romantic landscapes came into vogue. Andrew Mulholland planted over 90,000 trees and shrubs in landscaped grounds which merged into parkland and woods criss-crossed by woodland rides. His plantings included limes, laburnums and rhododendron hybrids. In the next generation his son John increased the shelter round the estate, planting Scots, Austrian and Corsican pines; and handsome conifers in the pleasure grounds.

The rock and water garden were added to the grounds by Henry, the second Baron Dunleath and his wife, Lady Norah. The third Lord Dunleath was a rhododendron enthusiast, subscribing to many of the plant expeditions, and he propagated his own hybrids including the rich dark red hybrid 'Lady Dunleath'. As part of the process he would place brown paper bags over the trusses of rhododendron blooms to ensure that insects didn't introduce other pollens. The results of his labours can be seen in the magnificent stands of rhododendrons in sheltered glades. There are some particularly fine big-leaved *R. sinogrande*, *macabeanum* and *falconeri*, and various hybrid crosses. The best time to visit this estate is in spring, and there is always a great deal to interest the dendrologist.

The late Lord Dunleath's interest tended more to landscape architecture and he carried out conservation and restoration work in both house and garden. New plants were propagated from the original rhododendrons to maintain the character of the planting. Glades and walks were reinstated among tender

Admission £2.00 with tour of the house included by special appointment, groups only by appointment, tel. (08) 012477-58203. There is a pick-your-own-soft-fruit scheme in season at the back entrance to the estate. Directions: Turn off the A20 between Newtownards and Portaferry at Greyabbey. Take the B5 Ballywalter Road, turn right at the T junction facing the estate gate and follow the wall around to the gate lodge on the right at Ballywalter farms.

trees which include pittosporums, embothriums and eucalyptus. Lord Dunleath became expert at striking a balance in the conflict between shelter and vista.

Within the grounds there is also a large walled garden, with some of the original glasshouses, a fine rose pergola with old rambling roses and an adjoining rose garden. The stream which runs through the grounds is crossed by several bridges designed by Lanyon and feeds an ornamental pool. The whole provides a charming insight into the changing tastes in gardening over 200 years.

At the end of a grass ride there are the remains of a curious structure made of plastic pipes where Lord Dunleath ingeniously constructed a full-scale model of a gothic gazebo. The trial folly stood for two and a half years before being blown down in a storm but Lord Dunleath abandoned the idea of a permanent replacement. In the present economic climate he decided the building of a folly is exactly that!

CASTLEWELLAN

National Arboretum,
Castlewellan, County Down

ARBORETUM, GARDEN, WILD GARDEN, HISTORICAL INTEREST

An exceptional garden offering hours of pleasure.

Castlewellan has three great things in its favour: beautiful surroundings near the Mournes, a superb arboretum created by Lord Annesley and a masterfully designed setting in a walled garden.

Although it is less well known, Castlewellan deserves to rank with Mount Stewart and Rowallane as one of the North's top gardens.

The Annesley garden was created by generations of the Annesley family. The 12-acre walled garden dates back to 1740 when the family first acquired the estate and the planting of the arboretum was begun around 1870 by the fourth Earl of Annesley after he built the baronial-style castle in 1856.

The garden is on a south-facing hill, sheltered by forest, a good walk from the lakeside car park. There is a truly spectacular vista down the central path towards the heron fountain circled by crimson maples. Huge topiaried yews shaped like drunken pears march alongside the gravelled walk and in the background are the vari-coloured towers and spires of century-old conifers.

Uphill the pathway leads to a charming mer-boy fountain, surrounded by dwarf conifers. Beyond this is a stunning double herbaceous border. Campanulas, acanthus, peonies and poppies, delphiniums, *Monarda didyama* and astilbes form part of a striking colour scheme of mauve and red against a yew hedge festooned with *Tropaeolum speciosum*, and the air is scented by towering eucalyptus trees.

The rest of the garden is divided by walks, each with a different theme. There is a eucryphia walk which becomes a mass of gold-stamened white flowers in August, there is the extraordinary

Sequoiadendron giganteum (var. 'Pendulum') looking for all the world like a giant hairy pencil, a pair of huge *Wellingtonia* – one of the earliest plantings in the country dating back to 1856, *Styrax japonica* clothed with a mass of delicate white bells in midsummer, and a giant Hondo spruce grown from seed brought back from the Himalayas in 1868.

In an age of instant effects this is a place to appreciate the worthwhile contribution mature trees make to a garden. It would be hard not to covet a *Picea breweriana* with its veils of weeping branches, or a golden-tipped *Picea orientalis* 'Aurea'. There are huge collections of different species from all over the world, with more than 50 types of *Picea*, 15 types of *Podocarpus* and 40 varieties of juniper.

Many of the specimens are the products of various plant expeditions. The coffin juniper (*Juniperus recurva* var. 'Coxii') arrived in a matchbox in 1932. The tallest tree in the garden is a western hemlock with a self-sown seedling growing underneath; the pair is known as the Mother and Child. The parent trees which produced the Castlewellan gold cypress, now planted around every second bungalow in the country, are in the Annesley garden.

Important specimens are clearly labelled and a helpful guide produced by the Forestry Service is available at the entrance to the estate. In the ideal conditions some of the trees have reached huge proportions. Beside the entrance a venerable *Acer palmatum* 'Atropurpureum', with a winter pool of snowdrops at its feet, is 23 feet/7 m tall, and the multi-stemmed Sierra redwood looks like

Admission £2.50 per car, open all year round, Annesley garden closed at dusk, tel. (08) 013967-78664. Alcohol-free area. Partially accessible to wheelchairs, great for children, special parking for disabled. Toilet facilities and pleasant restaurant in stable block. Caravan park and camping site. Directions: Three miles/4.8 km from Newcastle on the A25 Rathfriland Downpatrick Road, entrance via Castlewellan village.

a forest rather than a single tree. The garden is beautifully maintained with the exception of the old rose garden, which looks a little sad.

The glasshouses on a terrace looking towards the Mournes have been beautifully restored. Splendid examples of their kind, they house tropical birds, a collection of phormiums, ferns and all manner of luxuriant tender plants: passifloras, the Brazilian spider flower and the pink-trumpeted Chilean bellflower.

Planting has been extended beyond the walled garden by the Forestry Service to include new areas of interest. The spring garden with an attractive water feature is mainly planted with cherries and flowering crabapples. The dwarf conifer garden, interplanted with heathers, has some inspiring ideas for smaller gardens. In spring and early summer in the rhododendron wood the blooms of camellias and an extensive selection of rhododendrons and azaleas are reflected in an ornamental lake. Between the lake and the castle the autumn wood is not to be missed in late September and October when the trees turn scarlet and gold.

At the far end of the wood is the cypress pond in which a collection of *Chamaecyparis* or false cypress has been built up since 1969. The Castlewellan estate, now the centrepiece of the Castlewellan Forest Park, was purchased by the Forestry Service of the Department of Agriculture in 1967. The nearby hilly village of Castlewellan was partly laid out by the Annesleys.

SEAFORDE

Seaforde, County Down

WILD GARDEN

A romantically tousled garden featuring a maze and a butterfly house.

After half a century of somnolence, the walled gardens at Seaforde have been partially restored by Patrick Forde and are now open to the public. A maze, many tender shrubs and a pheasantry, with fine old trees and an ornamental pool, are the main features of four acres of pleasure grounds.

The surrounding walls are shown on a 1750 map and the Forde family built their first home at the estate around this time. What was the original fruit and vegetable garden has now become a popular nursery with six different varieties of tree ferns. There is also a butterfly house with exotic examples from South America, Africa and the Philippines. The largest specimens are Atlas moths with a 12-inch wing span.

Nearly 20 years ago Patrick Forde took over part of the stock of the celebrated Slieve Donard

Admission £2.00, OAP £1.50, open all year 10am-5pm, Sun. 2-6pm, closed weekends during winter. Tel. (08) 01396-811225. Butterflies and nursery accessible for wheelchairs. Children love the maze. The nursery is recommended by keen gardeners and has a fine selection of very reasonably priced shrubs with a good selection of magnolias, azaleas and rhododendrons. Directions: On the A24 Road, between Clough and Ballynahinch.

Nurseries when they closed down. He is a keen plantsman and took part in an expedition to Bhutan in the Himalayas, and recently went to North Vietnam where new plants are still being found in the wild. The material he brings back is propagated at Seaforde.

The first section of the pleasure grounds was once filled with the labour-intensive formal beds of annuals so beloved of the Victorians, and rows of glasshouses. Now the main attractions are a hornbeam maze with an eye-catching rose bower created from the skeleton of a Nissan hut at the centre, a summer house ingeniously built out of central heating pipes, and a fine assembly of shrubs. Two eucryphia *allées* flank the maze, and the garden houses the national eucryphia collection (this UK system involves keeping all the known cultivars of known species). There are 19 varieties of eucryphia at Seaforde. Dramatic spikes of Canary Island

Echium pininana go soaring up to eight feet/2.4 m and look as though they could turn into Triffids.

In summer peacocks, complete with families of peachicks, bask in the sun. Fountains of old roses grow through the trees, while *Podocarpus salignus*, *Melianthus major*, and a good selection of eucalyptus, hydrangeas, lilies and magnolias including the huge pink-flowered *campbellii* variety grow within the sheltering walls of the enclosed grounds.

Ornamental birds were once kept in the pheasantry and pheasants still stroll unconcernedly about the grounds. An ornamental pool has been restored and mirrors a great display of *Rhododendron arboreum* in spring. Some of the trees in the arboretum are over 150 years old. The gardens are approached by a magnificent avenue of ancient beeches, but sadly the early nineteenth-century house with views over ornamental lakes and the Mournes can't be seen.

TOLLYMORE FOREST PARK

Bryansfort, County Down

HISTORICAL INTEREST

Fine for forest walks and views, with notable reminders of the old demesne.

Tollymore Park was one of the earliest examples of an estate in the naturalistic manner made fashionable by William Kent. The estate was laid out by the first Earl of Clanbrassil in the mid eighteenth century and was greatly admired for its gothic follies and beautiful scenery with views of the Mourne Mountains and Dundrum Bay.

The gateways to the estate are especially pleasing: the castellated barbican gate leads to a splendid avenue of Himalayan cedars, while the gothic archway with pinnacles and buttresses frames a view of the Clanbrassil Barn (1757), which is totally convincing in its guise as a gothic church. Complete with tower and spire it is thought to have been designed by Thomas Wright. Other interesting features include a series of bridges across the Shimna and Spinkwee Rivers (the earliest, known as the Old Bridge, dates back to 1726), an obelisk, a grotto, and a rath known as the White Fort dating back to somewhere between AD 500 and 1000.

In the eighteenth and nineteenth centuries timber was planted not only for ornamental effect but as an important cash crop. The first Earl of Clanbrassil planted 60,000 trees a year, and Tollymore is still known for the quality of its timber; the Forestry Service, which has run the 500-hectare estate since 1941, produces 2,000 tonnes of timber a year. During the last war timber from the estate was driven into the sand on nearby beaches to deter German invaders and the tops of the poles can still be seen.

The first Earl also began the arboretum, which is carpeted with spring bulbs: daffodils, narcissi and snowdrops. He discovered the first dwarf Norway spruce (*Picea abies* var. 'Clanbrassiliana') and the original is still in the arboretum among a collection of fine trees. The Forestry Commission have added an azalea garden around a steep path which runs beside a tumbling stream. The house was demolished in 1952 and the site - sadly because it is a fine vantage-point - has been turned into a car park.

Admission £1.00 or £2.20 per car, open 10am to dusk. Great for children, good paths for wheelchairs in arboretum. Toilet facilities, restaurant for light meals. Directions: Tollymore, one mile/1.6 km from Newcastle, is signposted from Newcastle and from the A2 coast road.

KEADY RECTORY

Crossmore Road, Keady, County Armagh

FLOWER GARDEN
Wonderful old roses and herbaceous
plants in a well-planned small garden.

There can't be many vicars who admit to loving Lucifer. But the Lucifer in this case happens to be a fiery scarlet gentleman of the *Crocosmia* family who is a member of the richly varied flock assembled by the Rev. Dr W.G. Neely in the

garden of Keady Rectory.

When Dr Neely came to Keady eight years ago there was little more than a shelter belt of fir and cypress surrounding a lawn. Now there is an intriguing garden which offers a gothic walk, a rose bower, woodland shade and several dramatic borders in a relatively small space. And packed into every possible inch there are enviable plants.

The garden is planned as a series of rooms, each one an exercise in colour. The first - mainly pinks and reds - features old roses like 'William Lobb', 'Grootendorst' and 'Rambling Rector', mixed with choice shrubs, the ruby-coloured acer (*Acer palmatum* 'Dissectum Purpureum'), bronze *Pittosporum* and choice plants like pale pink *Dierama*, *Penstemon* 'Ruby Garnet' and *Potentilla* 'Miss Willmott'.

The small woodland walk shelters shade-loving plants, a variegated ponticum, *Hydrangea* 'Preziosa', the marching fern and the lovely hosta 'Frances Williams' among them. A huge pair of *Beschorneria yuccoides* plays a sculptural role at the entrance to a predominantly yellow and red area with *Lilium haemerocallis* planted together with *Alstroemeria*. New formal beds - there's nothing like a new bed - have just been claimed from a field and are planted with a rewarding combination of old roses and herbaceous plants.

Eye-catching plants to be found throughout the garden include *Salvia microphylla*, violas 'Irish Molly' and 'Jackanapes', a delphinium 'Alice Artingdale', a yellow hellebore, the cup-and-saucer campanula, *Dahlia* 'Bishop of

Llandaff', the vivid blue *Salvia patens* and the graceful white-flowered *Rosa glauca Hydrangea arborescens*. A chestnut - its feet carpeted with crocuses and snowdrops in spring - and the dark aisle of the gothic walk create contrasting quiet areas.

A collection of over 80 shrub roses - *R. rubrafolia*, 'Blush Noisette', 'Comte de Chambord', *moyesii*, 'Chapeau de Napoléon', 'Rose d'Amour', are among many favourites - make this a rose lover's heaven in June and July.

Admission £2.00, open to groups by appointment, tel. (08) 01861-531230. Difficult for wheelchairs.

Directions: The turning for Crossmore Road is opposite Keady fire station; the rectory is one mile/1.6 km up on the right.

BENVARDEN

Dervock, County Antrim

FLOWER AND WILD GARDEN
A beautifully maintained walled garden set in fine grounds.

Visitors to Benvarden may be a mite concerned to hear lions roaring from behind the rhododendrons. But despite the hair-raising sound effects there is no cause for alarm, the lions are a feature of the Safari Park on the far side of the River Bush.

Walled gardens are often the first casualty of changed times but at Benvarden the two-acre enclosure probably looks better than at any time in its recent past. Over the last 30 years Hugh and Valerie Montgomery have made a series of gardens within walls which are said to date back to the time of King Billy.

In midsummer the rose garden, laid out in a sunburst parterre around a fountain, is the most spectacular sight. The hybrid tea roses are planted in blocks of colour and the scent from a nearby collection of David Austin roses mingles with the sound of falling water.

Nearby is a new parterre, the centres of the pattern filled with silver foliage plants, lavender, rue

Admission £2.00, open to groups by appointment only, tours of the house by special arrangement, tel. (08) 012657-41331. Walled garden suitable for wheelchairs and well-behaved children. Teas in the stableyard by arrangement. Plants, fruit, vegetables for sale. Directions: Take the Portrush Road to Ballybogy, turn right onto the B67 to Ballycastle; the entrance gate is two miles/ 3.2 km out on the right.

and cineraria, with a silver weeping pear at the centre. The Blue Moon garden features box-hedged crescent beds filled with the Kingfisher daisy (*Felicia bergeriana*). Arches festooned with old-fashioned climbers like the Himalaya musk rose, gravelled walks, ancient apple trees and immaculately clipped box edging add to the Victorian feel of the place. Shrub borders filled with roses, cistus and azaleas, herbaceous borders with old favourites like white agapanthus, *Potentilla* 'Miss Willmott', *Veratrum album*, and a wonderful double pink-flowered tree peony are also features.

In a restored greenhouse ripening peaches and carefully tended vines make a rare sight. The kitchen garden is still in full production tended by Garry Curry with rows of perfect vegetables and huge strawberry and raspberry beds. Hugh Montgomery produces thousands upon thousands of hardwood saplings on the estate which are sold throughout the North of Ireland. He also produces thousands of fuchsias and geraniums for sale locally.

In the pleasure grounds near the river, a small pond sheltered by ancient Florence Court yews and a stream crossed by rustic bridges have been reclaimed from the undergrowth. A letter written from the Crimean War by a Montgomery ancestor sets the date of this part of the garden in the 1850s. The eighteenth-century house (once the home of the Macnaghtens, one of whom was hanged for shooting Mary Anne Knox of Prehen House) was enlarged by the Montgomery family in 1800.

DOWNHILL CASTLE

Downhill, County Derry

FLOWER GARDEN

An enchanting water meadow and flower garden beside an architectural gem.

Two memories of Downhill are indelibly printed on my mind. One is the sight of the Mussenden Temple in the dusk, a classical gem balanced improbably on the very edge of an enormous cliff with the sickle of Downhill Strand stretching away to the Donegal Hills on one side and the lights of Portrush winking across a silver sea on the other.

Inside the rotunda, where the sound of the waves echoes around the empty brick-lined interior, the effect is even more extraordinary. The building appears to be hovering high above the sea, with aerial views of the coast and of seabirds flying far below. In the twilit field scores of sheep are aahing much as the Earl Bishop's flock must have done when Frederick Augustus Hervey had this most extraordinary library built between 1783 and 1785.

The other memory is of the garden created by Miss Jan Eccles at the Bishop's Gate entrance to Downhill Castle. Where once the wind came howling up from Castlerock through the Black Glen to buffet the sandstone arch and gate lodge, there is now a romantic water meadow and flower garden in the shelter of a wood. In early summer the water meadow is lit with myriads of candelabra primulas and violet *Iris Kaempferi*. A colourful rock garden full of desirable plants like dwarf agapanthus and rock roses makes the gate lodge an eye-catching sight.

The headless statue of the second Earl of Bristol - known to his friends as George - stands guard over the avenue. Around him wafts the scent from roses fountaining over a pergola and a border filled with old favourites like the 'Queen Elizabeth' rose, phlox and tree peonies. Sad to say, plants are sometimes stolen; it would be much more appropriate if people were to bring lovely plants, for this garden has been created almost entirely with one pair of hands. Miss Eccles came as a warden

in 1962 and has reclaimed the formerly derelict spot, working from dawn to dusk. She is still planning additions to the garden: lovers' seats and steps made from fallen pieces of Downhill's masonry and a 'smelly bed' with aromatics like santolina, southernwood and camomile for blind people.

Miss Eccles's greatest love is for trees. At retirement age she began planting trees and shrubs in the glen: wingnuts, copper beech, Russian oak, a tulip tree, field maples, Indian chestnuts grown from conkers, Pyrenean oak, *Liquidambar*, a ginkgo and a blue cedar. Her saplings are now fine trees of three decades' standing. A *Metasequoia glyptostroboides* has special pride of place and thereby hangs a tale. It was grown by Miss Eccles from slips from a tree sent to Coleraine from China after the fabled fossil tree was rediscovered there in 1942. There are interesting things to be learned in every corner of this garden and if you are lucky Miss Eccles might tell you about them.

Beyond the garden are the gaunt ruins of Frederick Hervey's palace built in the 1780s, rebuilt after an 1851 fire to Charles Lanyon's design and partially demolished in 1950.

Hervey, a rich and worldly prelate with unbounded enthusiasm for building projects, chose the cliff-top site for its bleak grandeur. He had a wicked sense of humour and held races for fat clerics versus thin clerics after dinner at Downhill with rich livings as prizes for the winners. The Mussenden Temple (named indiscreetly for the Bishop's attractive cousin Mrs Frideswade Mussenden and based on the Temple of Vesta at Tivoli), the Lion's and Bishop's Gates and the Mausoleum (for the Bishop's brother George) - all part of the great estate - are now maintained by the National Trust.

Admission free, grounds always open, Mussenden Temple open Easter-Oct. 2-6pm weekends and weekdays in high summer. The drive through the garden is suitable for wheelchairs; this is a great spot for children; tel. (08) 012658-48728. Directions: Downhill is five miles/ 8 km from Coleraine on the A2 Road to Limavady.

O'HARABROOK

Ballymoney, County Antrim

**FLOWER AND WILD GARDEN,
HISTORICAL INTEREST**

*A romantic old-fashioned garden set in
an interesting estate.*

A spectacular beech avenue, a Quaker burial ground known as the Lambs' Fold, a riverside walk and a stackyard complete with rick stands are just some of the intriguing features to be found on a walk around the O'Harabrook estate.

On the approach to the house a shadowy gothic ruin - once a Quaker school - draped in scarlet *Tropaeolum speciosum* adds an exotic touch to the place. The mid eighteenth-century house was once a coaching inn on the old road from Ballymoney to Coleraine and is now owned by Sandy and Bridget Cramsie. The pretty conservatory filled with morning glory and geraniums was built in 1898 as a birthday present for a Cramsie great-grandmother.

The garden - fenced in corrugated tin at a time when the material was the very latest thing - is a bicycle ride away from the house. In the shelter of huge beeches and

---

Admission £2.00, open to groups by appointment, tel. (08) 012656-66273. Flower garden accessible to wheelchairs, woods wonderful for children. Teas by request for groups in the barn of the handsome old stableyard. Plants for sale. Directions: From the station at the bottom of Ballymoney take the road to the right (as you face the station). O'Harabrook is two miles/3.2 km out on the right-hand side. Look for white stones marking the entrance.

---

two towering tulip trees the layout of a formal garden has been redesigned to give a most romantic effect. Fountains of red and pink roses cover archways and drifts of frothy pink astilbe, hostas, *Alchemilla mollis*, and groups of white, pink, blue and silver plants spill over onto paths and crowd into corners sheltered by shrub roses and clematis where there are inviting seats. A huge old border is packed with *Alstroemeria*, peonies, delphiniums and hostas.

A new rose arbour pergola is already covered with swags of *R.* 'Rambling Rector' and 'New Dawn' and along one edge of the garden the tin fence is completely hidden behind burgeoning tree peonies, abutilon and *Viburnum* 'Mariesii'. There is also a very productive vegetable garden where you can pick your own raspberries.

The grounds are particularly lovely in spring when the rhododendrons and azaleas are out and there are carpets of daffodils, bluebells, primroses and orchids. Small streams run through the grounds to join the river and there is a pleasant path, known as the Well Avenue, which leads through the woods past a new pond.

BALLYLOUGH HOUSE

Bushmills, County Antrim

FLOWER AND WILD GARDEN
A marvellous profusion of flowers both wild and cultivated.

Four generations of passionate gardeners have contributed to a fine collection of plants grown within the sheltered walled garden at Ballylough. The Traill family have lived at the attractive eighteenth-century house with battlemented flanking walls for 200 years. But parts of the ancient walls of the garden may have belonged to the fortified bawn of the fourteenth-century McQuillan castle.

A bed beyond the garden doorway is packed with Alpines and choice plants guaranteed to delight enthusiasts. There are all kinds of eye-catching specialities in the garden: stands of the giant *Lilium cardiocrinum*, the green-flowered golden-leaved *Hacquetia epipactis*, a Russian almond producing deep pink buds in March, the pale blue-flowered herbaceous *Clematis* 'Wyevale'. The overall effect in June/July is of a riot of bloom with huge clumps of red, blue and pink penstemons, blue fountains of the chimney bellflower, pale lilac thalictrum, deep pink Japanese anemones and deep blue abutilons. The garden offers year-round interest. Earlier in the year there are peonies in every colour: yellow, white, palest pink and deepest red and choice spring flowers including fritillaries.

The huge vegetable garden (where there is a pick-your-own-soft-fruit scheme and fruit can be ordered in season or frozen) is

Admission £2.00, open to groups by appointment, tel. (08) 012657-31219. Suitable for wheelchairs and children. Plants for sale (including choice shrubs like Embothrium). Directions: Take the Dervock Road from Bushmills past the old distillery, the entrance to the Traills is one and a half miles/2.4 km on the right after a wooded area.

screened by a venerable beech hedge. Part of the two and a half acre site consists of informal lawns and shrubbery with a collection of old rhododendron hybrids and old shrub roses. Behind the house there is a wild garden where the Traills have counted 27 different varieties of wild flowers and there are carpets of bluebells underneath copper beech trees.

Richard Traill propagates all kinds of wonderful things in the greenhouse behind the attractive stableyard, including lilies and abutilons grown from seed and a handsome collection of *Streptocarpus*. In the vinery there are muscatel grapes and plumbago covered in delicate ice-blue flowers, and lemon and orange trees overwinter there.

ANTRIM CASTLE GARDENS

Antrim, County Antrim

FLOWER AND WILD GARDEN
The only example of a surviving seventeenth-century garden in the Six Counties, with a romantic setting on Sixmilewater River.

Y ou have to marvel at the optimism of English settlers like Sir Hugh Clotworthy. Once the native Irish had been dispossessed during the Jacobean Plantation of Ulster the planters set about making their mark on the landscape. Despite the fact that the country was torn apart by war for the rest of the century, or that attacks by Irish woodkerns and swordsmen made life a perilous business at Antrim Castle, the latest ideas - inspired by French, formal gardens - were being created before the end of the seventeenth century. In Ireland only one other of these baroque gardens - designed to reflect the authority of their owners in their ordered forms - survives intact at Killruddery, County Wicklow.

The all-important idea was to create a vista to be admired from the original castle - built by Sir Hugh in 1613 and enlarged by his son the 1st Viscount Massereene in 1662 - and enjoyed as an outdoor spectacle. The main vista is of a T-shaped canal flanked by dramatically high hedges. Walks cutting through formal blocks of woods are laid out in a grid pattern, like a mini version of Versailles. The walks lead to different features designed to excite admiration, including a round pond and a parterre - another favourite device of the period. Sometimes known as 'parterre de broderie' these elaborate designs were literally like embroidery on the ground. In France where the idea was brought to a fine art the designs were sometimes filled out with dyed clay rather than plants.

There is also the forerunner of an aerial view ingeniously provided by a mount (originally the remains of a Norman motte), with a spiral path to the top and splendid views over the garden. The garden with its towering hedges of yew, hornbeam and lime has recently been beautifully restored.

The original creation of such gardens could be ruinously expensive and involved a huge amount of labour. There is one cautionary French tale of Nicholas Fouquet who was angling after a ministry and hoped to impress Louis XIV by building a magnificent garden at Vaux-le-Vicomte, involving nearly 20,000 labourers. The plan misfired badly – the King was angry at his ostentation and Fouquet was charged with treason and spent the rest of his life in prison.

No such fate befell the Clotworthys, and their descendants built a grand Georgian gothic mansion which was eventually burned in the Troubles in 1922. Only a single tower remains, but the splendid 1840 Jacobean Revival stable block still stands as a reminder of aspirations of bygone grandeur.

The stables have now been converted to become the Clotworthy Arts Centre run by the Arts and Heritage Service of Antrim Borough Council, with an exhibition centre and an imaginative programme of drama, lecture and music events. Together with the garden it makes a great combination for a day's outing.

Open Mon.-Fri. 9.30am-2.30pm, Sat. 9am-1pm, Sun. 2-5pm. There is a charge for the guided tour for groups. Directions: Situated on the Randalstown Road just off the A26 Dublin-Ballymena Road, on the outskirts of Antrim town. Tel. (08) 01849-428000.

FAIR CITY

Dublin and environs

D ublin's Georgian heart still gives the city the essential character
which William Makepeace Thackeray noted in his 1842 Irish
Sketch Book. With a beguiling setting in the arms of Dublin Bay and
the Wicklow and Dublin Mountains a blue promise on the horizon, it is
a place which sidles subtly into the affections. The city has layers of
history and meaning: Viking Dublin, medieval Dublin, Georgian
Dublin, the literary Dublin of Joyce and O'Casey, all superimposed or
juxtaposed as in a collage. The grandest things about Dublin are the
wonderful collection of seventeenth and eighteenth-century set-piece
buildings, the Custom House, the Four Courts, King's Hospital, the
Bank of Ireland (once Parliament House) - and the Georgian squares and
streets. It is the scale and almost village-like intimacy of the place that
make it so pleasing.

It is very much a walkable city; most places of interest are within a
pleasant stroll of Trinity College, the routes punctuated with pubs. The
new Dart line now runs obligingly along the arms of Dublin Bay from
Howth with its harbour and restaurants, past Naples-like Killiney Bay to
the seaside resort of Bray, with numerous interesting stops in between -
Sandycove, Dalkey, Dun Laoghaire.

A very great deal has been written about Dublin but curiously little is
said about its gardens. The elegant squares and parks laid out in the
eighteenth century played an important part in the gay social life of one
of the larger European cities. Peter Somerville-Large in Dublin writes of
the Rotunda Gardens (now the site of the Rotunda Hospital extension),
where society paraded and where tea and coffee were served at tables at
the sound of a bell. The Ranelagh Gardens were another fashionable
spot where the *beau monde* assembled to hear music and to watch such

spectacles as balloon flights. Beaux Walk on the north side of St Stephen's Green was the place to be seen dressed to the very height of extravagant fashion.

In tandem with the tremendous surge in elegant building, gardening was extremely fashionable throughout the eighteenth century. Mrs Delaney's garden at Delville was one of the first to embrace the naturalistic style of gardening made popular by landscape designer Lancelot Brown (known as 'Capability' for his habit of telling his clients that their gardens were 'capable of great improvement'). In a letter of 1744 she describes fields 'planted in a wild way with forest trees and with bushes that look so naturally you would not imagine it a work of art'. Looking at the gardens and landscapes of estates was very much part of the entertainment for house parties and Mrs Delaney describes visits to Lord Orrery at Caledon in County Tyrone, as well as Lord Hillsborough's and the Annesleys' estate at Castlewellan, both in County Down, in her diaries.

Interest in matters botanical was fired by scientific expeditions which brought back new genera from countries such as New Zealand, and in 1790 the Royal Dublin Society acquired the site for the National Botanic Gardens at Glasnevin. Early in the 1800s Trinity College also set up a botanic gardens on the Shelbourne Road where the Berkeley Court Hotel now stands. After the Act of Union of 1801 closed the Irish Parliament Dublin never had the same glitter and gaiety.

Now, however, the wheel has come full circle. Dublin is one of the fun capitals of Europe and its gardens and parks are coming into their own again and provide the setting for music and concerts. Spaces which were private like Merrion Square have been thrown open to the public. Beside the City Hall Dublin Corporation has created a Millennium Peace Garden featuring a fountain, while Dublin County Council has a new park at Tallaght, and the Ranelagh Gardens have been restored and reopened. There are over 100 public gardens in the city ranging from the tiny Cabbage Garden off New Street, where Oliver Cromwell's men grew cabbages, to St Anne's Estate, Raheny, once the gardens of Lord and Lady Ardilaun. The Office of Public Works have become garden-conscious too and have recently taken in charge the Iveagh Garden, a remarkable secret garden at the heart of the city hidden away behind Earlsfort Terrace and the south side of St Stephen's Green. And the re-creation of a formal garden and parterre represents the final stage in the restoration of the wonderful seventeenth-century Royal Hospital at Kilmainham.

The major gardens ringing Dublin were once strictly private preserves but changed times have brought a new chapter in the fortunes of some of these previously hidden gardens. Dublin County Council have had the foresight to acquire a whole series of great houses and demesnes: Malahide, Ardgillan, Newbridge, Marlay Park, the Corkagh Demesne, Clondalkin, each very different and all of them adding greatly to the store of amenities for the Dublin area. And the increasing number of private gardens which are opening to the public around Dublin have wonderfully varied settings, including Fernhill on the side of Three Rock Mountain with views over Dublin Bay.

ROUND AND ABOUT

There are the most weird, wonderful and highly entertaining things to be seen in and around Dublin ranging from the mummified crusaders in the crypt of St Michan's Church to the ruins of the Hell Fire Club on Montpelier Hill, scene of naughty goings-on by the eighteenth-century 'hell rakers'. In the medieval/Viking area of Dublin you can discover why scholars were put in cages at Marsh's 1701 Library with its priceless collection of books just next to St Patrick's Cathedral. It is said that the expression 'chancing your arm' originated here, and Marsh's has a tiny, pretty garden. St Patrick's Park, beside the cathedral where Swift was once Dean, has a literary walk.

Francis Street (look out for the Old Dublin restaurant with a Russian twist to its cuisine) is the best possible place for browsing for antiques. Good places to mend the inner man are the Gallic Kitchen for mouth-watering pastries and Mother Redcap's Tavern for the music, craic and pub lunches, in Back Lane beside the 1706 Tailors' Guildhall (admission free).

The Viking presentation in St Audoen's, High Street (admission £1.50) takes you back to the Millennium (known to Dubs as the Aluminium). St Werburgh's Church (secret entrance through No. 8 Castle Street) had its steeple taken off to prevent snipers taking pot shots at the Viceroy in Dublin Castle; it is open 10am-12.15pm weekdays;

2-5pm Sundays. Thomas Read's cutler's shop in Parliament Street, which once sold swords, is the oldest shop in the city and is on the edge of the rejuvenated Temple Bar area, Dublin's Left Bank, with a good selection of inexpensive restaurants.

The most elegant cabbages in the world hang from the splendid ceiling of the Carolean chapel in the Royal Hospital Kilmainham, built by the Duke of Ormond, 1680. The building, based on Les Invalides, also houses the Irish Museum of Modern Art, open 2-5pm Tues.-Sat. and 12-5pm Sundays. My all-time favourite pub is Ryan's of Parkgate Street with restaurant upstairs and complete with snugs where the military from the nearby barracks entertained ladies.

The best place to get the feel of literary Dublin is in Bewley's Oriental 'lofty clattery' cafés (Grafton Street and Westmoreland Street). Dublin at long last now has a Writers' Museum at the top end of Parnell Square, and at the other end the Rotunda Lying-In Hospital's chapel has the most exuberant plasterwork in the city, featuring cherubs. The James Joyce Cultural Centre under restoration at 35 North Great George's Street nearby gives some idea of the splendour of Georgian houses. For the grandest of the grand, go to Newman House at 85 and 86 St Stephen's Green to see the utterly magnificent plasterwork by the Lafrancini Brothers in the Apollo room and the stunning staircase hall by Robert West. One of the nymphs in the salon was given a plaster bathing costume by the bishops when the building was the Catholic University. One of Dublin's best restaurants, the Commons, is in the basement.

It is now possible to see, at No. 29 Fitzwilliam Street, exactly what a Georgian house (complete with kitchen) would have been like (thanks to the ESB) in Georgian times. Admission free, open 10am-5pm Tues.-Sat. and 2-6pm Sundays. Powerscourt Town House, once the imposing town residence of Viscount Powerscourt, is a centre for shops and restaurants. Locks Restaurant, overlooking the Grand Canal at Windsor Terrace, is a favourite place for feasts, and the restaurants at the Point Depot, the Hugh Lane Gallery and the National Gallery are interesting and inexpensive. (Don't miss the hoards of Irish gold at the National Museum, Kildare Street.)

In the suburb of Cabinteely, Murphy and Wood on Johnstown Road just off the N11 is a place of pilgrimage for all serious plantspeople. Further afield Newbridge House, Donabate, County

Dublin, the Archbishop of Dublin's 1737 house, can be visited 10am-5pm Tues.-Sat. and 2-6pm Sundays, while Ireland's equivalent of the Parthenon, the magnificent Palladian palazzo of Castletown House just across the county border at Celbridge, County Kildare is open 10am-5pm Mon.-Fri., 11am-6pm Sat. and 2-5pm Sundays.

Drimnagh Castle, a feudal stronghold surrounded by a moat, has just been opened to the public; its garden has been laid out in the seventeenth-century manner with formal parterre and walks. Open April-15 Oct. 10am-5pm Wed., Sat., Sun. Admission £1.50.

The most exotic jewel on Northside Dublin, the Casino Marino, was built in the ground of the Earl of Charlemont's house and is the most perfect example of a small Palladian villa. It is just off the Malahide Road, Fairview. Open 10am-7pm May-Sept.; 10am-4pm April, Oct.; and 2-4pm Sundays.

PLACES TO STAY

J ust ten minutes by car from the centre and near Phoenix Park (the largest enclosed park in Europe incidentally) is a charming eighteenth-century lodge run by Frank and Josie Carroll. Avondale House was once a hunting lodge on the Earl of Granard's estate. The two double rooms have the most original decor, one with an ecclesiastical theme, the other in a chinoiserie style. B & B £35.00, dinner £20.00, tel. 8386545.

A handsome double-fronted Regency terraced house, Chestnut Lodge, Vesey Place, run by Mrs Nancy Malone, overlooks a green square between Dun Laoghaire and Monkstown. The sea, the Dart line, restaurants, pubs and the ferry are all just a short distance away and there are four double rooms. B & B £25.00, tel. 2807860.

Just off St Stephen's Green and right in the heart of Georgian Dublin the Georgian House at No. 20 Baggot Street is an elegant 200-year-old terrace house. B & B £94.60 for 2 sharing, tel. 6604300.

Leeson Court, Lower Leeson Street, is another centrally situated guesthouse. Composed of two terrace houses it has some charming touches, bookcases in the hall, a bar like a country pub and a cosy breakfast room. Twenty rooms, B & B £74.00 (double room), tel. 6763380.

Michael and Marese O'Brien recently added the next-door house to their charming Victorian terrace house at 52 Lansdowne Road, Dublin 4. There are now 12 Victorian bedrooms. Ariel House is furnished with antiques and there is a garden restaurant. B & B from £34.00, tel. 6685512.

At Glenveagh, 31 Northumberland Road, Dublin 4, Joe and Bernadette Cunningham offer the friendliness of a family house with all the convenience of a hotel. The Georgian house retains its original character, and is minutes away from the city centre by Dart and bus. Six double rooms, three twin, B & B £65.00 for 2 sharing, tel. 6684612.

THE TALBOT GARDENS

Malahide Castle, County Dublin

SCIENTIFIC INTEREST

A collector's garden but with something for all the family.

The Talbot Gardens seem to have a particular air of serenity about them. Perhaps it is the legacy of generation upon generation of Talbots who loved Malahide, for the castle is the longest in continuous family occupation in Ireland; Talbots lived there since Richard Talbot was granted land in 1185 - with a brief absence in the Cromwellian period - until the death of the seventh Baron Talbot of Malahide in 1973.

The 20 acres of ornamental garden which Milo Talbot created from 1948 are his living monument. Lord Talbot de Malahide was a dedicated plantsman with a special interest in the plants and shrubs of Australasia, which he helped to popularise in Ireland. His is primarily a collector's garden of historical and scientific interest and the walled gardens were used in an experimental way to prove his theory that many delicate plants could actually be grown outdoors in sheltered conditions.

The gardens surrounding the castle with its Georgian gothic exterior and medieval heart are on the principle of Russian dolls. Within the sweep of parkland and playing fields are the castle grounds with appealing vistas of a Lebanon cedar, its feet carpeted in autumn with dwarf cyclamen, and a *Quercus petraea* whose boughs dip to touch drifts of snowdrops. Lord Talbot's favourite Australian genera olearia, pittosporum, acacia, hoheria and grevillea are represented here.

Two rides and an area of walks and shrubberies contain many rare and interesting species, my own particular favourite being an *Acer griseum* with dark chocolate-coloured curling bark, the weeping coffin juniper (*Juniperus recurva* 'Coxii'), and *Abies spectabilis* with its violet cones. Dwarf *Parrotia persica*, *Onopordum arabicum*, *Photinia serratifolia*, the 'potato climber' *Solanum crispum* 'Glasnevin' and Malahide's own hybrid of the tassel bush *Garrya* 'Pat Ballard' are among the many intriguing specimens.

The inner sanctum of the walled garden is open for accompanied tours and groups. Within this are the holiest of holies: the greenhouses, the enclosed garden with the wonderful violet Chinese *Clematis macropetala*, the pond garden – almost Mediterranean in its luxuriance – and the south-facing Tresco wall where the most exotic plants – like the South American *Bomarea caldasii* and *Lyonothamnus floribundus* – are grown. At the heart of this area is a tiny high walled garden once known as the chicken run which now shelters a collection of Alpines and tender plants like *Aristotelia chilensis*.

Dublin County Council courageously acquired Malahide Demesne in 1977 and the estate is now a national park. Their Parks Department are doing a valiant job maintaining the gardens in the spirit intended by Milo Talbot. While part of the original collection has been lost, many of the plants are gradually being replaced thanks to Lord Talbot's many connections in botanical circles as the plants he once gave to friends and fellow enthusiasts are returned to their source.

Admission free to demesne, daily 10am-dusk, castle open daily May-Sept. 2.30-4.30pm, or by appointment to groups; walled garden open Wednesdays only, conducted tours 2pm, admission £1.50. Suitable for wheelchairs and children (except walled garden). Castle restaurant with home-made goodies, souvenir shop, adventure playground, the Fry Model Railway exhibition, and nearby attractions - pitch and putt, golf, cricket, football, tel. 8727777. Directions: Malahide Castle is on the outskirts of Malahide, coming from Dublin.

RATHMORE

Westminster Road, Dublin 18

FLOWER GARDEN

A wonderful herbaceous collection in a rewarding small garden.

The gardeners who face the greatest challenge are those who set out to create interesting gardens in small suburban spaces. Mary Simpson has done exactly that, and her Foxrock garden contains most rewarding colour and variety.

A botanist who did research work at Kew, Mrs Simpson has grown plants ever since she was a child and her particular enthusiasm is for herbaceous plants. While the builders were still in her home 18 years ago Mrs Simpson went out armed with canes, string and paint and boldly drew out her design for the small back garden.

Triangular in shape, it is dominated by two deep herbaceous borders which in early September still display magnificent colour. One border, backed by a pergola covered

with great swags of clematis, is filled with gloriously contrasting hues and forms, with purples and oranges, yellows and mauves juxtaposed in a planting scheme reminiscent of Mount Stewart in County Down. Bronze/pink *Alstroemeria* 'Princess Lily' vies with the black and red of Dahlia 'Bishop of Llandaff'. A feathery mauve *Aster sedifolius* 'Nanus' is beside a canary yellow *Coreopsis grandiflora* and a dusky indigo herbaceous *Clematis integrifolia*. A similar colouring is repeated with the deeper mauve *Aster frikartii* 'Monch' and lemon yellow *Anthemis tinctoria* 'E. C. Buxton' and again with *Osteospermum* 'Sparkler'. In the centre of the bed is the rare hybrid *Magnolia grandiflora* 'Maryland' with scented cup-size blossoms and a mauve drift of thalictrum growing through its branches.

A keen plantswoman, Mrs Simpson knows every plant and is particularly fond of salvias, lobelias, clematis and hostas. Choice plants greet the eye throughout the garden: *Cardiocrinum* lilies, the Arum lily 'Green Goddess' with trumpets which last the whole summer, a pot filled with scarlet nerines, the variegated *Phlox paniculata* 'Norah Leigh', the chocolate plant *Cosmos atrosanguineus* and the handsome little *Tulbaghia violacea*. Another bed punctuated with shrub roses contains quieter compositions: pinks, dusky pink/mauve monardas and silvery artemisias.

In a shady area under a cherry tree a statue makes a good focal point. Elsewhere containers hold combined plantings of Swan River daisies, osteospermum, helianthemum and diascia. The front garden has a quieter theme with shrubs and trees providing the framework for a tremendous collection of hostas, with *Lobelia tupa* and *cardinalis* growing among the greenery, echoed by a *Berberis thunbergii* 'Rose Glow' and ropes of *Tropaeolum speciosum* trailing brilliant scarlet blossom.

The garden has a good spring display with unusual daffodils and hellebores. Later there are peonies, while its colourful herbaceous peak is from mid June to August.

Admission price discretionary, open, by appointment only, to small groups, tel. 2895101. Not suitable for wheelchairs or children. Directions: Turn off the N11 at Westminster Road (a turning to the right before Cornelscourt). Rathmore is on the corner at the first turn left.

71 MERRION SQUARE

Dublin 2

TOWN GARDEN

An exquisitely designed urban garden.

Designer Sybil Connolly loves flowers. Blooms proliferate in her fabric designs, plants decorate her designs for Tiffany plates, and flowered chintzes and papers – some of her own design – adorn her Merrion Square home. Mrs Delaney, who was still creating wonderful studies of flowers in embroidery, shells and *découpage* in the 1760s when she was in her seventies, has always been a source of inspiration.

Number 71 Merrion Square became Ireland's first couture house when Miss Connolly moved there in 1953. The lower three floors acted as a salon and workshops while the top two storeys, with views of the Dublin mountains and an aerial view of the garden, were transformed into the designer's private quarters. But the long-

awaited opportunity to create a garden only became possible 14 years later.

Narrow and over 100 feet/ 30.5 m long, the garden was not an easy shape to design for, especially since it had to appeal both at ground level and when seen from Miss Connolly's favourite room on the fifth floor. Her solution was to use simple dramatic lines with a strong structure and to cover the high walls with a profusion of roses, clematis and climbing shrubs.

The garden is divided into three sections, a formal terrace outside the main house, a small formal garden behind the mews guest house and the central area with velvety lawn, shrubs and flowers. Here the graceful curves of a brick path running between a formal terrace and the mews, and the rounded shapes of a silver pear and an *Acer pseudoplatanus* 'Brilliantissimum' have been used to counteract the severe lines of the garden. Curving borders with flowering shrubs like *Viburnum plicatum*, a pink-flowered tree peony and festoons of clematis and old-fashioned roses like 'William Lobb' and 'Variegata de

Bologna' soften the high stone walls. In spring and summer this central section is filled with scent and colour. The mauves of bearded irises planted under a blue clematis, the perfume of double white lilac in spring and *Nicotiana* and lily of the valley in summer are some of the delights here.

Among Miss Connolly's favourite flowers are the hybrid tree peony 'High Noon' planted under a mauve *Wisteria sinensis, Meconopsis* 'Slieve Donard' and the *Viola* 'Irish Molly'. Architectural trellis-work, inspired by a Gertrude Jekyll design, gives the terrace a formal French air and makes a framework for wreaths of roses and clematis, among them *C.* 'Madame le Coultre', *R.* 'Madame Alfred Carrière' and *R.* 'Gloire de Dijon'. Versailles tubs and urns filled with fuchsias, petunias and geraniums provide a movable feast of colour. Steps lead down to a small paved area with spring bulbs planted between the stones and a herb garden at one side where lovage, lemon verbena and French tarragon are grown.

The formality of the small garden behind the mews is reinforced by trellis work carrying espaliered cherries and morning glory and by topiaried box trees. And the tinkle of a small dolphin fountain makes an idyllic addition to the scents and colour of fruit and flowers. The whole garden must be a delightful inspiration for town gardeners. It is featured in *In an Irish Garden*, edited by Sybil Connolly and Helen Dillon, and the house appears in *In an Irish House* edited by Sybil Connolly.

Admission charge discretionary, open by appointment only, to small groups April-end August, weekdays only 10am-3pm, tel. 6767281.

45 SANDFORD ROAD

Dublin 6

A wonderfully rewarding garden for plantspeople and aspiring amateurs.

Some of the happiest plants I encountered were in this lovely town garden. But that is hardly surprising since the garden - described by Roy Strong as the best of town gardens - is the creation of Helen Dillon, one of Ireland's leading plantswomen.

The most important thing about gardening, says Helen, is deciding where to put a plant. And her interest in plants and desire to know their habits better has taken her to some very remote places including the Himalayas and the Andes. Her plants are carefully sited with due regard to their preferences and planted with a bucket of whatever they fancy.

The garden is a most rewarding illustration of the point that having a collector's garden and having a garden which is a pleasant place need not be mutually exclusive aims. There are several thousand plants in her collection, where Alpines, bulbs and herbaceous plants are especial favourites.

Unusually for Dublin, where gardens are often long and skinny, this one is a generous square shape and its layout has been completely changed since Val and Helen Dillon moved there 20 years ago. The front and back gardens present striking contrasts. In the front, gravel paths winding around raised rock beds full of sheltered niches allow the admiration of individual treasures - it might be a Pasque flower, *Pulsatilla vulgaris* in spring, or an autumn crocus (*Colchicum agrippinum*), a clump of golden oats (*Stipa gigantea*) in summer or different families of the silvery New Zealand daisies, *Celmisias*.

In the back garden - where beds are laid out around incredibly velvety lawns - individual star plants also pull their weight as members of teams where colour counts. Imagine an early autumn bed of blues and lilacs, in their midst the most intense blue of *Salvia patens*. Or think of hot autumn colours, with the red and black of the 'Bishop of Llandaff' dahlia blazing away beside the burnished crimson leaves and bronze seed heads of *Rodgersia pinnata* 'Superba'.

A south-facing corner has raised beds of Alpines and an elegant greenhouse holds tender plants like *Lapageria*, with its showy waxy pink bells. A circular fountain backed by a rose arbour provides a focal point in the centre of the garden.

A wrought iron trellis, draped in autumn with delights like the double crimson *Clematis viticella* 'Purpurea Plena Elegans' and a purple vine complete with grapes, hides a series of smaller gardens within the garden. A little formal garden of raised beds guarded by a statue holds smaller plants from all over the world: New Zealand, South Africa, South America. And an intimate area partially shaded by an old apple tree has beds of shade-loving plants and smaller herbaceous plants: perfect little pets like *Kniphofia* 'Strawberries and Cream' and 'Apricot'.

Among the huge collection are tender plants like, *Melianthus major* in a sheltered spot by the house, the plumed poppy, *Macleaya cordata*, the *Cornus controversa* 'Variegata' – one of the most admired plants in the garden – willow gentians, the Chatham Island forget-me-not *Myosotidium* and *Lilium henrii* which has a special association since it was introduced from China by the botanist Augustine Henry, who lived in the house next door. While some of the plants are very unusual – like a lovely bronze-leaved form of *Corydalis* only recently discovered in China, others, like a white willowherb, are pleasing forms of reassuringly everyday plants.

Plants have a place in this garden first and foremost because Helen loves them, secondly they have to earn their keep and are chosen for their sterling qualities. The garden has an almost miraculous capacity to change its appearance over the months thanks to dense planting and clever planning, and merits several visits during the year. Helen Dillon's accumulated wisdom can be found in her book *The Floral Garden*, Conran Octopus. Together with Jim Reynolds, Helen Dillon also runs occasional series of garden courses, tel. 046-36017 for details of the Irish Garden School.

Admission £3.00, OAP £2.00, open Mar., July., Aug. daily 2-6pm, April, May, June, Sept. Sun. only 2-6pm, tel. 4971308. Directions: Situated in a cul-de-sac off the Sandford Road on the right-hand side just after Merton Road and church.

RATHMICHAEL LODGE

Rathmichael, County Dublin

FLOWER GARDEN
Exuberant cottage-style garden with old
roses a speciality.

This small cottagey garden is a riot of colour and is full of those happy effects which look accidental but are really quite hard to achieve. The borders are planned so that different plants grow through each other, roses ramble through old apple trees and clematis romp through shrubs and climbing roses.

The present incarnation of the garden is quite recent and, like many a mum whose family have grown up, Corinne Hewat found something new to nurture in plants and began replanting the garden six years ago. A pair of curving beds creates a division between a small lawn near the house and the rest of the garden. A grassy path guarded by urns leads off invitingly to the dappled shade of apple trees and a rose pergola. At the end of the garden flowers screen a vegetable plot.

Corinne Hewat loves old roses and herbaceous flowers and being guided around her plants is rather like being introduced to favourite friends at a party; 'This is someone called "Lavender Lassie", this is "Pearl Dawn" who is a sister of "Margaret Merril" and here is "Adelaide" romping up a tree.' In

Admission £3.00, by appointment, June/July, tel. 2822203. Directions: Take the N11 to the start of the Bray by-pass, go left off the round-about for Shankill village, take the first right turn at the petrol station, continue to Rathmichael church, turn sharp left down Ballybride Road, and the house is third on the left-hand side.

June there is a wonderful display of damask, moss and centrifolia roses with pink-flowered scented varieties predominating: 'Madame Isaac Pereire', 'William Lobb', 'Felicia'.

Her garden is a cheerful assembly of colourful characters and old favourites. Yellow scabious, red Maltese cross (*Lychnis chalcedonica*) and prussian blue delphiniums shout cheerfully at each other in the herbaceous border. An army of bright violas, valerian, pelargoniums and geraniums overflows the terrace and a 'bed of thugs', as Corinne calls them – those obliging invasive plants like *Alchemilla mollis*, catmint, poppies and foxgloves – is planted under curtains of the old shrub rose 'Felicia'. The garden is full of interesting planting effects, blues, silvers and pinks or yellows and blues.

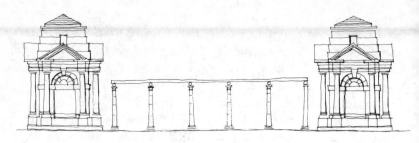

WAR MEMORIAL GARDENS

Islandbridge, Dublin

ORNAMENTAL GARDEN,
HISTORICAL INTEREST
A splendid Lutyens-designed garden.

To my shame I discovered this garden only recently and it turned out to be a most wonderful treat. The name has a sad ring to it and on the map of Dublin it doesn't look anything special, but this garden on the banks of the Liffey is one of Dublin's unsung treasures.

Inky autumn clouds were boiling up as I climbed up from the riverside and against them the avenues of poplars shone acid yellow and the groves of greeny black service trees were hung with scarlet berries. Approached from below, the sheer scale and grandeur of the garden came as a stunning surprise.

The garden was designed by Sir Edwin Lutyens and was begun in 1931. It is the largest of his gardens in Ireland; the others are at Heywood, Lambay Island and Howth Castle. The memorial is an architectural garden on a heroic scale. Based on circles and ovals it has at its centre the war stone, flanked by two round fountains, while a huge oval lawn surrounds these features with pairs of temple-like bookrooms linked by stone pergolas. In one of these rooms are volumes filled with the names of 49,400 Irish soldiers who died in World War I.

At either end of the oval are two

identical sunken gardens, their central ponds surrounded by ascending terraces and rose beds. The hybrid tea roses, planted in solid blocks of colour, were flushed with bloom in September, the wells of the garden filled with their perfume. Their colours go from pale pinks and creams in the outer circles to deepest red in the centre of the gardens. The outermost circular beds of these gardens are filled with Jekyllesque planting. In autumn the colour scheme was a rich combination of purples, reds and pinks, with massed asters, Japanese anemones, dahlias and dark-leaved shrubs. Avenues radiate out from the central features and the garden is guarded by the Great Cross. The Memorial was restored by the Office of Public Works in 1987-9.

Admission free, open all year round during daylight hours. Suitable for wheelchairs and children. No facilities. Directions: Not an easy garden to find. Going down the South Circular Road towards Phoenix Park, just before the Islandbridge the gardens are signposted to the left. The entrance to St John of God's on the same side also leads to the gardens.

NATIONAL BOTANIC GARDENS

Glasnevin, Dublin

HISTORICAL INTEREST
Full of interest and splendid reminders of its Victorian heyday.

Northsiders are lucky to have this fascinating and venerable garden on their doorsteps. Founded in 1795 by the Dublin Society it is full of all kinds of wonderful things: where else in the 26 counties could you find an Amazonian waterlily or see bananas ripening?

This is a garden which works on many different levels - for teaching, research, conservation and for pleasure. Seeds and plants are sent from Glasnevin to 700 botanical gardens around the world, 150 students are taught there and there are over 20,000 different plants in the collections.

The first thing that greets visitors is an enormous *Parrotia persica* coloured gold and amber in autumn.

To the north the River Tolka flows around the garden forming an island. Nearby there is a pleasant waterlily lake overlooked by a delightful chain tent wreathed in *Wisteria*. Near the gates is the Students' Walk where plants are grouped botanically in family beds and at the far end of the garden is the arboretum. The jewels in Glasnevin's crown - the range of glasshouses - are in the centre of the garden. These include Richard Turner's magnificent curvilinear glasshouses (1843-69) which have been beautifully restored. The Great Palm House (1884) - a fascinating steamy jungle - contains the banana tree which intrigues many people but by far the rarest plants there are the primitive cone-bearing cycads - one of which, *Encephalartos woodii*, is now extinct in the wild. The Victoria House (1854), filled with aquatic and damp-loving plants, was specially created to house the giant Amazonian waterlily. There are also fern and orchid houses, with a collection of urn plants. Orchids were raised from seed and grown to the flowering stage for the first time in the gardens in 1840. The handsome new Alpine House was awaiting its collection when I saw the gardens.

Everyone who visits has their own favourite areas; mine are the collection of bearded iris and the collection of peonies (May/June), including the lovely red streaked *Paeonia* 'Anne Rosse' from Birr Castle, and the collection of dark, sighing yews including the yellow-fruited yew (*Taxus baccata* 'Fructo-luteo'), hung with Christmassy golden berries. And the family of *Bromeliaceae* plants with brilliantly coloured rosettes in the midst of their spiny leaves (beside the Victoria House) have a fascination of their own.

The most colourful parts of the garden are the enormous double curving herbaceous borders, at their most glorious in July and August. Among the curious trees are the handkerchief tree *Davidia involucrata*, the 'living fossil tree'- one of the first to be grown from the seed of the *Metasequoia glyptostroboides* discovered in 1948, the Caucasian elm (*Zelkova carpinifolia*) - surely one of the most beautifully shaped trees, and the graceful weeping cedar (*Cedrus atlantica* 'Pendula').

There is now a guided walk to plants from China with an accompanying leaflet. Included in the tour are the Old Blush rose introduced in 1789 and immortalised by Thomas Moore as the Last Rose of Summer and the lavender-flowered *Rhododendron augustinii*, one of the many lovely plants introduced by Dundee-born Dr Augustine Henry. More such walks are planned.

The botanist William Farrer once described the rock garden unkindly as a 'Devil's lapful'. It may look a little dishevelled - the original dwarf conifers are no longer dwarf, but it contains some rare plants: for example, a new *Cotoneaster* which grew there and is still awaiting a name.

A book has been written about the National Botanic Gardens, *The Brightest Jewel* by Charles Nelson and Eileen McCracken. Beautifully illustrated, it is full of insights into the colourful history of the gardens. I liked the story of Frederick Moore

---

Admission free, open daily all year except Christmas Day, during daylight hours, tel. 8374388. Directions: Situated in the north Dublin suburbs between Finglas Road and Botanic Road.

(father and son, Dr David Moore and Frederick William, were directors in turn during the heyday of the gardens 1838-1922), who was bullied on his appointment at the tender age of 22 by the opinionated horticulturist William Gumbleton, who beat to bits with his umbrella a 'tosh plant' to which he took exception .

The book also chronicles the exciting and previously unknown plants which were sent by explorers to Glasnevin. Pampas grass was sent by John Tweedie in 1840; Edward Madden, a Kilkenny man serving with the Bengal Artillery, introduced the spectacular giant *Cardiocrinum* lilies from the Himalayas; Henry Travers collected the Chatham Island forget-me-not among many other New Zealand plants; and amateur botanist Lady Charlotte Wheeler Cuffe sent back the yellow-flowered *Rhododendron burmanicum* from Burma.

Glasnevin, controlled by the State since 1877, has suffered from lack of funds. It doesn't have a much-needed car park, visitor centre or restaurant. Hopefully with a new management plan all these improvements will come on stream.

AYESHA CASTLE

Killiney Hill, County Dublin

WILD GARDEN

Early Victorian garden with romantic woodland paths.

Ayesha Castle adds an interesting architectural flourish to Dublin's answer to the Bay of Naples. From the brow of Killiney Hill the neo-gothic castle has an enchanting view of the crescent bay sweeping around to the jagged outline of Bray Head.

The small area of formal garden was laid in 1840 when the castle was built, with flights of granite steps, lawns and herbaceous borders set into the steep hillside. The appeal of the grounds at Ayesha lies more in the surroundings, the castle looming from its granite perch, the view of Killiney Bay and the paths which burrow through woods and shrubbery down towards the beach.

Once named Victoria Castle in honour of the Queen's accession in 1837 the building was renamed for Rider Haggard's *She* after it had been gutted by fire. Built by Robert Warren, at one time the residence of a former Provost of Trinity, the Rev. Humphrey Lloyd, restored by the Thomas Power of whiskey fame, Ayesha has belonged to the Aylmer family since 1947.

Admission, tour and tea £5.00, 1-31 March daily 10am-2pm, April-May Tues.-Fri. 2-6pm, June-July Sat.-Mon. 11am-3pm; other times and groups by appointment, tel. 2852323. Justin and Bridget Aylmer provide entertaining tours of castle and gardens. There are small lace and historical exhibitions. Directions: Just below Killiney village, turn down the hill under the gothic arch and Ayesha is on the right.

PRIMROSE HILL

Lucan, County Dublin

FLOWER GARDEN

A plantsperson's garden and a great treat for genuine enthusiasts.

The existence of this secluded haven just off the busy road running through Lucan comes as a delightful surprise. At the top of a narrow laneway a stone gateway opens onto an avenue of beeches; in autumn a scattering of pink and white dwarf cyclamens grows at their feet. The formality of the Regency house with its handsome doorcase and sentinel Florence Court yews is in total contrast to the riotous assembly gathered inside the walled garden.

Like a party with a thoroughly successful guest list the company of plants in this old-fashioned garden are all colourful and interesting and invite conversation and further acquaintance. Mrs Cicely Hall began to restore the neglected garden in the 1950s and many of the plants came from now vanished gardens where an endangered species of gardeners were kept up to the mark by grand old gels who knew their stuff. Mrs Hall and her son Robin wanted to create a truly Irish garden and many of the specimens are variations special to Ireland. Their brilliant colours - reds, purples, pinks, oranges and yellows - make

Admission £2.50, group rate £2.00. House and garden open Feb., July, Aug. daily 2-6pm, open to groups by special arrangement at other times, tel. 6280373. Not suitable for children or wheelchairs. Directions: On the main road from Dublin into Lucan look for a narrow turning on the left after bridge and traffic lights. Primrose Hill is at the end of the lane.

an exhilarating change from fashionably pale-flowered plants and the all too familiar specimens available at contemporary nurseries.

To hear Mrs Cicely Hall talk about her garden is to gain a delightful insight into the sex lives of plants. Perhaps the hot, dry nature of the garden, sheltered to the north by beeches planted by Gandon, provides an encouraging climate for colourful liaisons. The plants hop in and out of bed with each other, interbreeding in an uninhibited way; some unions have resulted in unreliable offspring who don't reproduce true to type, other crosses have produced new hybrids, some of them unique to Primrose Hill.

There are two named lobelias: the handsome 'Pink Elephant' and showy 'Spark'. Among the many plants are a miniature astrantia of which the Halls are particularly proud, 'Old Irish Blue', double green and old red auriculas, *Testaceum* lilies, *Kniphofia* variants, the nut rose 'Roxburghi roxburghii' and happily interbreeding *Roscoea*. There is one of the finest collections of snowdrops in Ireland, including some Primrose Hill specials. The headache-inducing *Lobelia tupa* with its handsome red stems and scarlet flowers, the shimmering *Cornus controversa* 'Variegata' are among the choice plants. Tremendous work is still being put into developing the garden by Robin Hall, who feels that Primrose Hill should be on a par with National Trust gardens in Britain. (I think its charm surpasses them.) A new arboretum has been planted, arthritic old outhouses have been swept away and a charming 'fore garden' has been created outside the entrance which acts as an appetiser for the delights inside the walls.

In the former kitchen garden the original grid of paths has been softened and the happiest looking plants drift merrily into central grass areas. One of the great pleasures here is the striking contrast in plant forms - burly *Onopordums* offset ephemeral white willowherb, punchy fists of yellow centurion offer strength beside delphiniums weeping blue tears.

The smaller treasures - armies of fierce looking *Roscoeas* and chalky blue *Codonopsis* among them - reside in the informal garden beside the house which is attributed to Gandon. The cottage-style house, which matches a drawing by Gandon found at Clonbrock, the architect's nearby home, is also open. There are plants for sale including some Primrose Hill specials.

Every single plant in the collection has been catalogued with the exception of a small double daffodil which no one has been able to name.

FAIRFIELD LODGE

Monkstown Avenue, Monkstown,

County Dublin

FLOWER GARDEN AND ROCKERY
Small inspirational, town garden packed with interest.

Rather like an alpine plant, the garden at Fairfield Lodge is tiny and perfectly formed. But that said, it provides a wealth of inspiration in three gardens - each with a very different character - which have been created either side and in front of the 1780s lodge.

The white garden which greets visitors as they enter the wicket gate has been created recently by John Bourke. Two formal, box-edged beds have been given an added dimension, with raised compartments ingeniously formed with railway sleepers. Iceberg roses, a pair of weeping pea shrubs and silver foliage plants make up the main elements of the scheme. *Romneya coulteri* - the horned

California poppy discovered by Thomas Coulter, the Dundalk botanist, in the 1870s - has been planted to frame the gate with its spectacular golden-hearted white flower and silver leaves.

In June the west side of the house is in a spectacular curtain of wisteria blossom and fragrant cup-shaped flowers of *Magnolia sieboldii.*

In the shady courtyard - filled with golden plants and shrubs - it seems as though the sun is always shining. A sea sprite with a dolphin presides over a corner fountain and the terra cotta painted walls are lined with Versailles trellis to encourage climbing plants. Among the especially eye-catching plants here are the gorgeous yellow peony, Molly the Witch, yellow lantern flowered *Clematis orientalis* and, covering the conservatory walls, the yellow splashed leaves of an *Abutilon.*

The courtyard is an exercise in the use of foliage, running from the vivid green yellow of golden hop, through the rich golds of the maple 'Brilliantissimum' to dark leaved, variegated ivies striped in cream. There's a shade bed with lots of examples of good plants for dry, sunless spots, including one of John's prize plants, *Kirengeshoma palmata*, with its cream bells and black stems.

The main garden gives the illusion of being much larger than it actually is. At one end there is a raised terrace and lily pool, backed by a little, oriental, bamboo garden and framed in desirable shrubs: camellia, *pieris* (there's a particularly good *forrestii* variety, which carries bright bronze new foliage and clusters of lily of the valley type flowers simultaneously), and old shrub roses like the deep pink *Rosa de la Haye*.

At the end of a vista down a velvety lawn the eye is drawn to what John calls 'Pope's urn' - a copy of an urn design by the poet Alexander Pope - and to the wedding cake layers of *Viburnum plicatum* 'Mariesii'.

In June the side of the house is smothered in the lacy cream flowers of climbing hydrangea and the unfurling leaves of a colourful vine. And in the deep herbaceous border which runs the length of the garden there are two particularly eye-catching plants - one is a tree peony with silky apricot flowers which no one has been able to name, the other is a magnificent clump of the plumed poppy which rockets up to ten feet.

Two of the questions John is asked most often are how he keeps his plants in such good condition and how he gets the lawn so perfect. The answer is TLC. He mows the lawn twice a week and feeds it once a week, while his plants are fed special goodies once a week!

Admission £2.50, Wed., Sun. and Bank Holidays, May-Sept. 2-6pm, tel. 01-2803912. Plants and brochure on sale. Look for a pale pink-washed house with the name on the gate on the left-hand side near the top, going up Monkstown Avenue.

KNOCKREE

Glenamuck, Carrickmines, County Dublin

FLOWER GARDEN

An unusual garden centred on a rocky outcrop with a wonderful collection of plants.

There are some gardens where you simply have to sit and gaze in sheer enjoyment at your surroundings and this unusual garden in the foothills of the Dublin mountains is one of them.

The bones of the garden were created in the last Ice Age when retreating glaciers exposed the underlying rock which gives Knockree its special character. A dramatic granite outcrop forms the main focus of the garden and, obligingly, provides not only the perfect setting for rhododendrons but basins for two pools: one surrounded by a host of Himalayan primulas, the other acting as a mirror for the mound forming *Acer A. palmatum* 'Dissectum Atropurpureum'.

The untamed rock – with a backdrop of pine and larch – also makes a fabulous contrast to the unusual herbaceous plants at its foot, which look for all the world as though they were growing in a garden of paradise planted by nature. In fact, the garden was first started about seventy years ago, but is largely the creation of Mrs Shirley Beatty who has lived there with her family for the last thirty-four years. 'It is very much a spring garden and the rock is really what makes it,' says Mrs Beatty. The garden is also very much a plantsperson's heaven, filled with wonderful collections of hardy

Admission £2.50, groups £1.50.

Open 1 April-16 July by appointment only, tel. 01-2955884.

South west of Foxrock and Cabinteely villages, one-third way up the Glenamuck Road which runs between the Enniskerry and Brighton/Brennanstown Roads.

geraniums, roses, clematis, rhododendrons, ferns and unusual shrubs and herbaceous plants.

Mrs Beatty's descriptions of her protégés sound like a collection of colourful party guests - with geraniums Mrs Kendal Clarke, Sue Crug and Mavis Simpson, and sweet little Bill Wallis, very blue and eaten by rabbits, alas! And then there are the rhododendrons who sound terribly grand - Countess of Derby and the very fragrant Princess Alice who is quite happy out-of-doors in a sheltered corner and the lovely *azaleadendron*, Martha Isaacson, with her coral tipped, pink flowers set against bronze foliage.

Plants are used to create almost painterly colour compositions throughout the garden, usually in pale shades. One lovely combination includes the yellow day lily *Hemerocallis flava*, the showy comfrey *Symphytum uplandicum* 'Uplandicum' and geranium 'Kashmir Purple'. Another combines a deep crimson flowered *Astrantia* 'Ruby Wedding' with pink flowered lamium and a golden holly and double lilac in the background.

Beyond the rock there is a caged vegetable garden and greenhouse, and rock steps leading to a hidden destination. Climb them and you find yourself in a wild area with panoramic views of the mountains. Nearby, pockets in the rock create a perfect environment for different heathers.

A peaceful green garden, island beds and old-fashioned roses scrambling up mature trees provide a complete contrast where plants which like shade and cooler conditions, like hellebores and Himalayan poppies, prosper. The house is almost invisible behind a wonderful profusion of climbers like the yellow 'Canary Bird' rose and clematis 'Carnaby' with its huge white flowers.

Plant fanciers tend to depart in an inspired condition, their heads filled with several plants they simply *must* have - like hosta 'Snowden' with its huge bluey green leaves, or the wonderful, blowsy, blue-pink climbing rose 'Madame Caroline Testot', or a *Rhododendron griersonianum*, or the frivolous pink peony 'Do Tell'. But many of the plants at Knockree are not easily come by, since they were gifts from fellow plant enthusiasts or came from specialist nurseries outside the country. The *Trilliums*, for instance, which have spread in the shelter of a rhododendron glade, were a gift from another garden enthusiast, Mrs Gaisfort St Lawrence. There are treasures to be seen everywhere, so that visitors proceed at a snail's pace - although snails are probably the last thing you would find in this garden.

KILBOGGET

Church Road, Killiney, County Dublin

FLOWER GARDEN

A plantsman's dream on two-and-a-half acres filled with rare shrubs and rhododendrons.

Like the most intriguing mystery plots this two-and-a-half-acre garden on the south-west slope of Killiney Hill does not reveal everything at once. The view from the terrace is breathtaking: first the eye is drawn up to the panorama of the Wicklow and Dublin Mountains which fills the horizon and then to a great sweep of sloping lawn surrounded by the contrasting colours and forms of trees. The boundaries are hidden and grass paths wind off mysteriously behind island beds and shrubs: an open invitation to discover the secrets of the garden which lie waiting to be explored.

The garden was originally the creation of the late Sydney Maskell and his wife Grace, who chose the site to build a home in 1949, partly for its proximity to Killiney Golf Course. While working on the garden with his wife, Mr Maskell, an architect and landscapist with the Office of Public Works, became hooked on plants and lost interest in golf. Having created shelter, the Maskells took full advantage of the local micro-climate on the south-west facing hillside and planted a

Admission £3.00. Open from the beginning of April to the end of Oct., Sun. and Bank Holidays, 2-6pm; to groups by appointment, tel. 01-2852542 or 088-574338. Directions: The turning for Kilbogget is on the left-hand side of Church Road going towards Bray, just a few hundred yards before Killiney Church.

huge range of trees and shrubs from all over the world, many of which would not survive if planted just a few miles away.

The result has been described as a plantsman's dream which is at its most spectacular in spring and autumn. In mid May when I saw the garden the rhododendrons were in their final flush of glory. Someone once unkindly described rhododendrons as 'about as interesting as a wallpaper catalogue'. Whoever it was can't have had the pleasure of seeing, touching and smelling a collection of shrubs as varied and distinguished as those at Kilbogget. The range of colour alone is huge, moving through the spectrum from lavender blue *Rhododendron augustinii* to apricot 'Goldsworth Yellow', to waxy deep red *R. cinnabarinaum*. Some are deliciously perfumed: *R. crassum*, blushing *R.* 'Princess Alice' and the intoxicating scent trapped in the shell-coloured trumpets of *R. loderi*. Other blooms change colour as they open, so that buds and flowers form a contrast. *R. 'Idealist'* for instance starts on an apricot note and blossoms into pale yellow.

Rhododendrons may be the spring stars of the garden, but there is a huge variety of other flowering shrubs and plants: the Canary Bird rose fountaining gold; lavender blue and purest white flowered *Abutilons*;

scarlet tassels of the *Embothrium coccineum* towering up to fifty feet; *Magnolia wilsonii* with its fragrant, white, crimson-stamened flowers. The changing foliage of the dozens of different conifers and deciduous trees add their own more subtle interest.

For anyone who has not fully realised the glory of trees and shrubs Kilbogget is a revelation. Many are rare and tender, like the beautiful *Cupressus cashmeriana* with its weeping habit and the strange spiney *Olearia lacunosa*; others like the Snow Gum and the cinnamon-stemmed myrtles have fascinating bark; still others like the *Eucryphias* produce wonderful displays of flowers. Some are the kind that regular visitors enquire after like old friends: 'And how is the *Dicksonia antarctica* or the Libocedrus?' Others are worthy of a special visit - like the conifer *Picea likiagensis* which is covered with maroon cones in spring.

There are dozens of unusual plants to excite connoisseurs - the Chilean bromeliad *Puya alpestris*, the yellow African heather *Erica pageana* and the New Zealand conifer *Libocedrus plumosa* among them.

In late September and October the garden produces an autumn symphony of colour, copper *Parrotia persica*, fiery maples and golden and scarlet sorbus and cornus. The terrace backing the house provides shelter for all kinds of tender treasures like *Fremontadendron* and the lobster claw plant. My eye was especially caught by the little climbing nasturtium, *Tropaeolum polyphyllum*, scrambling through a cushion of the miniature spruce *Abies* 'Nana'.

The second chapter of Kilbogget has a romantic twist. Patricia and Michael Troughton-Smith, who had each lost their previous partners, met and fell in love. Shortly after, they also fell in love with Kilbogget, which had come on the market. It seems they were destined to have the property, and moved in following their honeymoon. It is quite a challenge to become the custodians of a famous, well-loved garden and has, the couple admit, been a learning experience. After nearly a decade Patricia and Michael have restored and nurtured the garden and compiled a computerised catalogue of all the plants. Having realised that gardens do not stand still but change and grow, they are making their own additions to the planting. Kilbogget is now designated a heritage garden and is a member of the Gardens of Ireland group.

ARDGILLAN DEMESNE

Balbriggan, County Dublin

DEMESNE

An eighteenth-century estate with a rose garden and a four seasons walled garden.

The gardens at Ardgillan are the kind that offer something for everyone, from those who want inspiration to brighten up a small front garden to rose enthusiasts. Curiosities at the estate include a hidden ice-house - precursor of the modern refrigerator - and the ghost of Edith Shackleton who was drowned in a bathing accident and is said to haunt the Lady's Stairs pathway to the sea. The house - originally known as Prospect House - has the most appealing setting on land sloping down to the coast, with a stunning view of the Mourne and Cooley Mountains.

The story of the estate provides a neat object lesson in the chequered nature of Irish history. In 1737 the land, originally held by the O'Caseys, was bought by the Rev.

Robert Taylour, descendant of Thomas Taylour who came to survey the land confiscated following Cromwell's campaign. It is sobering to reflect that Robert bought the land for just 21p per acre and paid labourers 1p a day plus a meal and a tot of whiskey (price two shillings and two pence a keg from Bushmills) to clear the woods and make way for his new house on Ard Choill (high wood), which has

Admission free. The park and garden are open daily 10am-6pm. The castle is open Tues.-Sun., 11am-6pm, with guided tours £2.00. Directions: Ardgillan is between Skerries and Balbriggan and is signposted from Balrothery on the main road to Belfast.

become anglicised to Ardgillan. After 200 years the estate passed out of the hands of the Taylour family and was eventually bought in 1982 by Fingal Council from the German Pott family.

By the time the Council came on the scene the main features of the landscaped pleasure grounds had been lost and the walled garden, which once provided vegetables, fruit and cut flowers for the house, had become derelict.

Over the years new features have been created, more in keeping with the times. Flanking the house a modern rose garden has been laid out with geometric beds filled with hybrid tea-roses like golden 'Whiskey Mac' and the scarletissimo 'Alex'. A circular lily pond provides the main focal point and, in time, the climbing roses fountaining up their supporting posts will be grown over loops of chains to form graceful swags.

Rose lovers might prefer the more subtle charms of the old-fashioned roses planted around the walls of this garden. Among them are 'Souvenir de St Annes', a pale Irish beauty with a golden heart, which originated in St Anne's Park, plump magenta 'Empress Josephine' and velvety carmine 'Henri Martin'.

The satisfying herbaceous border beside the castle and the row of Florence Court yews, dating back to the 1840s, with their pinnacled tops guarding the 'ha ha', are suggestive of relics of 'old decency'. A 'ha ha' was a concealed drop designed in the eighteenth century to allow uninterrupted views of parkland, and caused a great ha ha if an unwary wanderer fell over it. The Florence Court Yews are all descended from cuttings from one freak tree at Florence Court, County Fermanagh.

The gardeners of Fingal Council have gone to a great deal of trouble to create four contrasting gardens within the old walled garden. The first of these (not for plant connoisseurs) is full of brilliantly coloured flowers like African marigolds and gladioli to gladden the hearts of suburban gardeners. Then there is an herbaceous and shrub garden with a central walk between double borders. This is a very good place to get to know plants better, since everything is clearly labelled and there are some choice plants like the handsome black-leafed *Cemicifuga ramosa*, the thistly *Eryngium oliverianum* with its startling blue stems, *Mandevilla sauveolens*, an evergreen climber with white flowers trumpeting rich perfume, and *Hydrangea villosa* with its big, quilted leaves and furry stems.

The potager laid out with beds enclosed in neat box hedges shows just how decorative vegetables can be when they are grown in geometric patterns. Fruit - including companionable male and female Chinese gooseberries or Kiwis - is still grown in the sheltered niches along the walls. Among the more eye-catching vegetables are black French beans and spaghetti marrows.

The area where visitors seem to linger longest is the herb garden, where old-fashioned herbs like Penny Royal, Salad Burnett and Lemon Thyme surrounded by box edging are laid out around a central bed of fragrant lavender in hues from white to midnight blue.

Deepest purple flowered *Buddleias* provide a butterfly paradise along the sunny walls. The glasshouse beside the walled garden has been magnificently restored and no doubt will offer all kinds of exotic treats by the time it is opened to the public.

Ardgillan is a great place for a family outing. There are tours of the house pleasant tea-rooms and miles of walks in the 200-acre park, including the Lady's Stairs - the private bridge to Barnageera Beach built for the Taylour family in exchange for allowing right of way for the Dublin-Belfast railway line.

FERNHILL

Sandyford, County Dublin

WILD AND FLOWER GARDEN

A romantic garden, made for strolling, within a 40-acre hillside setting.

May and June are the best months for the larger Irish gardens in the Robinsonian style, which depend on naturalistic planting and flowering shrubs and trees for their effect. One of the loveliest of these is Fernhill, 500 feet up the side of Three Rock Mountain, with panoramic views over Dublin Bay.

This is a garden full of 'oh wows', the kind of spectacular natural displays guaranteed to stop anyone in their tracks. Among them are the handkerchief tree, fluttering with hundreds of snowy white bracts, and the ethereal *Magnolia wilsonii* hung with ballerina-like flowers, once described by a farmer as fairy cups hanging on a tree instead of a dresser.

Prince Charles isn't the only one to talk to plants. This is the garden where Sir Frederick Moore, curator of the Botanic Gardens at Glasnevin from 1879, used to raise his hat when he greeted a specially fine specimen of *Rhododendron arboreum* given to Judge Darley by his father David. The aptly named tree rhododendron is still there today, roofed in May with deep pink flowers and appreciative of a word or two from visitors.

The forty acres of ground were originally laid out by Judge William Darley in the last century, and the wonderful broadwalk of conifers - Sequoias, Tsugas and Deodaras - were planted by him in 1860. Sequoias are sometimes known as 'Wellingtonias' and were introduced to Ireland in the 1850s from California. They were often planted in avenues in belated celebration of the Duke of Wellington's victory at the battle of Waterloo. The Walker family have owned the estate since 1934. It is still very much a family garden, currently kept up by Mrs Sally Walker with the assistance of just three other pairs of hands. Now, thanks to the Heritage Council and a mile of fencing, it is free from the deer that used to come down from the mountains to munch on precious plants.

The tour begins at the kitchen garden, enclosed by high beech hedges. Beside the entrance is a romantic little cottage-style garden punctuated with deep blue delphinium spires. The main section is planted in the traditional way, with paths lined with ornamental herbaceous borders full of old favourites like peonies and shrub roses where the Victorians liked to walk and admire the neat rows of fruit and vegetables destined for the dinner table. Espaliered apple trees and a parterre filled with old roses provide other old-world touches.

A path seemingly lit by scores of candelabra primulas and the brilliant yellow green of skunk cabbage meanders over a stream and through shrubs to what, for many regular visitors, is their favourite part of Fernhill. The Edwardian rockery with its charming pools and cascades is full of dwarf shrubs, unusual bulbs and a collection of heathers or ericas.

Near the house there is a hidden spring garden with *Trilliums*, hostas and hellebores planted under *Cornus*, *Acers* and a magnificent *Camellia reticulata*, first introduced to Ireland by the plant explorer, George Forrest, from China in 1924.

The main part of the grounds are laid out with number trails which wind around the hillside where magnificent displays of rhododendrons merge perfectly with the rocky hillside and trees, just as though they were in their native habitat in the Himalayas. From the higher paths you can look down on a wonderful patchwork of blossom formed by flowering shrubs planted under a sheltering canopy of beech and pine. Don't miss the fernery or the path from the broadwalk which leads up through spectacular rhododendrons like the deliciously perfumed *R. dalhousie*, named for

Admission £2.50, open March-Nov. Tues.-Sat. 11am-5pm; Sundays, garden only, 2-6pm; advance notice required for groups and guided tours, tel. 2956000. Suitable for children, and wheelchairs in the lower sections, toilet facilities, plant sales including species propagated at Fernhill. Directions: Two miles/3.2 km from Dundrum on the Enniskerry Road.

some reason after a particularly nasty Governor of India and dazzling scarlet Mayday rhododendrons. There's even a rhododendron reputed to be an aphrodisiac. 'It hasn't done anything for me yet!' says Mrs Walker.

The sheltered frost-free slopes also allow the sub-tropical tree fern *Dicksonia antarctica* to flourish, while the grounds provide interesting insights into past garden fashions, like the laurel lawn below the broadwalk.

INDEX